THE PROMS IN 2017

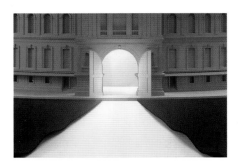

29 JULY

The first Relaxed Prom welcomes audiences who might benefit from a more informal atmosphere

19 AUGUST

Sir Simon Rattle makes his 72nd appearance at the Proms – his first with the London Symphony Orchestra, of which he becomes Music Director this year

16 JULY

The Proms Extra Family series begins: workshop-introductions to the music of the following Prom

5 AUGUST

BBC Proms Inspire hosts a day of interactive workshops and creative sessions for young composers, coinciding with the annual appearance of the National Youth Orchestra of Great Britain

9 SEPTEMBER

Audiences across the world can share the Last Night of the Proms celebrations, with TV and radio broadcasts in countries across Asia, Australasia, Europe and the USA

14 JULY

The First Night of the Proms begins a season that welcomes artists and ensembles from more than 36 countries, from Australia to Uzbekistan

22 JULY

The 'Proms at ...' series explores venues never previously visited by the Proms, including Stage@TheDock in Hull – the

13 AUGUST

Ninety years since the BBC took over the Proms, every Prom is broadcast live on BBC Radio 3 and in HD Sound online,
ие globe

CONTENTS

4
WELCOME
BBC Proms Director **David Pickard** introduces the 2017 festival

8
MY PROMS
Audience members share their Proms memories *(see also pages 54 and 79)*

20
RUSSIAN REVOLUTIONS
One hundred years after the October Revolution, **Gerard McBurney** explores the musical legacy of 20th-century Russia

26
TO SING A NEW TUNE
In the 500th anniversary year of the Reformation, **Paul Griffiths** looks at how Luther's changes to the Church were reflected in music

32
MAXIMAL MINIMALISTS
Pwyll ap Siôn contrasts the careers of Minimalist composers John Adams and Philip Glass on their 70th and 80th birthdays

36
THE FIRST LADY OF SONG
Stuart Nicholson pays tribute to Ella Fitzgerald in the centenary year of the jazz singer's birth

40
OPEN TO ALL
The benefits of relaxed performances are hailed by **Suzanne Bull**, ahead of the first Relaxed Prom

42
FROM SEED TO FRUITION
Cellist **Alisa Weilerstein** shares her diary of musical creation with **Helen Wallace**

46
DARKNESS AND LIGHT
Elgar's three symphonies feature in this year's Proms – **Stephen Johnson** considers how the works reflect the paradoxes of the composer

50
NATURAL REFLECTION
Toks Dada considers how the Proms is addressing diversity in classical music

66
NEW MUSIC
Tim Rutherford-Johnson profiles the British composers whose music is given world, European, UK or London premieres at this year's Proms

72
PROMS EXTRA

A round-up of this year's free pre-concert talks, workshops and events, by **Amanda Holloway**

74
PROMS POTENTIAL

Three young musicians explain how they have benefited from participating in Proms Learning projects

76
SUMMER ADVENTURES

Rick Jones outlines the range of free events and activities aimed at families at this year's Proms

80
STAFF SARGENT

Fifty years after Malcolm Sargent's death, **Leanne Langley** traces the career of one of the Proms's most popular conductors

84
WATER MUSIC

Anna Picard revisits Handel's *Water Music*, 300 years after its first performance

88
BROADWAY'S GIFT TO OPERA

Tim Carter on the success of Rodgers and Hammerstein's first collaboration, *Oklahoma!*

90
MAESTRO MUSINGS

Photographer **Andrew Hayes-Watkins** captures four conductors as they prepare to perform

94
LIGHTS! CAMERA! ACTION!

Behind the scenes during Proms 'rig week' at the Royal Albert Hall with **Clemency Burton-Hill**

98
BRINGING THE PROMS TO YOU

The Proms on TV, Radio and Online

117
CONCERT LISTINGS

Full listings and details of Proms Extra events

158
BOOKING

Royal Albert Hall Seating Plan   158
Tickets and Discounts   158
How to Book   160
How to Prom   162
The Last Night of the Proms   163

164
VENUE AND ACCESS INFORMATION

Royal Albert Hall   164
Beit Venues, Imperial College Union   165
Cadogan Hall   166
'Proms at …' venues   166

180
INDEXES

Index of Artists   180
Index of Works   182

The BBC Proms 2017 Festival Guide is also available as an audio book, in Braille and as a text-only large-print version. See page 168 for details.

Chris Christodoulou/BBC (Proms Potential); Andrew Hayes-Watkins (Maestro Musings)

WELCOME TO THE 2017 BBC PROMS

One of the great pleasures of 2016, my first season as Director of the BBC Proms, was the opportunity to attend every concert and to experience, at first hand, the range and variety of this remarkable festival. In particular I treasure the days that threw up strange contrasts – such as moving from an afternoon of Purcell at the Sam Wanamaker Playhouse to an evening of Gershwin at the Royal Albert Hall, or Mahler's Symphony No. 3 followed an hour later by a celebration of David Bowie. I can think of no other festival in the world that offers such an astonishing range of music over an intensive eight-week period and I would like to pay tribute to the extraordinary teams at the Proms and BBC Radio 3 who work tirelessly to make it all happen.

My first year at the Proms has also confirmed for me that the founding principles of the opening season in 1895 still hold good today. This is truly a festival that offers the best of classical music for the widest possible audience. In 2017 we are once again presenting the finest orchestras from across the UK alongside the pick of visiting ensembles from abroad. The BBC Orchestras and Choirs form the backbone of the festival, performing in 29 concerts, but we also celebrate the vitality and vibrancy of the wider UK orchestral scene. We look forward to the regular visits of some of this country's finest orchestras alongside Proms debuts by groups such as Chineke! and the Dunedin Consort. Similarly, we are delighted to welcome back top international orchestras such as the Vienna Philharmonic, the Staatskapelle Berlin and Amsterdam's Royal Concertgebouw Orchestra, alongside first-time visitors such

BBC Creative/BBC (season identity); Chris Christodoulou/BBC (Pickard)

as the Cincinnati Symphony Orchestra, the Orchestra of La Scala, Milan, and the French period-instrument ensemble Pygmalion.

Founder-conductor Henry Wood's vision of serving the widest possible audience grew significantly in ambition with the arrival of the BBC's involvement 90 years ago. (Some objectors at the time saw radio broadcasting as a threat to the entertainment industry, but Wood firmly believed in its democratising effect, and by 1929 there were already 2.25m radio licence-holders.) Low-priced 'Promenade' tickets remain a key part of our offer, but the audience opened up through broadcasting has extended the reach of the Proms way beyond that envisioned by its founders. 122 years ago around 125,000 people might have attended the first Proms

Nicholas Collon (*centre*) returns with the Aurora Orchestra to perform Beethoven's 'Eroica' Symphony from memory

season at the Queen's Hall. In 2016 we performed to more than 300,000 at our live concerts, with millions more enjoying the Proms on radio, television and online – with every concert, as ever, broadcast live on Radio 3.

We continue to expand our offering for audiences new to classical music. Family Proms are now an established part of our programme, not least thanks to the huge impact of the BBC's Ten Pieces scheme, and we have a number of additional activities specifically designed for young people and their families. Following the success last year of its explanatory concert based around Mozart's 'Jupiter' Symphony, the Aurora Orchestra presents a dissection of Beethoven's 'Eroica' Symphony – a fascinating experience both for those new to the piece and for regular concert-goers. In a similar vein, the Hallé's presentation of Dvořák's 'New World' Symphony will bring Gerard McBurney's Beyond the Score® programme from Chicago to the Proms for the first time – with a dramatisation that provides a historical context for the piece. For audiences more comfortable in an informal atmosphere we present our first Relaxed Prom, with the BBC National Orchestra of Wales, allowing people with a disability – including autism, sensory and communication challenges and learning disabilities – to enjoy orchestral music in an accommodating setting. The 'widest possible audience' grows ever wider.

One of the most inspirational events at the Proms is the annual appearance of the National Youth Orchestra of Great Britain (this year conducted by Thomas Adès, a former member of the orchestra), and putting new talent and young performers centre-stage

Wilton's Music Hall in London's East End: the intimate venue is one of five – including Stage@TheDock in Hull – to play host to this year's 'Proms at …' series

remains a key part of our programme. Our own Proms Youth Choir takes pride of place on the First Night, tackling their most ambitious project to date: John Adams's epic *Harmonium*. Later on, members of the Proms Youth Ensemble play alongside the dazzling US ensemble Bang on a Can All-Stars in a Late Night Prom including the world premiere of a new piece for the Proms Youth Ensemble by Michael Gordon (the third commission for the ensemble in as many years). We also continue to offer young people access to some of the world's leading performers and composers through our Proms Sessions and the Inspire scheme for young composers.

Two pivotal moments in history provide inspiration for this year's programme. The 100th anniversary of the Russian Revolution allows us to explore not just those composers

Backing our most precious resources.

The arts.

The arts are something our nation does brilliantly. No wonder millions of
visitors fill UK art galleries, theatres and concert halls. It's an integral part
of our culture that helps promote us to the rest of the world. That's why we have
supported the arts for over 50 years with long term support for the
Royal Opera House, the National Portrait Gallery, the British Museum and the
Royal Shakespeare Company. Over that time, more than 50 million people
have experienced a BP supported event and we will continue to help bring
what the UK does so well to a wider audience.

Find out more at bp.com/arts

who lived through that seismic change and reflected it in their music, but also the ways in which politics has inspired and influenced composers across the ages. Our three operatic offerings this summer (Beethoven's *Fidelio*, Mussorgsky's *Khovanshchina* and Mozart's *La clemenza di Tito*) all explore political power as a central theme. The 500th anniversary of the Protestant Reformation provides an opportunity to see the many ways in which the Lutheran chorale has inspired composers through the ages, culminating in a special Reformation Day with the chance for members of the audience to participate in a performance of Bach's *St John Passion*.

Cultural identity also forms a running theme – whether in the celebration of Finnish Independence, our Late Night Prom marking the 70th anniversary of Partition through the classical music of India and Pakistan or the Bohemian nationalism of Dvořák, Smetana and Janáček. We also embark on some longer-term projects: the start of a series of Handel oratorios and the first instalment

of a two-year plan to present Bach's complete *Well-Tempered Clavier* with Sir András Schiff, and the continuation of a multi-year Berlioz strand with the Orchestre Révolutionnaire et Romantique and Sir John Eliot Gardiner.

Expanding on last year's exploration of a variety of venues across London, we return to Peckham's Bold Tendencies Multi-Storey Car Park as well as discovering some new spaces in 2017 – Wilton's Music Hall for Peter Maxwell Davies, Southwark Cathedral for Renaissance and modern choral works, and the striking underground Tanks at Tate Modern for a late-night exploration of contemporary and experimental works. To mark the 300th anniversary of the first performance of Handel's *Water Music* we go to Hull – UK City of Culture 2017 – for three waterside performances at the new Stage@TheDock under early-music specialist Nicholas McGegan. Other anniversaries we celebrate this year include the centenaries of two jazz legends – Ella Fitzgerald and Dizzy Gillespie – both represented in a Prom with the BBC

Concert Orchestra; the 450th anniversary of the birth of Monteverdi with a performance of the *Vespers* and a lunchtime concert of choral and vocal music given by I Fagiolini; and the birthdays of two pioneers of American Minimalism – John Adams (70 this year) and Philip Glass (80). It is also 50 years since the death of one of the great figures in Proms history, Malcolm Sargent, who succeeded Henry Wood in 1948 as chief conductor of the Proms. Not only do we recreate Sargent's 500th Prom from his final season in 1966, but we also reprise works by Walton and Vaughan Williams whose world premieres he conducted, as well as Sargent's own *An Impression on a Windy Day* on the Last Night.

I hope you will find much to inspire you, and that you enjoy a thrilling summer of world-class music-making. ●

David Pickard, Director, BBC Proms

Welcome to the 2017 Proms, where once again we invite the world to enjoy the greatest classical musical festival in the world and to explore both the familiar and the new. The Proms reaches hundreds of thousands of people in the Royal Albert Hall and other venues, and is an important part of BBC Radio 3's mission to connect audiences with the best music and the best performances of classical music all year round.

Every Prom is broadcast live on Radio 3 and available in HD Sound online and for

download 30 days afterwards, and 25 Proms are broadcast on BBC TV as part of BBC Music. This year marks 90th anniversary of the Proms being run by the BBC, and the coverage is as broad and deep as ever. As well as connecting people to the remarkable music that is the very essence of the Proms, we also connect to the talks and ideas that further enhance the experience of encountering music in this unique, democratic setting – one that was at the heart of Henry Wood's vision.

The themes this year include Revolution – how humans continue to evolve thought and action in breaking free from oppression, and

how this is reflected in music. We've had a great deal of revolution in how we do things in broadcast terms over the years and that doesn't stop this year. Whether you listen or watch online or on the airwaves, the BBC continues its proud, 90-year tradition of giving everyone everywhere the best seat in the house. Have a lovely Proms 2017.

Alan Davey, Controller, BBC Radio 3

TARIQ KHAN
customer service manager

I have been going to the Proms for 23 years – I love hearing live music and, living in London, it would have been silly not to go to a British institution like the Proms and hear world-class orchestras and soloists for next to nothing! It cost only £3 to Prom when I first went, but what keeps me coming back year after year is the variety of music, from standard repertoire and neglected pieces to contemporary music and new commissions. I buy a season ticket for the Gallery every year. I love the relaxed atmosphere of Promming and seeing my fellow regular Prommers.

AT THE MOMENT I'M ENJOYING ...

A lot of contemporary music, by composers such as Magnus Lindberg, Colin Matthews and Steve Reich. I love the breadth of contemporary music – there is a piece to suit any mood and with so many different styles I am discovering something new all of the time. I also didn't realise that Florent Schmitt's *Antony and Cleopatra* suites were so stunning until I heard the BBC Symphony Orchestra performance at the Barbican last year.

MY MOST RECENT MUSICAL 'DISCOVERY'

My most recent discovery was not so much musical but more the way in which to present a concert. I loved the way the Proms at ... Roundhouse, Camden, last year included live projection that worked with the music, as well as the introductions to each piece by Andrew McGregor. I thought it would be a great way to get a younger audience interested in classical music.

MY PROMS HIGHLIGHTS

There are so many highlights to choose from – an amazing concert by the Singapore Symphony Orchestra in 2014, the debut of the Simón Bolívar Symphony Orchestra in 2007 and a Late Night Prom featuring Steve Reich's *Music for 18 Musicians*. The Prom that really stands out for me, though, is the BBC Scottish Symphony Orchestra's performance of Vaughan Williams's Fourth, Fifth and Sixth Symphonies in one concert in 2012. Andrew Manze's conducting was just stunning and I heard the symphonies in a new light – it was an inspired piece of programming.

Matthew Lloyd

JUDI THOMAS
travel writer and performer

When I moved from Germany to England in 1999, the Proms gave me the chance to hear live music that I only knew from recordings. My first Proms were in the Gallery, including the Last Night in the Royal Albert Hall in 2001. I bought my first season ticket, for the Arena, in 2006. For the past 16 years the Proms has been my summer; without it I would never have seen the world's best orchestras and soloists and heard such a variety of repertoire. It's also a social event – I've met some of my best and closest friends at these concerts and, after all these years, being at the Proms feels like coming home.

AT THE MOMENT I'M ENJOYING …
Violin concertos by Beethoven, Brahms, Bruch and Mendelssohn. Although, when I'm travelling as part of my job, or working on a boat, for example, I don't have much time to listen to music.

MY MOST RECENT MUSICAL 'DISCOVERY'
Ray Chen at last year's Proms, performing Bruch's Violin Concerto. I was standing in the first row of the Arena, right in front of him. It felt like he was playing for me. Also steel bands! During the past two years I spent time as crew on a sailing boat in the Caribbean and I heard a lot of steel drums. The repertoire goes from Latin and jazz to film and popular songs – whether it's a single drum or a big band, the sound is unique and joyful.

MY PROMS HIGHLIGHTS
At last year's Last Night I threw a Paddington Bear to Juan Diego Flórez onstage and he serenaded him. The previous year, again on the Last Night, I pinged my knickers at Jonas Kaufmann, who replied with a pair of Union Jack boxer shorts. Who said we Germans don't have a sense of humour?

ON THE TOWN

music by **LEONARD BERNSTEIN**

book and lyrics by **BETTY COMDEN** and **ADOLPH GREEN**

based on a concept by **JEROME ROBBINS**

7 Jul — 5 Aug

OLIVER TWIST

CREATED FOR EVERYONE AGED SIX AND OVER

adapted by **ANYA REISS**

from the novel by **CHARLES DICKENS**

A TALE OF TWO CITIES

a new play by **MATTHEW DUNSTER**

adapted from the novel by **CHARLES DICKENS**

11 Aug — 16 Sep

JESUS CHRIST SUPERSTAR

lyrics by **TIM RICE**   music by **ANDREW LLOYD WEBBER**

REGENT'S PARK
OPEN AIR THEATRE

0844 826 4242*

openairtheatre.com

*9am – 9pm; calls cost 7pp plus your phone company's access charge

THE ROYAL PARKS

Season Partners

BRITISH AIRWAYS

CLASSIC *f*M   The Telegraph

Jesus Christ Superstar 2016. Photo David Jensen.

"If I am to play my best, there is no way but STEINWAY."

LANG LANG
STEINWAY ARTIST

STEINWAY HALL LONDON 44 MARYLEBONE LANE, LONDON W1U2DB

FOR MORE INFORMATION OR TO ARRANGE A PRIVATE APPOINTMENT
AT OUR LONDON SHOWROOMS, PLEASE CALL:

0207 487 3391 OR EMAIL INFO@STEINWAY.CO.UK

STEINWAY & SONS

BIRMINGHAM **CLASSICAL**

Hear the world's greatest musicians in one of the world's best acoustics

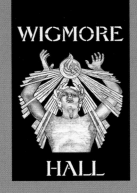

£5 tickets for Under 35s at Wigmore Hall

www.wigmore-hall.org.uk/u35

'I think the impact is much greater in a direct performance scenario... it's exciting and fun, and you never quite know what is going to happen!'
Anna Sideris, young audience member

'When performers open up and release that barrier... that's when the magic happens.'
Rannveig Káradóttir, young audience member

Buy a ticket to selected concerts throughout the season for just £5!

DIRECTOR: JOHN GILHOOLY OBE
36 WIGMORE STREET, LONDON W1U 2BP
REGISTERED CHARITY NO. 1024838

Department for Culture Media & Sport | LOTTERY FUNDED | ARTS COUNCIL ENGLAND

Photograph © Benjamin Ealovega

CLASSICAL SEASON
2017/18

BELIEF AND BEYOND BELIEF
Explore what it means to be human, in partnership with the London Philharmonic Orchestra and featuring the Emerson Quartet playing Beethoven's late quartets.

LIGETI IN WONDERLAND
Step inside the adventurous world of this pioneering composer as programmed by Artist in Residence Pierre-Laurent Aimard.

BERNSTEIN'S MASS
Celebrate the spirit of idealism, protest and questioning of the mid-20th century, as embodied by Leonard Bernstein. Features performances of Bernstein's masterpiece Mass, plus an updated, 21st century take on his Young People's Concert.

INTERNATIONAL ORCHESTRAS
Featuring Daniel Barenboim conducting the West-Eastern Divan Orchestra and Sir Simon Rattle with the Berliner Philharmoniker.

RESIDENT ORCHESTRAS

London Philharmonic Orchestra
Changing Faces: Stravinsky's Journey, explores his life and music with Vladimir Jurowski.

Philharmonia Orchestra
Celebrating 10 years with Principal Conductor Esa-Pekka Salonen, and marking the centenary of the Bolshevik Revolution in *Voices of Revolution: Russia 1917*, with Vladimir Ashkenazy.

Orchestra of the Age and Enlightenment
Dive into *Visions, Illusions and Delusions* and the music of Mozart, Bach, Handel and more.

London Sinfonietta
Celebrate the orchestra turning 50 with landmark commissions including Hans Werne Henze's *Voices* and groundbreaking new projects.

THE HOME OF CLASSICAL MUSIC

SOUTHBANK CENTRE

LOTTERY FUNDED

Supported using public funding by
ARTS COUNCIL ENGLAND

southbankcentre.co.uk
020 79604200

THE FUTURE OF MUSIC

Top conservatoire for Performing Arts in the UK*

Diverse programme of public events

World-leading research

Internationally successful alumni

ROYAL
COLLEGE
OF MUSIC
London

   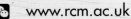 www.rcm.ac.uk

EDINBURGH INTERNATIONAL FESTIVAL

4–28 AUGUST

PERFECT SCORES

With many of the world's finest performers the classical music line-up during the International Festival's 70th Anniversary is unmissable.

Highlights include **Bryn Terfel, Iván Fischer** and **Budapest Festival Orchestra,** Joshua Bell, **Mikhail Pletnev, Gianandrea Noseda** and **Teatro Regio Torino,** Mitsuko Uchida, Riccardo **Chailly** and **Filarmonica della Scala,** Karen Cargill, René Pape, Edward Gardner and **Bergen Philharmonic Orchestra** and many more.

EIF.CO.UK
#EDINTFEST

·EDINBVRGH·
THE CITY OF EDINBURGH COUNCIL

CREATIVE SCOTLAND
ALBA | CHRUTHACHAIL

THE ELEVENTH

ENGLISH MUSIC FESTIVAL

In 2017, the BBC Concert Orchestra returns to The English Music Festival with world première performances of important works by Vaughan Williams, Stanford and Montague Phillips, while other events range from major orchestral and choral concerts in Dorchester Abbey, through the soaring voices of choristers and English piano trios, to a late evening guitar recital and the dapper New Foxtrot Serenaders. Join us for another Festival full of exquisite music-making, fascinating talks and bubbling conviviality!

For further information contact Festival Director Em Marshall-Luck at English Music Festival, Suite M0222, 265-269 Kingston Road, Wimbledon, London SW19 3NW or by email to: em.marshall-luck@englishmusicfestival.org.uk.

26-29 MAY 2017
DORCHESTER-ON-THAMES, OXFORDSHIRE
www.englishmusicfestival.org.uk

EM RECORDS

EMR CD037-38

NOW COMES BEAUTY
commissions from The English Music Festival

BBC Concert Orchestra
Gavin Sutherland (conductor)
Owain Arwel Hughes (conductor)
Rupert Marshall-Luck (violin)
Roderick Williams (baritone)
David Owen Norris (piano)

EMR CD036

HERACLEITUS
GURNEY, WARLOCK and BUTTERWORTH

The Bridge Quartet
Michael Dussek (piano)
Charles Daniels (tenor)

EMR CD023

THE FIRE THAT BREAKS FROM THEE: Stanford and Milford Violin Concertos

BBC Concert Orchestra
Rupert Marshall-Luck (violin)
Owain Arwel Hughes (conductor)

Join us as a Foundation Subscriber to receive a free copy of each disc as soon as it is released, individual disc subscription benefits and a pair of free tickets to all recitals, launches, receptions, parties and events that EM Records organises.

Visit **www.em-records.com** for further details of subscription schemes, audio-clips and to purchase discs or contact Director **Em Marshall-Luck** at **em.marshall-luck@em-records.com** or on **07808 473889**.

EM Records is distributed in the UK by Discovery and world-wide by Launch Music International

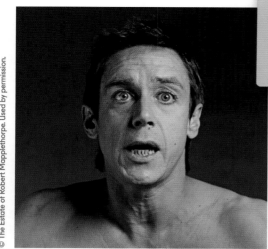

National Art Pass_____ _can give you lust for life

Luke Judlin
Individual

Please show your card for free admission and reduced price entry to participating museums and galleries

See more art for less. Search National Art Pass.

_with Art Fund

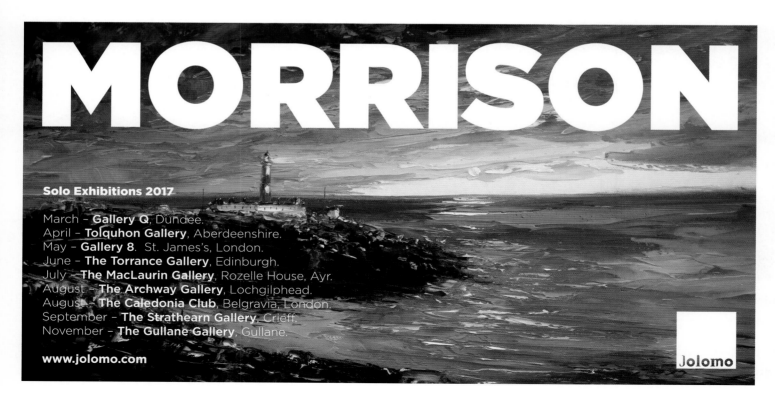

MORRISON

Solo Exhibitions 2017

March – **Gallery Q**, Dundee.
April – **Tolquhon Gallery**, Aberdeenshire.
May – **Gallery 8**. St. James's, London.
June – **The Torrance Gallery**, Edinburgh.
July – **The MacLaurin Gallery**, Rozelle House, Ayr.
August – **The Archway Gallery**, Lochgilphead.
August – **The Caledonia Club**, Belgravia, London.
September – **The Strathearn Gallery**, Crieff.
November – **The Gullane Gallery**, Gullane.

www.jolomo.com

Jolomo

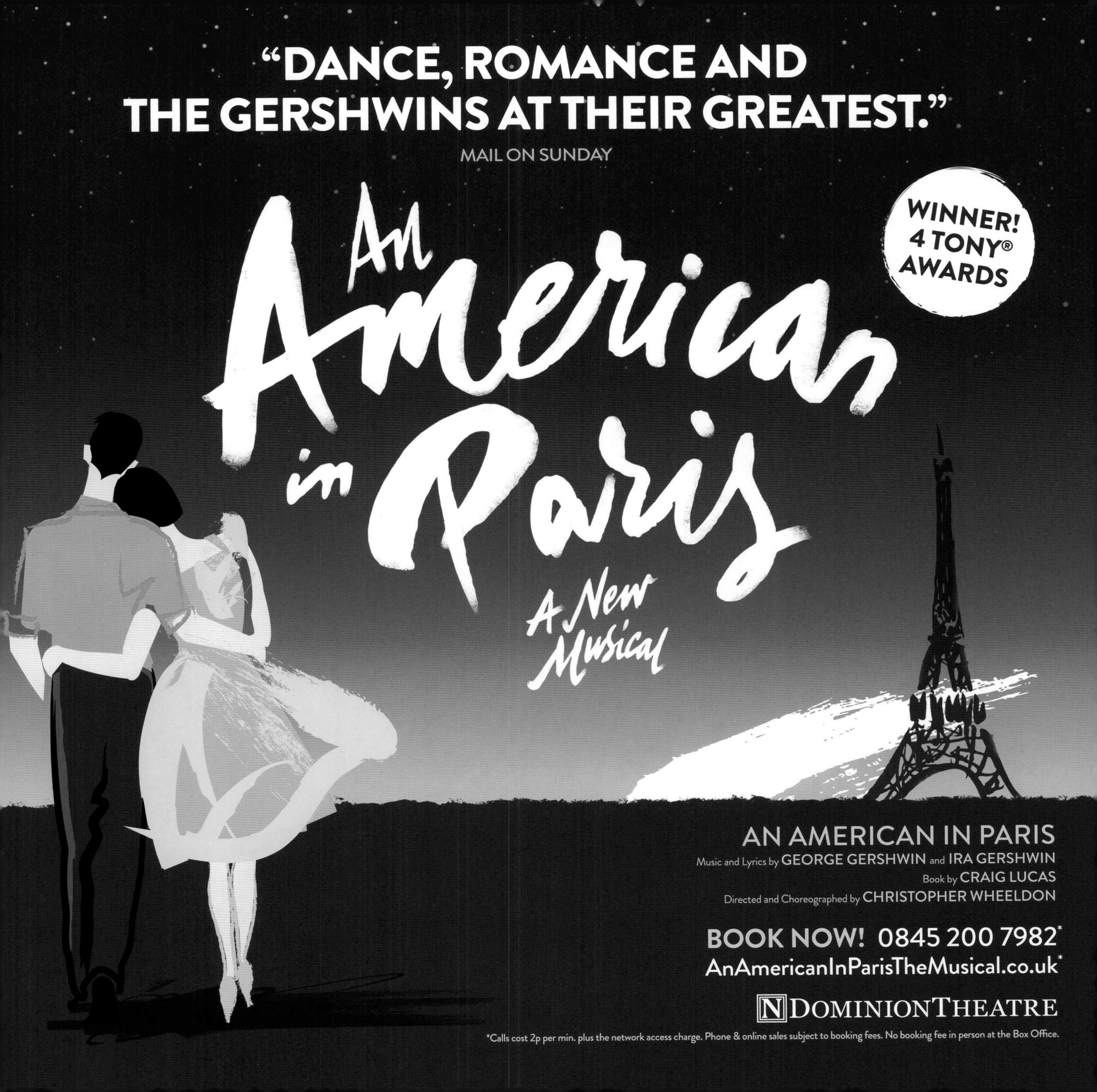
"DANCE, ROMANCE AND THE GERSHWINS AT THEIR GREATEST."
MAIL ON SUNDAY
WINNER! 4 TONY® AWARDS
An American in Paris
A New Musical
AN AMERICAN IN PARIS
Music and Lyrics by GEORGE GERSHWIN and IRA GERSHWIN
Book by CRAIG LUCAS
Directed and Choreographed by CHRISTOPHER WHEELDON
BOOK NOW! 0845 200 7982*
AnAmericanInParisTheMusical.co.uk*
N DOMINION THEATRE
*Calls cost 2p per min. plus the network access charge. Phone & online sales subject to booking fees. No booking fee in person at the Box Office.

RUSSIAN REVOLUTIONS

As the Proms marks 100 years since the October Revolution of 1917, **Gerard McBurney** explores how subversive, progressive and revolutionary ideals were reflected in the music of 20th-century Russia

History happens. But we can also make it happen, look at it from a distance or from close up, remember it vividly or vaguely, re-invent it, or simply be completely unaware of it, even when it swirls around us. If we want, however, history can be something we anticipate.

In Russia, 100 years ago or more, anticipation was a tempting option. As the long 19th century unfolded, the paralysingly inert Romanov empire seemed to many people destined to be overthrown in an act of dreadful violence. That's why they kept asking the same question made famous in the title of Nikolay Chernyshevsky's 1863 novel: *Chto delat'?* ('What Is to Be Done?').

In pre-revolutionary days, this question was posed by philosophers and dreamers, conservatives and revolutionaries, and chewed over by characters in novels by Dostoyevsky and Turgenev and plays by Chekhov. It was also reused by Lenin as the title of a pamphlet. No surprise, then, to find echoes of it also in music.

We can hear those echoes already in Mussorgsky (*Khovanshchina*, left uncompleted at its composer's death in 1881) and implicitly in the symphonies of Tchaikovsky (the Fourth, 1878, and Sixth, 1893, especially). But it was really in the so-called Russian Silver Age – approximately 1890–1920 – that a stark and simple question was transformed into an elaborate and almost mystical rhetorical trope surfacing all over the work of poets, novelists, playwrights, painters, choreographers and others.

The obvious musical example from that period is Stravinsky's and Roerich's self-consciously apocalyptic *The Rite of Spring* (1913), although it's often forgotten what an ambiguous piece that ballet really is. It looks backwards to a mythic, utopian, peasant past – and is in that sense deeply conservative and nationalistic – but also forwards to a violent and brave new world. That's why, despite Roerich's prehistoric village set and costumes, the original Nijinsky choreography and the Stravinsky score reminded many early listeners of modern cities and machines. What was clearest to everyone, though, was that the message of *The Rite* – from all three of its authors – was that only a violent cataclysm can ensure the world will be renewed and life will continue.

You can find quite different views of the same impending catastrophe in nearly contemporary works by Rachmaninov and Scriabin. Rachmaninov's 1902 cantata *Spring* sets visionary lines by the 19th-century writer Nekrasov, in which violence and disaster are averted by 'the humming of the green sound' of spring. More than a decade later, by the time of his Edgar Allan Poe-inspired symphony *The Bells* (1913, the same year as *The Rite*), Rachmaninov had changed his tune:

> *Hear ye the howl of the alarm bell?*
> *Truly groans a hell of bronze!*
> *These sounds of wild agony*
> *Tell a tale of horrors!*

Rachmaninov's erstwhile classmate Scriabin took another approach. Apocalypse, often with a heavily sexualised undertow, was the diminutive pianist-composer's post-Wagnerian stock-in-trade. Already in his *Poem of Ecstasy* (1908), he was using the instruments of the orchestra to dramatise his own decidedly overheated verse:

> *The universe*
> *Is embraced in flames …*
> *That which menaced*
> *Is now seduction.*
> *That which frightened*
> *Is now pleasure.*
> *And the bites of panther and hyena*
> *Are now caresses*
> *And the serpent's sting*
> *Is but a burning kiss.*

Seven years later, shortly before his death, with a World War raging and two 1917 Revolutions not far off, and with his vast and never-to-be-written *Mysterium* raging in his imagination, Scriabin issued a shocking proclamation:

> The masses need to be shaken. In this way they can be rendered more perceptive of finer vibrations than usual. How deeply mistaken it is to view war merely as discord between nations ... Upheavals, cataclysms, catastrophes, wars, revolutions, all these shake the souls of peoples and force them to perceive the idea hidden behind the outer event.

Understandably, Rachmaninov disagreed. His *All-Night Vigil* (*Vespers*), from the same year as Scriabin's grandiloquent announcement, ends with an appeal to the Virgin Mary: 'As you possess invincible might, set us free from all calamities!'

The moment when real revolution actually erupts – the economy in collapse, bullets flying, people dying – is not usually a good time to sit down to musical composition. But Prokofiev managed it. In May 1917, about 10 weeks after the February Revolution that ousted Tsar Nicholas and brought in the Provisional Government, Prokofiev noted in his diary:

> I returned to my dacha on the 10th to warm weather and the unequivocal arrival of spring ... [and] settled down to work: thinking out every last detail of the Violin Concerto [No. 1], an easy and pleasant task, and also, as I walked through the fields, composing the 'Classical' Symphony.

By September, as the political situation worsened, he was in an even better mood:

> Strolling through the countryside, I thought how beautiful was the northern autumn ... and with a light heart I savoured all the loveliness around me. Every five days or so I journeyed to the city ... to buy sweetmeats and English cigarettes.

He knew what his priorities were:

> The most significant event of this September was the composition of [my cantata] *Seven, They Are Seven*. I became engrossed in the work to the point of obsession ... My other occupation was reading Kant ... I also meticulously took cold-water showers with the window open.

In October, with still barely a thought to the tumult in Moscow and Petrograd (St Petersburg), Prokofiev set off for the warm south and a health resort in the Caucasus, where he worked on the lyrical slow movement of his Fourth Piano Sonata, gave piano recitals and dreamt of an operetta. Suddenly, just as he was about to return back north, reality got through to him, and he changed his plans:

Shostakovich addresses a meeting of the Communist Party of the Soviet Union in 1960. Whether his joining the Party was a free decision or the result of political pressure is unclear, but his membership was a prerequisite for his appointment by the government as General Secretary of the Composers' Union.

MUSIC AND REVOLUTION

An interpretation of the 'diabolical festivities and orgies' in Berlioz's *Symphonie fantastique* by Spanish-American artist Julio de Diego (1900–79)

The various connections between Western music and the great upheavals of history are tangled but fascinating.

For example, the 16th-century Protestant Reformation (*see also pages 26–31*) was obviously an outstanding revolutionary event, albeit of an unusual kind, and we can hear its multitudinous effects on the language of European music from the 16th-century English composers (for and against) right through to Bach. By contrast, the later English Cromwellian Revolution seems to have led more to musical suppression than encouragement, but its counter-revolutionary overthrow in 1660 and even more the Glorious Revolution of 1688 provided wonderful opportunities for Purcell.

It's curious that the American Revolution had so little effect on European composers, given that it was well talked about on both sides of the Atlantic, but there are hardly any echoes of it in serious music until Charles Ives. But this post-American silence was more than made up for by the immediate and noisy effects on composers of the French Revolution.

The great Viennese Classical masters were certainly all touched by it. The social tremors can be heard in Mozart's comedies, especially *The Marriage of Figaro*, based on Beaumarchais's notorious and subversive play and composed in 1786, just one year before the Revolution began. Haydn's two trips to London between 1791 and

1795 involved taking the long way round from Austria to England to avoid the fighting and his late symphonies and Masses echo with 'ancestral voices prophesying war' (interestingly, Coleridge's *Kubla Khan* itself was written in 1797). And nearly every music-lover can sense that Beethoven's most famous symphonies – and a lot of his other pieces too – are laced with revolutionary idealism and disillusion, both emotions centred on the emblematic figure of the age, Napoleon.

In Paris, during these years, actual revolutionary music flourished, with grand anthems, marches and cantatas for the innumerable open-air public ceremonies of the period. And these sometimes elephantine pieces laid the foundations for the more public works of Berlioz, especially his *Requiem* (1837), itself a memorial to the July Revolution of 1830.

Some Paris composers espoused a new genre: the 'rescue opera', which – depending on taste and occasion – could be revolutionary or counter-revolutionary. Cherubini's *Lodoïska* (1791) and *The Water Carrier* (1800) were hugely successful at the time, and even inspired Beethoven's *Fidelio* (1804–5, rev. 1806 and 1814; Prom 9, 21 July).

A little later came Auber's heroic opera *La muette de Portici* (1842), in which the main character's rousing cries of 'Aux armes!' are said to have detonated the Belgian revolution of 1830, rather as Verdi's 'Chorus of the Hebrew Slaves' from *Nabucco* (1842) was once said to have unleashed revolution in Italy just six years after the opera's premiere.

But perhaps the most famous and vivid depiction of revolutionary turmoil in the 1830s is Berlioz's *Symphonie fantastique* (Prom 7, 19 July). The last two movements of that piece, in particular, firmly established the idea of diabolical festivities and orgies as a cipher for the bloodthirsty chaos of modern revolution.

News of the Bolsheviks: their victories and vandalism are spreading all over Russia. Slaughter on the streets of Moscow. A shell has fallen on the apartment I would have been staying in. How clever of me not to have gone at all!

My state of mind? A strange serenity. I finished *Seven, They Are Seven* and began work on my new [piano] concerto.

And [then] it struck me there was no need to stay in Russia.

Go to America! Of course! Here, slaughter and barbaric rhetoric; there, cultivated life. Here, shabby concerts in Kislovodsk; there, New York, Chicago!

Unsurprisingly, repeated aftershocks of the Bolshevik Revolution can be traced down the history of Soviet music, from the bang of 1917 to the collapse of 1991. Probably the first really impressive orchestral response to the upheaval was the Sixth Symphony of Nikolay Myaskovsky, completed in 1923. A choral and orchestral epic, it was inspired by the composer's experiences of the post-Revolutionary Civil War, and – in its melancholy finale – by his memories of wild crowds in 1917 shouting revolutionary songs in the street, tunes which he skilfully interwove with a haunting chant of a traditional Russian village funeral:

What have we seen?
Wonder of wonders, a dead body,
The soul separating from the body,
Saying farewell to it.

Four years later, as the 10th anniversary of the 1917 Revolution approached, lamentations were not what the young Soviet government had in mind. More in the

A propaganda poster by Abram Lvovich Starchevsky (1896–1969) celebrating the 10th anniversary of the October Revolution

....

mood was the 21-year-old Shostakovich's experimental Symphony No. 2, 'To October', with its poster-like choral finale:

Struggle! You led us to the last battle!
Struggle! You gave us the victory of Labour!
Let all in this struggle be young and bold:
For the name of this victory is … October!

By the time of the 20th-anniversary celebrations in 1937, the situation was changed again, with show trials and the Great Terror in full swing, and strident modernism out of favour. Shostakovich's Symphony No. 5 dates from this terrible year but was given no overt connection to the occasion, although there

were those who heard an implicit, dark connection all the same.

Instead, it was left to the newly returned and cocksure Prokofiev to try to seize the public moment with one of his most ambitious and preposterous undertakings, his *Cantata for the 20th Anniversary of the October Revolution*. He threw everything he had at it: double chorus, four orchestras (including one for firearms, sirens and the tramping of a million feet of the victorious proletariat), an orator howling through a loudhailer, and an ear-popping text drawn by the composer himself from Marx, Engels, Lenin and Stalin. Alas, the result proved *too* ear-popping for the committee of commissars to whom the composer played and sang it ('very badly', according to his friend Myaskovsky), and this monster piece was summarily banned. Shostakovich is said to have commented: 'Prokofiev fell like a chicken into the soup.' The outraged senior official in charge of the case (who himself was shot, only a few months later) was blunter:

How dare you, Sergey Sergeyevich, take words which belong to the people and set them to this kind of music?

Wisely, Shostakovich took a more discreet course. Occasionally, he would announce a forthcoming massive choral and orchestral 'Lenin Symphony' (to be modelled on Beethoven's Ninth), but none appeared. For the 40th anniversary of the October Revolution in 1957, he produced his purely instrumental 11th Symphony, neatly deflecting the demands of the occasion by making it a memorial to the victims of the 1905 Revolution – and therefore presumably to victims of revolutions in general.

Shostakovich (*front, centre*) and Prokofiev (*front, far right*) photographed in Moscow in 1946 with other contemporary composers, including Dmitry Kabalevsky (*back, second from left*), Aram Khachaturian (*front, far left*) and Reinhold Glière (*front, second from right*)

In 1961, soon after Shostakovich had joined the Communist Party, he followed up with his dark and sinewy 12th, 'The Year 1917'. Finally, in 1967, for the Revolution's 50th anniversary he produced a short and little-known tone-poem, *October*. In between its noisy outer sections, it quietly quotes a patriotic song he wrote originally in 1937 for a film score, *Volochayev Days*, completed around the same time as his Fifth Symphony. The words make curious and ambiguous reading:

Where waters splash, where blue
*   horizons lie,*
Where the Pacific Ocean roars,
For the Motherland we gave our lives …

Our native country will remember us.
And in songs, comrade, the people will
*   write down*
Our names, yours and mine. ●

Gerard McBurney is a composer, arranger, broadcaster and writer with a special interest in Russian music. He was Artistic Programming Advisor of the Chicago Symphony Orchestra, of whose *Beyond the Score*® series he was Creative Director (2006–16).

Shostakovich
Symphony No. 10 in E minor
PROM 5 • 17 JULY

Shostakovich October
PROM 6 • 18 JULY

Stravinsky The Rite of Spring
PROM 28 • 5 AUGUST

Mussorgsky, orch. Shostakovich
Khovanshchina
PROM 29 • 6 AUGUST

Prokofiev Seven, They Are Seven
PROM 30 • 7 AUGUST

Rachmaninov All-Night Vigil (Vespers)
PROM 38 • 13 AUGUST

Shostakovich Ten Poems on Texts by
Revolutionary Poets – excerpts
PROMS AT … CADOGAN HALL, PCM 5
14 AUGUST

Shostakovich Symphony No. 12
in D minor, 'The Year 1917'
PROM 60 • 29 AUGUST

Prokofiev Cantata for the 20th
Anniversary of the October Revolution
Shostakovich
Symphony No. 5 in D minor
PROM 68 • 3 SEPTEMBER

Prokofiev
Violin Concerto No. 1 in D major
arr. Stravinsky
Song of the Volga Boatmen
Shostakovich Symphony No. 11
in G minor, 'The Year 1905'
PROM 71 • 6 SEPTEMBER

TO SING A NEW TUNE

As the Proms marks the 500th anniversary of the Reformation, **Paul Griffiths** investigates how Luther's rethinking of the church service resonated across the musical world, both within and outside of worship

Contrary to the popular image, Martin Luther probably did not decide one morning to bang up sheets of religious propositions on the doors of the castle church in Wittenberg. What he did, in October 1517, was publish his *Ninety-Five Theses* as a pamphlet, in Latin, because his intended audience was not the local townspeople but rather his fellow clergy far and wide, whom he was inviting to debate the topics with him. Yet the myth contains a grain of truth. Luther may not have nailed his theses to the church door, but certainly, with this pamphlet, he nailed his colours to the mast.

> 66 Luther aimed his theses at one particular abuse in religious life: the Church's sale of indulgences. 99

Also true to the case is the old story's dramatically public version of the event, with the populace craning to see what the young monk was putting on display. The Reformation was not the creation of one individual, however intelligent, charismatic and energetic (all of which Luther evidently was, if also woefully anti-Semitic). There was a general urge for the Church to change, a pressure coming as part of a still wider phenomenon – one to which we are heirs, and which we are in some respects replaying: a growing resistance to authorities and hierarchies in order to assert the full rights and status of the individual.

This great and continuing waterfall of all the old systems and certainties gave Luther the power to achieve as much as he did: a new religious dispensation in place across northern Europe by the time of his death, less than 30 years after he had published his theses, plus a translation of the Bible into German, together with new orders of service and hymn books, to which he contributed texts and perhaps also tunes. From the waterfall he engineered a river, which was to flow through – and partly shape – western culture over the next five centuries.

That may not have been what he had in mind in 1517. He aimed his theses principally at one particular abuse in religious life: the Church's sale of indulgences, or pardons, by which the purchaser would be let off a certain number of years in Purgatory and so whisked more swiftly to Heaven. You could buy indulgences for yourself or for your ancestors, and the newly prosperous tradespeople of the cities provided a ready market – a ready source of funds, therefore, to be channelled into the rebuilding of St Peter's in Rome. Thus was the work of Bramante and others realised by means of a continent-wide hoax.

Luther's challenge to this practice, for all his academic courtesy and his Latin, did not go down well. There were indeed debates, but the outcome for Luther in 1520–21 was denunciation by both the Pope and the imperial parliament, the Diet of Worms. A century beforehand, the career of the Bohemian priest Jan Hus had followed a similar course, ending rapidly in a heresy trial and execution by burning at the stake. Luther, however, had two advantages: he was protected by the ruler of Saxony, his home region; and there were now printing presses in practically every big city, so that his ideas were widely disseminated. There were also other Reformers at large, including his Wittenberg colleague Philip Melanchthon and, very soon in Switzerland, Huldrych Zwingli and John Calvin. Even if Luther had been eliminated, the river was unstoppable.

Luther saw it had to be controlled. The spirit of reform, insisting that each person could

Johann Gutenberg standing by a printing press with workers reading a proof sheet: Gutenberg's invention of the press in c1440 greatly impacted on the spread of ideas across Europe, including those underpinning Luther's Reformation

have direct contact with God through prayer and the Bible, risked letting loose religious and political anarchy; and, though Luther might have preferred each local church to come up with its own doctrines and forms of worship, he was obliged to participate in creating, within German-speaking territories, a national Church for what was not yet a nation. What he put forward as merely one possibility for the eucharistic ceremony, his *Deutsche Messe* of 1526, thus became the general standard.

If the new Church was becoming as orderly as the old, it still differed crucially in treating its adherents as readers and understanders. Printing brought Luther's translation of the

Bible, as well as his theological polemics, into the hands of the multitude. And, though the Mass in German lands had been partly worded in the language of the people for generations, the new services were entirely so. They were also celebrations enacted not by the priest for the people but by priest (renamed 'pastor', shepherd of the flock) and people together, addressed to God by a collective 'we'.

Accordingly, congregational singing of chorales (Lutheran hymns, *see panel opposite*) was these services' chief musical adornment. In composing chorales, Luther and his allies drew on sacred songs in German that already existed, on Latin hymns and on

folk songs, choosing, adapting or devising tunes that are strong, memorable and thereby well-suited to Luther's congregational understanding of worship. In parallel, Calvin adapted psalms to regular metres for congregational singing (a practice later emulated in Scotland), though his ban on musical instruments was to limit the development of music within the Calvinist tradition.

"In composing chorales, Luther and his allies drew on sacred songs in German, on Latin hymns and on folk songs. "

Luther, more positive on music's place, had no objection to polyphony, the first book of chorales set for several voices appearing in 1526. There is also a tradition that he himself would accompany chorale singing on the lute, though he could hardly have predicted the effect his nurturing of the chorale would have on music for another instrument: the organ.

Singing in Roman Catholic worship had been the province of the clergy and of regular choirs, well practised and requiring no instrumental support. The Lutheran congregation, by contrast, would have needed help, and help from something louder than a lute. Hence the importance in Lutheran churches, at least from the next century onwards, of the organ, to keep the congregation in tune and in time, and perhaps to remind them of the melody beforehand, a necessity out of which there developed the

LUTHER'S CHORALES

The hymn's the thing

'A mighty fortress': *Ein feste Burg*. The words were among those that came into Martin Luther's mind when, in the 1520s, he began writing hymns for the new Church then rapidly growing up around his tenets. For him the fortress was God, but the phrase could be applied equally to the whole body of hymns, or chorales, that he and his successors created: a mighty, invisible fortress of stirring words and tunes. The chorales, always in German, strengthened the identity not only of the Church but of the nation. Singing them, you belonged. Singing them, too, you were taking items of faith not just into your head but into your lungs and throat, not just learning the faith but embodying it.

Strictly speaking, the term 'chorale' applies only to the tune. Generally, though, the term is used for the whole hymn, words and melody combined. Luther and others of his time produced enough to fill the earliest hymn books, but Lutheran pastors went on composing chorale texts and tunes for a century after his death, to the time of Johannes Crüger in the mid-17th century. Crüger wrote some of the most cherished chorale tunes, including that for Martin Rinckart's poem *Nun danket alle Gott*, which, when Protestant hymn-writers in Britain and the USA began to discover their German heritage, in the 19th century, became 'Now thank we all our God'.

By Bach's time the repertoire was considered complete, at several hundred, a decent number of which Bach used elsewhere in his works. His church cantatas customarily end with a chorale verse sung in four-part harmony, and some offer much more thoroughgoing treatments of chorales, such as the cantata on *Ein feste Burg* (BWV 80), which includes all four of Luther's verses in different settings. Also,

chorales proceed as pillars through the Passion settings and feature strongly in Bach's organ music, notably his chorale preludes, where chorale tunes are couched in contrapuntal decoration.

If Bach's prolific and incessantly inventive use of chorales had no equal, *Ein feste Burg* in particular has had a notable history in the music of Handel, Mendelssohn (the 'Reformation' Symphony), Wagner, Debussy and Vaughan Williams, to name but a few. Other chorales feature in works by Berg (Violin Concerto), Hindemith (*Mathis der Maler*) and many more. Quotations, though, are the least of it. Bach's chorale settings provide examples of harmonisation that have been taught to student musicians for generations, fixing in their minds an image of chords in stout progression that, in the case of composers, is almost bound to recur in their works. In that sense, the progeny of the chorale is infinite.

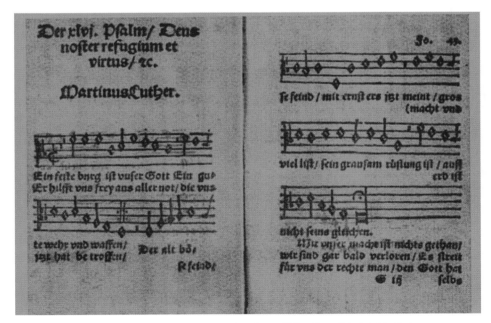

The notation of Luther's chorale *Ein feste Burg ist unser Gott*, from a 1533 edition of his *Geistliche Lieder* ('Sacred Songs') printed in Wittenberg

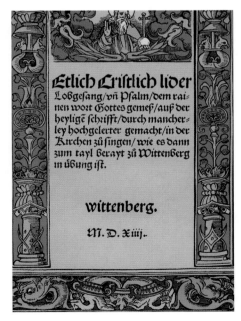

Title-page of the first edition of the first Lutheran hymn book, published in 1524 in Wittenberg

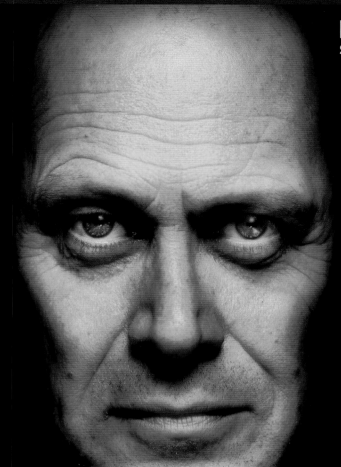

RSC
ROYAL
SHAKESPEARE
COMPANY

ROYAL SHAKESPEARE THEATRE
STRATFORD-UPON-AVON

WILLIAM SHAKESPEARE
JULIUS CAESAR

WILLIAM SHAKESPEARE
ANTONY & CLEOPATRA

WILLIAM SHAKESPEARE
TITUS ANDRONICUS

SEASON OPENS 3 MARCH

ROME
MMXVII

TICKETS FROM £16
WWW.RSC.ORG.UK

Supported using public funding by
ARTS COUNCIL
ENGLAND

Facsimile of a 16th-century engraving satirising the sale of indulgences, a practice that inspired Luther's reforms

chorale prelude as an organ fantasy on the tune. Unthinkable, therefore, without the Lutheran Reformation was the whole school of North German organist-composers, down through the generations to J. S. Bach.

Many of those composers, Bach certainly included, did not have to confine themselves to the organ loft, for the early emphasis on congregational singing had soon become supplemented by music for trained choirs. The chorales – sanctioned by Luther himself, and in some cases written by him – remained central, but, from the beginning of the 17th century onwards, they were elaborated in all kinds of ways, sometimes polyphonically, sometimes with their verses set for different combinations of choir, solo singers and instrumentalists. Starting at the same time, Lutheran musicians began creating settings of the climactic moments in the Gospel narratives, those of the Passion.

All this, too, was inherited by Bach, whose life in some respects followed the pattern of Luther's. Their birthplaces, Eisenach and Eisleben, are not only similar in name but also under a hundred miles apart. Less distance separates the city of Bach's longest residence, Leipzig, from Luther's Wittenberg. The two men were both Saxons, and in Saxony they largely stayed. They were both, also, vastly productive. And they were both not only founders but finishers of a tradition. Luther's Bible, Luther's services and Luther's chorales were to remain the foundation stones of Lutheranism, and Bach's immense musical achievement outfaced any successor.

Even though in modern times the music of Dietrich Buxtehude, from the generation before Bach, has begun to make its quieter way, Bach still represents the full musical flowering of Luther's Reformation. To Luther's Bible, Bach adds indelible illustrations, not only in his two Passions, recounting the story as given by St Matthew and St John, but also in many of the 200 cantatas he wrote for church services as contemplations on New Testament stories and promises, musical dramas of the soul.

As for the enormous edifice of Luther's theology, Bach brings to it a witness, an inhabitant. Luther was all about the individual's relationship with, and responsibility to, the Divine; Bach individualises the individual. The solo singers of his Passions and cantatas are people whose lives depend on the doctrines and events they are expounding.

Luther nailing his theses to the door of the church in Wittenberg, an act popularly taken to mark the start of the Reformation and the beginnings of Protestantism

They suffer and rejoice in accordance; they watch and pray. They are also people whose existence is grounded in the community of faith that expresses itself in the chorales punctuating almost all these works. Through Bach we can all, whatever our beliefs, hear the Reformation as our own. ●

A critic for over 30 years, including for *The Times* and *The New Yorker*, Paul Griffiths is an authority on 20th- and 21st-century music. Among his books are studies of Boulez, Cage and Stravinsky as well as *A Concise History of Western Music* and *The New Penguin Dictionary of Music*. He also writes novels and librettos.

Works by J. S. Bach and Schütz
PROM 25 • 2 AUGUST

Reformation Day
PROMS 47, 48 & 49 • 20 AUGUST

Works inspired by the Bohemian Reformation
PROM 56 • 26 AUGUST

See also works by J. S. Bach, orch. Stravinsky (Prom 24), J. S. Bach, orch. Bantock (Proms at … Bold Tendencies Multi-Storey Car Park, Peckham), Hindemith (Prom 33) and Mendelssohn (Prom 67)

Torker/private collection/Bridgeman Images (left); akg-images (right)

MAXIMAL MINIMALISTS

John Adams and Philip Glass (70 and 80 this year respectively) are often mentioned in the same breath as key figures of musical Minimalism, but **Pwyll ap Siôn** traces their independent journeys

Adams and Glass may have taken divergent paths down the road of Minimalism, but there are parallels between the two. Both made their mark on opera in the 20th century, producing arguably two of its most important works: Glass's genre-bending *Einstein on the Beach* (1975–6) and Adams's *Nixon in China* (1985–7). The latter was just as innovative as the former in its presentation of recent historical and political events on stage. Equally, both composers have embraced established musical forms – symphony, concerto and string quartet, for example. The orchestra has often served as a vehicle for some of their most ambitious and imaginative creations, often with the addition of choral forces, such as Adams's *Harmonium* (1980) and *El Niño* (1999) or Glass's symphonic cantata *Itaipú* (1989) and Symphony No. 7, 'A Toltec Symphony' (2004).

However, whereas Adams arrived early on at a distinct language based on the forms and structures of the Western classical tradition, Glass quickly moved away from these, to return much later on. Glass's musical upbringing and education – an unorthodox mix of traditional theory and unconventional practice – occurred against the backdrop of 1950s European Modernism. Composition lessons with William Bergsma and Vincent

Persichetti at the Juilliard School in New York (1958–62), followed by two years of intense study in Paris with Nadia Boulanger (1964–6), laid the foundations for a solid technique, rigorous discipline and keen musical ear. Soon enough, however, Glass realised that the music he was writing wasn't his: he was struggling to find his own voice at a time when young composers felt pressured to adopt the 12-tone techniques that had stemmed from Arnold Schoenberg.

The unlikely breakthrough moment for Glass came in 1966, when he was asked to transcribe sitar player Ravi Shankar's music for Conrad Rooks's psychedelic film *Chappaqua*. Through his sudden initiation into North Indian classical music (to which he would return when collaborating with Shankar on the 1990 album *Passages*) Glass was introduced to completely new concepts relating to rhythm, time, structure and musical perception. It forced him to rethink the musical elements that had been eschewed by the avant-garde, such as regular pulsation, repetition and consonance.

Upon returning to New York in 1967, Glass and fellow composer Steve Reich became part of a thriving, 'back to basics' downtown arts scene. A new aesthetic emerged, which favoured straightforwardly tonal lines instead

of chromaticism, harmonic consonance instead of dissonance, rhythmic and formal simplicity rather than complexity. Minimalism was born.

Musical Minimalism had already shed its more radical and uncompromising elements by the time Adams emerged on the scene in 1977 with his important solo piano composition *Phrygian Gates*. Glass's monumental *Music in Twelve Parts* (1971–4) and Reich's *Music for Eighteen Musicians* (1974–6) had by then seen the style metamorphose into a dynamic, dazzling musical language – visceral, vivid, colourful and capable of stirring the emotions too.

> ❝ Glass discovered his voice while tapping into non-Western traditions, while Adams drew on an eclectic mix of largely Western traditions. ❞

There was no need for Adams to wipe the slate clean, as Glass had done before him. The style was already fully formed. However, Adams also underwent a period of musical

HOW WE GOT INTO MINIMALISM AND HOW WE GOT OUT

Philip Glass disliked it ('the term doesn't describe the music well'), Steve Reich steered away from it and John Adams was at best circumspect towards it ('it's only a fraction of my musical life'): almost 50 years after first appearing in print, 'Minimalism' remains the go-to term when describing the music of Glass, Reich and Adams too – embracing anything from gentle, almost ambient sounds to driving, aggressive patterns and more besides. So how did we get into it in the first place – and is it time we got ourselves out?

The term didn't appear out of the blue. It was already established in the art world when critic turned composer Michael Nyman first applied it to music in 1968. Certainly, Minimalist art's aesthetic of radical simplification and reduction of materials rubbed off on Glass and Reich, who worked with artists such as Sol LeWitt, Donald Judd and Richard Serra, and whose music was often performed alongside exhibitions of Minimalist art.

With the publication of Nyman's book *Experimental Music: Cage and Beyond* in 1974, it seemed that Minimalism as a musical description was here to stay. Yet, by this time, Glass and Reich had moved on quite considerably. 'Minimalism' hardly encapsulates the sheer richness and diversity found in Glass's first opera, *Einstein on the Beach* (1975–6), for example.

Having emerged from an aesthetic movement and created its own musical language and techniques, Minimalism had come of age. So, if this music was no longer Minimalist, then what was it?

Some have adopted the term 'post-Minimalism' to describe the music of composers who, like Adams, have appropriated some of Minimalism's techniques without necessarily buying into its aesthetic *in toto*.

Given the influence of this important movement on the history of 20th-century music, are we all post-Minimalists now?

John Adams conducting at the BBC Proms in 2012

experimentation and self-discovery during the mid-1970s, before finding his own voice. Having enrolled first as a talented clarinettist and promising conductor at Harvard University, he received counterpoint lessons from David Del Tredici and studied composition with Leon Kirchner and Earl Kim – both of whom had been taught by Schoenberg – but he remained discouraged by the stuffy academicism that underpinned the new music scene of the time.

A more congenial creative milieu greeted Adams upon arriving at the San Francisco Conservatory in 1972, where he taught composition and conducted the New Music Ensemble in concerts ranging from Cage and Stockhausen to Machaut's *Messe de Nostre Dame*. The Mass was performed with an electronically generated soundscape assembled by Adams, much to the chagrin of early-music purists. Electronic music offered an escape route for the composer away from 12-tone serialism, and his 'waveform' concept of musical structure owes as much to synthesizer technology as it does to shapes and objects found in the natural world.

Adams's interest in combining tape and live performance can be heard in 'Christian Zeal and Activity' (the middle movement of his

1973 work *American Standard*), which draws inspiration from Gavin Bryars's *Jesus' Blood Never Failed Me Yet* (1971). But he soon fell under the spell of the emerging Minimalist aesthetic. In 1974 Adams organised a concert that included Reich's then-new *Music for Mallet Instruments, Voices and Organ* – one of the first performances of the work to be given by anyone other than the composer's own ensemble. Having grown up listening to jazz, Adams was immediately drawn to Minimalism's use of regular pulsation, tonal harmony and motivic repetition.

Adams has continued to draw on Minimalist style throughout his career, but to varying degrees. In his *Naive and Sentimental Music* (1997–8), the first two movements don't appear outwardly Minimalist, while the third ('Chain to the Rhythm', a cheeky allusion to Grace Jones's 1985 pop hit 'Slave to the Rhythm'), carries references to a whole panoply of Minimalist devices – ranging from Reich (*City Life*, *New York Counterpoint* and *Music for Mallet Instruments, Voices and Organ*) and Terry Riley (*In C*) towards the beginning, to Adams's own Minimalist fingerprint (the end of his *Short Ride in a Fast Machine* in the middle section), before co-opting Louis Andriessen into the stylistic jamboree for a final rallying cry featuring dirty hocketing brass. 'Chain to the Rhythm' acts as a kind of farewell symphony at the end of the 20th century to a musical style that provided Adams's music with much-needed sustenance over the years.

At the same time, Adams has identified certain weaknesses in the Minimalist aesthetic: 'I missed the shock of the unexpected, the possibility of a sudden revolution in mood

Chris Christodoulou/Lebrecht Music & Arts

or coloration,' he has said. Glass discovered his voice while tapping into musical forms and structures of non-Western traditions, while Adams was more willing to find his voice by drawing on an eclectic mix of largely Western traditions that ranged from the orchestral music of Mahler, Debussy, Ravel and Charles Ives to Minimalism via jazz, pop and other forms of vernacular music.

A comparison between Adams's choral-orchestral *Harmonium* (1981) and Glass's third opera *Akhnaten*, composed two years later, reveals some of these differences. In *Akhnaten*, every scene forms a self-contained building block upon which the opera's entire edifice is constructed. Once established, the overall mood and tone of each scene never vary. Dynamic changes occur between, rather than within, these block-like sections. The effect is like standing in front of an enormous monolithic structure or edifice;

Ravi Shankar (*left*) and Philip Glass (*second left*), working on their collaborative record *Passages* at Living Room Studios in New York on 27 April 1990

or maybe, since this is an opera about an ancient Egyptian pharaoh, one of the country's imposing pyramids.

On the other hand, in *Harmonium*, Adams generates large architectonic structures through musical waves that rise and fall, creating a series of overlapping peaks and troughs. Even in the very opening of the first song, 'Negative Love', which gives the impression of near-stillness, the music is seldom static. It slowly comes into being from near-silence – even words are gradually formed from the stuttering syllables of 'never' and 'nothing'. Rather than the dark, menacing shapes that impel the music in *Akhnaten*, short repeating patterns are combined in 'Negative Love' to create a shimmering effect, like tiny ripples on the surface of a lake. It takes Adams almost the same amount of time to get to the first line of Donne's poem as it does for Glass to finally wrench away from the grip of A minor in the prelude to his Egyptian opera (around four minutes), but in 'Negative Love' the music evolves as if from nothing in front of our very eyes. As Adams notes, the music is 'brought to life and impelled forwards by an inner pulse and by a constantly evolving wave-like manipulation of the surface texture'.

For Glass, his musical language has remained largely fixed, and his aim is often to explore the various possibilities that arise from this language: to draw from a large pool of ideas and patterns that provide him with an infinite set of meta-variations. Adams's musical language exists in a more fluid state. Of course, each composition possesses Adams's own fingerprint, and there are certainly works (such as *The Chairman Dances* or the *Doctor Atomic Symphony*) that rework previous

ideas (in those two examples, from the operas *Nixon in China* and *Doctor Atomic* respectively). However, in the spirit of the American pioneer, Adams continues consciously to push the boundaries in his music, exploring previously uncharted areas in the hope that they will reveal new musical pathways.

Adams and Glass have clearly arrived at different destinations, but there has been some fascinating overlap in their chosen routes. ●

Pwyll ap Siôn is Professor of Music at Bangor University, and has published a number of books on Minimalist music. Last year he was the recipient of a Leverhulme Research Fellowship on the music of Steve Reich. He writes regularly for *Gramophone* magazine.

Adams at the Proms

Harmonium
PROM 1 • 14 JULY

Naive and Sentimental Music
PROM 24 • 2 AUGUST

Harmonielehre
PROMS AT ... BOLD TENDENCIES MULTI-STOREY CAR PARK, PECKHAM 26 AUGUST

Lollapalooza
PROM 69 • 4 SEPTEMBER

Lola Montez Does the Spider Dance
PROM 75 • 9 SEPTEMBER

Glass at the Proms

Passages (composed with Ravi Shakar)
first complete live performance
PROM 41 • 15 AUGUST

THE FIRST LADY OF SONG

As the Proms celebrates the centenary of the birth of jazz singer Ella Fitzgerald, **Stuart Nicholson** charts the evolution of her career, from taking part in talent contests in Harlem to becoming one of the most celebrated artists of the 20th century

Ella Fitzgerald lived to sing. It was the focus of her whole being, sustaining her at the top of her profession for seven decades. Her vocal style, widely admired for its purity of tone, clarity of diction, harmonic imagination and a highly refined sense of swing, is still universally acknowledged as a touchstone of musical excellence. Few artists have ever been admired so unanimously – for example, the great Dietrich Fischer-Dieskau, one of the most famous Lieder singers of the 20th century, having just given a recital in Washington DC, rushed to the airport and took the first plane to New York to hear Ella perform with Duke Ellington at Carnegie Hall on 6 April 1958. 'Ella's singing with Duke,' he exclaimed, as he rushed past startled well-wishers after his recital. 'You just don't know when there may be a chance to hear her do that again!' To paraphrase Robert Graves, Ella Fitzgerald was really very good, despite all the people who said she was very good.

Today, Ella is best remembered for her incomparable *Song Book* series, part jazz art-song and part personal artistic statement.

Comprising eight albums recorded between 1956 and 1964 that included such classics as *Ella Fitzgerald Sings the George and Ira Gershwin Song Book*, *Ella Fitzgerald Sings the Cole Porter Song Book* and *Ella Fitzgerald Sings the Rodgers and Hart Song Book*, the series reawakened songs from the canon of the Great American Songbook in a way that proved hugely successful to a wide public. In so doing, Ella enhanced her artistic stature in a way that has proved timeless – today, any singer contemplating material by the likes of George Gershwin, Cole Porter, Jerome Kern or Harold Arlen instinctively turns to Ella's versions to listen and learn.

Ella Jane Fitzgerald was born out of wedlock on 25 April 1917, in Newport News, Virginia. Within four years, her mother Tempie had responded to stories then rife in America's southern states of better employment and housing prospects in the northern urban centres and had moved to the city of Yonkers in New York State. After her mother's unexpected death in a road accident in 1932, Ella was almost certainly physically abused by

her stepfather, an incident that might help to explain the low self-esteem that haunted her throughout her life. Running from harm's way, she sought her fortune on Harlem's streets, entering talent contests for small cash prizes, culminating in winning the Apollo Theater's famous Amateur Nights on 21 November 1934. There she was spotted by Charles Linton, then vocalist in drummer Chick Webb's Orchestra, who persuaded Webb to add her to the band. In no time her easy swinging style had connected with the bobby-soxers and jitterbugs, earning her the nickname 'First Lady of Swing'.

In 1939 Webb died and Ella's career stalled. She continued to front the band into the 1940s, but wartime restrictions triggered the demise of the big bands, and so Ella was out on her own touring seedy dance halls and dingy nightclubs in a segregated America that still tottered on the racial divide. Her lifeline was a recording contract with Decca and, when producer Milt Gabler took over her career, her fortunes took off. Gold record followed Gold record and, while it's true many were novelty numbers with

LOVE
MUSIC
HELP
MUSICIANSUK

Knowing I had the support
of Help Musicians UK was
incredibly reassuring during a
volatile and unpredictable time.

Your support means we can help
more musicians like Oli make
the transition from student to
professional.

Donate at helpmusicians.org.uk
or call 020 7239 9100

Backing musicians throughout their careers.
Registered Charity No. 228089

the likes of Louis Armstrong, Louis Jordan, the Ink Spots and the Delta Rhythm Boys, several sides, such as 'Lady, Be Good', 'Flying Home', 'How High the Moon' and 'Lullaby of Birdland', were out-and-out jazz performances, where it was clear she had been listening to the latest jazz craze, bebop. As a result she was invited to tour with the newly formed big band of trumpeter Dizzy Gillespie, which culminated in their Carnegie Hall debut on 29 September 1947. Subsequently, their affection and regard for each other as a result of touring together lasted their lifetimes – their musical relationship acknowledged in this year's Proms tribute featuring singer Dianne Reeves and Australian trumpeter James Morrison.

" The mere mention of Ella's name was enough to sell out concert halls around the world. "

In 1949 Ella, now known as 'The First Lady of Song' after swing went out of fashion, was invited to join impresario Norman Granz's Jazz at the Philharmonic, a novel idea that brought together jazz stars of the day onto the concert hall stage in informal jam sessions. Granz recorded the concerts; the success of the records boosted the concerts and the success of the concerts boosted the records. By the time Ella joined the venture as star of the show, it had been going for five years and was a hugely popular attraction in America. In 1953 the JATP troupe were among the first American jazz musicians to tour Japan and were greeted by a ticker-tape welcome in Tokyo, such was their popularity.

In 1955 Granz took over the management of Ella's career, forming Verve Records to feature her, and she debuted on the label with *Ella Fitzgerald Sings the Cole Porter Song Book,* which became one of the most popular recordings of 1957. The *Song Book* cycle established Ella as an international star. Never happy unless she was working, she toured extensively for the greater part of each year, the mere mention of her name enough to sell out concert halls around the world. In Europe she would often play two cities in one night, her capacity for work astonishing all around her. As one musician who toured with her for years observed, 'Her marriages have failed, she doesn't have an awful lot of the normal activities most women have, such as home life, so she wraps herself up entirely in music. She wants desperately to be accepted.'

Ella's final concert was at Michigan Music Hall in the autumn of 1992. A journey that had begun in wretched poverty ended in Beverly Hills luxury in her $2 million pink-washed, Spanish-style mansion on 15 June 1996. In her own unassertive way she had defied the expectations of a black person in a predominantly white society; she had endured discrimination with dignity but gave herself equally to black and white audiences, who took her into their hearts. One of the most celebrated artists of the 20th century, she had collaborated with the very best artists in jazz and popular music, from Louis Armstrong to Duke Ellington and from Frank Sinatra to Nat King Cole, had been feted by the rich and famous and been presented to heads of state. She topped countless prestigious critics' and readers' polls, not just once or twice but year after year, was presented with the Presidential Medal of Freedom and National Medal of

Ella Fitzgerald and Louis Armstrong during a recording session at the Decca studios in New York in 1950

Arts, and was the recipient of 13 Grammy Awards, plus several honorary doctorates from America's top universities. She appeared in four Hollywood feature films, sold over 40 million albums and performed for tens of thousands of delighted fans night after night, year after year. One of the great and enduring figures of 20th-century music, she once said, 'It isn't where you've come from that matters, it's where you're going to that counts.' And, if anyone could embody that simple motto through a realisation of the American Dream, then it was that enigmatic, self-effacing lady known around the world by one simple word, Ella. •

Stuart Nicholson has written eight books on jazz, including acclaimed biographies of Ella Fitzgerald, Billie Holiday and Duke Ellington. His journalism has appeared in magazines and newspapers all over the world. He is Visiting Professor at Leeds College of Music.

Ella and Dizzy: A Centenary Tribute

Dianne Reeves *singer*, James Morrison *trumpet*, BBC Concert Orchestra, John Mauceri *conductor*

PROM 27 • 4 AUGUST

OPEN TO ALL

With the introduction of the first Relaxed Prom – offering an informal atmosphere suitable for people with a wide range of sensory and physical challenges – **Suzanne Bull MBE**, Chief Executive of Attitude is Everything, reveals the benefits of relaxed performances

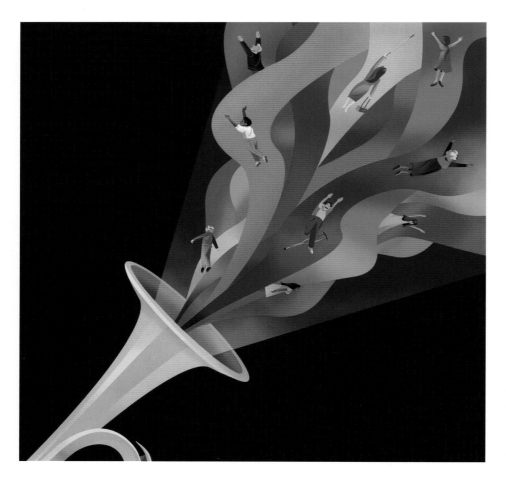

Everyone should have the right to enjoy the arts in a way that is accessible and inclusive to them. While 3.6 million disabled people in the UK attend live music events each year (DCMS *Taking Part* survey 2014/15), there are many people who are still not engaging with the arts due to the barriers they face. Increasingly, theatres, cinemas, music venues and festivals are recognising the value of 'relaxed' events designed to address the issue of this 'missing' audience.

A 'relaxed' concert is designed to provide a comfortable environment for all audiences, with a focus on seeking to include children and adults with autism, sensory and communication impairments and learning disabilities.

Relaxed concerts welcome people who might need to move about, or make noise, during a performance. The underlying philosophy is that people should be empowered to act naturally during a performance, free of the restrictions and barriers that might result from 'regular' rules of concert etiquette. A relaxed concert embraces diversity and allows people to express their enjoyment in their own unique way. So it's no surprise that they tend to be joyous, fun, celebratory occasions that create a valuable experience for everyone attending.

The Relaxed Prom to be performed by the BBC National Orchestra of Wales on 29 July is designed to be inclusive and is for all of the family to enjoy, with simple changes, such as auditorium doors being left open to facilitate coming and going, alongside dedicated 'chill-out' spaces to enjoy away from the action.

The Relaxed Prom will also provide a bespoke pre-event pack with venue and facilities information, as well as background information on the music and the performers. The orchestra will wear colour-coded shirts according to the instrumental groups. Each piece will be introduced from the stage by conductor Grant Llewellyn and musician Andy Pidcock, who will encourage audience participation. There will also be picture communication systems projected on large screens during the performance.

The BBC National Orchestra of Wales has been delivering an extensive Learning and Outreach programme for more than 20 years, featuring inclusive activity for children and young people with autism, sensory and communication impairments and learning disabilities, as well as individuals who are Deaf, deafened and hard of hearing. But the Relaxed Prom is a first for the orchestra in terms of its scale and it's an event that excites Suzanne Hay, the orchestra's Head of Partnerships and Learning. 'We are passionate about finding new ways of making music inclusive,' she says. 'This concert offers an accessible introduction to the orchestra in an atmosphere that is fun, relaxed and welcoming.'

Access to performance is central to the organisation that I lead, Attitude is Everything, which helps break down the barriers that prevent Deaf and disabled people from accessing live music. There are now over 125 venues and festivals which have been awarded Bronze, Silver and Gold awards on our Charter of Best Practice, including the Royal Albert Hall. In recent years we have worked with the BBC Proms to implement best-practice queueing systems and provided access consultancy for Proms in the Park.

The BBC Proms and BBC National Orchestra of Wales in partnership with the Royal

Anyone for owl ice-cream? Audience members enjoying a relaxed performance of *The Gruffalo* in Mousetrap Theatre Projects' 2015 production at the Lyric Theatre in London's West End

Albert Hall Education & Outreach team have joined a small but growing number of music venues and promoters that have started to incorporate relaxed concerts and performances. Charter venues include the Liverpool Philharmonic, Wigmore Hall, The Lowry, Brighton Dome and Nottingham Theatre Royal. The classical music world is embracing this new model of performance, with Orchestras Live's current Sound Around project including a tour of six relaxed concerts in 2016–17.

An important aspect of a relaxed concert is that everyone attending is aware of what to expect. The prospect of experiencing a classical concert in a relaxed environment is appealing to many people beyond the core target audience, which is why the event is open to anyone who wishes to experience an orchestral performance in this type of informal setting. The Relaxed Prom aims to be a rich, enjoyable and fun experience for everyone. ●

Suzanne Bull MBE is CEO of Attitude is Everything, which works in partnership with audiences, artists and the music industry to improve Deaf and disabled people's access to live music.

Relaxed Prom Including the *Doctor Who* theme, Pharrell Williams's 'Happy' and classical favourites

PROM 19 • 29 JULY

Suitable for children and adults with autism, sensory and communication impairments and learning disabilities, as well as individuals who are Deaf, hard of hearing, blind and partially sighted.

For more information about access at the Proms, see pages 162–168.

FROM SEED TO FRUITION

In recent years, American cellist Alisa Weilerstein has championed new cello works by Osvaldo Golijov, Lera Auerbach and Joseph Hallman, and at last year's Proms presented Matthias Pintscher's *Reflections on Narcissus*. This summer she gives the UK premiere of *Outscape* by Pascal Dusapin. In interview with **Helen Wallace** she describes her two-year journey with the work, from project proposal to world premiere

MAY 2014

I hear from the Chicago Symphony Orchestra that they're commissioning a cello concerto from French composer Pascal Dusapin, and he wants to write it for me – which is thrilling. I don't know his music at all, so I listen to everything of his I can find, including the beautiful violin concertos and his first cello concerto, *Celo* (1996). I find in his music a perfect combination of cerebral drive and emotional directness: there's real substance to hold onto but, equally, the music has a special language and an ethereal, spiritual quality.

SEPTEMBER 2014

I start receiving emails from Pascal, saying he's listened to practically every note I've recorded – even files on YouTube that I probably haven't even heard myself! He has a wonderfully flamboyant way of expressing himself.

MAY 2015

Pascal and his wife come along to a performance I give in Paris of Dvořák's Cello Concerto. We connect immediately; he's a kindred spirit: passionate, curious and imaginative – the music is the man. He's almost completed the concerto and I learn that it will form the second part of a cycle about nature, which started with *Morning in Long Island* (a BBC co-commission given its UK premiere at the 2011 Proms), inspired by a sleepless night he spent at the beach in winter.

JULY 2015

Two months have gone by since that Paris concert, but it seems to have made an impact. Pascal confides in me that, when he heard me play the Sarabande from Bach's C major solo Cello Suite as an encore, he decided to change the concerto's ending completely. Right before the conclusion there's a really wild, extremely virtuosic passage and it was going to end that way. Now he's brought the music down and marked it 'calm and a little sad', inspired by the solemn quality of the Bach. (I later learn just what a powerful, almost tragic, ending he generates by doing this.)

AUGUST 2015

He's finished the concerto, and explains that it's called *Outscape:* he wanted the cello to be escaping the orchestra, finding its own nature – it's almost overwhelmed but then flees and follows its own path. It's a fascinating idea. He was thinking of a concept related to the poet Gerard Manley Hopkins's idea of 'inscape' in nature I'm longing to make this drama a reality.

SEPTEMBER 2015

The score arrives by email and Pascal's publishers send me a hard copy. I begin by looking at it away from the cello, absorbing the orchestration, the harmonic language, so I can get a feel of the character and atmosphere. I love reading scores – I've no desire to become a conductor, but I can hear everything in my head. The solo part is very virtuosic, but also exploits the instrument's lyrical, expressive voice. It's almost neo-Romantic in that it's emotionally very open, yet its orchestration and language are absolutely of today. It's structured as a very long *crescendo* that turns into something quite wild and frightening … After taking it all in, I start going through the mechanics of my part – the notes, the choice of fingering and strings. I integrate it into my own practising until it becomes part of me.

MARCH 2016

It's normally impossible for me to focus on just one piece, but I'm expecting my first baby

Down-time: taking a break during recording sessions for her CD of cello sonatas by Rachmaninov and Chopin with pianist Inon Barnatan (Teldex Studio Berlin, November 2014)

at the end of the month, so have the luxury of having a little more time without any concerts immediately ahead of me. I give my last public concert at 35 weeks and then have a few weeks at home to go through the score. I'm huge and uncomfortable, but I have that most precious resource, time.

I give birth to my daughter (31 March)! My husband (conductor Rafal Payare) and I name her Ariadna. When I go back to practising, I play Bach and Dusapin – two bookends of my repertoire to put my playing back together again.

MAY 2016

I leave Berlin and fly to Chicago. Ariadna sleeps on my chest all the way over. *Outscape* will be the first piece I perform since her birth. I start rehearsing with Cristian Măcelaru: the

players of the Chicago Symphony Orchestra are so fantastic we are able to play the whole concerto through the first time. Of course, there are details to be worked out, but this is an exhilarating start. *Outscape* will always be connected in my mind with the heightened atmosphere of the time: the birth of a new piece, and I'm suddenly living a completely new life. I have my daughter with me backstage. It makes it so intense in the most wonderful – and challenging – way.

JUNE 2016

Fortunately, five concerts were lined up in Chicago, so performances got progressively more comfortable. The first is always harrowing, and you can't necessarily bring out everything you want to, because we're all on our toes, but by the third things settle and

Cello by
Matthew Hardie
Edinburgh c.1800

F.N. Voirin, Paris, c.1875-78

Cello by
Joseph Hill, London
c.1770-1780

Eugene Sartory
Paris, c.1930

Tom Woods

LONDON'S DEDICATED CELLO SHOP -
IN THE HEART OF THE WEST END
www.tomwoodscellos.com
+44 (0)20 7362 1812

Nicolas Leonard Tourte
Paris, c.1785-80

Cello by
Albert Caressa
Paris, c.1926

Victor Fetique, Paris, c.1925

Cello by
Louis Guersan
Paris, c.1760

I am far freer. I imagine the piece in four continuous movements, with the third being the most intimate. Here the cello seems to be protesting in a very private way, crying out against the deep, mournful bass and cello sounds. I want as much freedom as possible, but, of course, that can only happen if everyone feels free. We get there in the end and I feel it really makes musical sense.

AUGUST/SEPTEMBER 2016

When I look back at those days in May, I can't wipe the smile off my face. It was the greatest feeling to integrate my life as a new mother with my artistic life. I always planned to do it, but I didn't ever fully believe it could happen.

Now I've come to Stuttgart to give the European premiere of *Outscape* with Markus Stenz and the Stuttgart Opera Orchestra. We have more time to rehearse and I know the concerto better now, so we can go further. We've been able to work on the balances, and bring out more subtleties, producing intensity through detail. This is infinitely flexible music; both performances are valid. It's a strong, expressive piece and I feel both audiences have reacted warmly: there has been a real sense of engagement.

FEBRUARY 2017

After Stuttgart I put *Outscape* away. I like to let things leaven and then come back to them afresh with a new perspective. Inevitably it's growing in my subconscious. Meanwhile, I've been working on a new concerto dedicated to me by Matthias Pintscher, *Un despertar* ('An Awakening'), which I'm premiering in March with the Boston Symphony Orchestra. It couldn't be more different to Pascal's piece. Whereas in

'An exhilarating start': Alisa Weilerstein performing in the world premiere of Pascal Dusapin's *Outscape* with the Chicago Symphony Orchestra in May last year

Outscape Pascal wants the cello 'to sound like a cello' – which I really appreciate – Pintscher is pushing it to extremes. It's a big challenge and very exciting. There's room for both approaches with this chameleon-like instrument. I'm lucky to be performing right now, when there's an outpouring of new concertos and so many extraordinary colleagues able to play them. It's a great moment for the cello.

APRIL 2017

I'm about to give the French premiere of *Outscape* with Susanna Mälkki and the Orchestra of the Opéra de Paris, which will be a very significant moment for Pascal. I'm so much looking forward to reprising it again in the summer at the BBC Proms, with the BBC Symphony Orchestra – and my younger brother, Joshua, conducting. It's always a joy to work with him; he's so natural and professional, a special conductor and a great accompanist. And a hop to London is no big deal for Ariadna now: she's flown to 12 countries already and is excited to get on a plane! ●

Helen Wallace is a music critic, writer and broadcaster, and Creative Consultant at Kings Place Music Foundation.

Pascal Dusapin Outscape
BBC co-commission with the Casa da Música Foundation (Porto), Chicago Symphony Orchestra, Opéra de Paris and Stuttgart Opera: UK premiere
Alisa Weilerstein *cello*
PROM 7 • 19 JULY

Erin Hooley/Chicago Tribune

DARKNESS AND LIGHT

As all three of Elgar's symphonies appear at the Proms – including Anthony Payne's haunting completion of the unfinished Third – **Stephen Johnson** considers how personal insecurities and emotional grey clouds contributed to these works, whose moods range from the fleet-footed to the funereal

No composer's symphonies have suffered more radically different fates than Elgar's. When, after long struggles, Elgar presented his Symphony No. 1 to the world in 1908, it was cheered to the rafters, hailed internationally as 'the first great British symphony' and performed nearly a hundred times in its first year of existence. Three years later, its successor landed with a dull flop. According to Elgar, the audience 'sat there like stuffed pigs', and the critical response ranged from lukewarm to hostile – one even accused the composer of 'pessimism and rebellion'.

Two decades after that, in 1932, following a long creative silence, Elgar began work on another symphony, but only about half of it was sketched by the time of his death in 1934. Those surviving fragments were routinely dismissed – they were incoherent, sad reworkings of old, stale ideas, it was claimed – until in 1997 the composer Anthony Payne showed just how wrong the detractors were *(see panel overleaf)*. What's now routinely referred to as the 'Elgar–Payne Symphony' is still performed all over the world, and the widespread verdict seems to be that it equals the first two in power and originality.

> 66 In their very different ways, each of Elgar's three symphonies reflects the paradoxes of the man with a special intensity. 99

So how does Elgar's symphonic 'cycle' look, after that startling posthumous 50 per cent growth? Well, for a start, the three symphonies

are all clearly products of the same creative mind. Fortunately it is no longer quite so necessary to argue that Elgar was, behind the carefully crafted Edwardian gentlemanly mask, a very complicated man. In his darker moments he recalls the leading character in Ford Maddox Ford's novel *The Good Soldier* (1915), another 'Edward' – outwardly a distinguished, charismatic, upstanding military man, who turns out to be both tormented and destructive to others, 'romantic' in the worst, self-deluding sense, and who ends up committing suicide. Elgar never quite got that far but, according to his wife Alice, he was 'constantly talking of making an end of himself'. Mystifyingly to others, Elgar's bouts of despair and self-hatred would sometimes follow his greatest successes, like the First Symphony's spectacular triumph. That may well be a symptom of some kind of mood-disorder, evidence for which has been presented by several specialists. Winston Churchill's notorious 'Black Dog' – the term he used to describe his depression – certainly made a point of circling Elgar and, when it did, no amount of success, or of repeatedly avowed loyalty from his many friends, could appease the sense of isolation and emptiness that possessed him.

In their very different ways, each of Elgar's three symphonies reflects the paradoxes of the man with a special intensity. They are perhaps the most complete, all-embracing self-portraits he ever composed. Elgar's sense of humour could be delightfully spontaneous, but it could also disguise complex truths. When asked about the strikingly original structure of his First Symphony, Elgar stated breezily that it began as a kind of wager. A friend, he said, had challenged him: 'Bet you can't write a symphony in two keys

Queen's Hall, London (c1905), where Elgar's First and Second Symphonies received their London and world premieres, respectively, in 1908 and 1911; the hall was also home to the Proms from 1895 to 1941

at once.' Talk of key relationships in music can be tedious even for musicians, but in the case of Elgar's First Symphony the two-key – it's tempting to call it 'bipolar' – aspect is as much about emotional character as about abstract symphonic concepts such as form and development. The First Symphony begins and ends in the key of A flat, with a theme Elgar aptly described as conveying 'massive hope'. It is both shamefully and gloriously Edwardian and English, opulent and grandly ceremonial – the effect rather as if the Knights of the Grail from Wagner's *Parsifal* were processing into the House of Lords.

But between these two splendidly heraldic statements comes some of the most restless, impassioned, turbulent and at times heart-achingly nostalgic music Elgar ever created. The 'glad, confident' (another Elgar description) mood of the First Symphony's start and finish is more like a misleading frame: the 'Once upon a time …' and '… happily ever after' of a deeply unreliable narrator. The fact that the symphony spends more time in the remote key of D than in its purported 'home key' heightens the sense of two spiritual worlds in seemingly irreconcilable conflict. Yet somehow the symphony's sweeping energy – its intricate, arc-like overall structure, transcending its seemingly conventional four-movement layout – gives the impression that it is possible to hold both extremes in a kind of dynamic balance. Elgar the man may have been unable to reconcile his inner conflicts, but as a composer he shows that he could at least compel them to coexist. It's one of the things that make this symphony so fascinating and exhilarating: neither side 'wins' – or, as Beethoven put it in an enigmatic little note on the manuscript of one of his songs, 'Sometimes the opposite is also true.'

After the First Symphony's stunning overview, the apparent discontinuity of Symphony No. 2 can be unsettling, even disappointing for the newcomer. It isn't just that the individual movements – and especially the enigmatic finale – are precisely that: 'individual', seemingly apart from each other. There are also strange changes in emotional perspective within each of the four movements. The first springs into being like a greyhound out of the trap, bounding forwards with a typically Elgarian rhythm, repeated obsessively for page after page of score. It's one of those features of Elgar's symphonic thinking that, in an unsympathetic performance, can become wearyingly repetitive but, when played with understanding, takes on a quality the composer-conductor Oliver Knussen has described as 'flying'. It sounds as though, as

the composer claimed, it was written 'at fever heat'. But, for all Elgar's airborne exuberance, there are moments where he can't help looking down anxiously, if only for an instant. Then, when the energy is allowed to flag, as flag it surely must, out from the shadows stalks what Elgar compared memorably to 'a sort of malign influence wandering thro' the summer night in the garden'. The luxurious nocturnal beauty is all there, but so too is the menace. Is this also a self-portrait? In one of his worst Black Dog moments Elgar speculated that his own 'influence' on others was 'only for evil'. Extreme, of course, but clearly rooted in *something* authentic.

Later, at the heart of the second movement's nobly elegiac funeral music, comes another moment of discontinuity. A solo oboe is directed to play in its own free tempo, as though independent of the sombre ceremonial tread. One voice stands out, lost and lonely, amid all the trappings of collective mourning. Then, in the rondo third movement, comes a passage which in some performances can be genuinely terrifying. Amid the prevailing mercurial humour and wistful lyricism, the first movement's 'malign influence' theme returns on full brass, massively underlined by pounding percussion. Elgar compared this to a nightmarish episode in Tennyson's poem *Maud*, in which a would-be suicide imagines himself buried alive beneath a road, where horses' hoof-beats pound 'into my scalp and brain'. How are we supposed to relate this to the contentedly strolling theme that begins the finale, or the attempted re-evocation of the First Symphony's 'massive hope' in the more substantial theme that follows? The answer is, we can't. Did Elgar ever fully intend us to do so? There are more enigmatic, shadowy moments, but none more disquieting than the

Nigel Luckhurst/Lebrecht Music & Arts

FINISHING THE UNFINISHED

Twenty years after its first performance, composer Anthony Payne looks back at his completion of Elgar's Third Symphony

Two decades after completing Elgar's Third Symphony, do I still take pride in it? Absolutely! It sounds arrogant but, if people ask me if there's anything I'd like to change, I say, 'No, I got it pretty well right!' There are no moments where I think, 'Oh God, if only I'd done that differently.' I still find the whole thing exhilarating. I remember when I went to the first rehearsal, I knew the sound of it would blow me away, and it did. It still does. I've reckoned up how much of the overall music is by me, and it's around 50 per cent – not including the orchestration. The biggest challenge was the ending. Elgar left no clue as to how to finish the symphony, so I had to work out where it was going emotionally. Using his 'The Wagon Passes' from his late *Nursery Suite* as a model – that marching that fades up and down – made sense to me then, and it does now too. Afterwards I was seriously worried about whether I'd be able to be myself again as a composer after spending 18 months inside Elgar's head. But my own voice came back very quickly. I felt like I'd been an actor acting the role of Elgar, who then had to throw it all off. Fortunately for me, it worked.

exquisitely scored return of the symphony's opening theme at the end – a theme Elgar characterised with a quotation from Shelley: 'Rarely, rarely comest thou, Spirit of Delight!' Recalling a theme from an earlier movement ought to enhance the sense of connection, integration; instead, this return actually undermines it. At the same time, it is music that manages to say both 'Delight' and 'Rarely'. Like his idol Schumann, Elgar is often at his most heart-breaking when he seems to smile. Whatever the meaning of the Shelley reference, the Second Symphony seems in the end to confront the First's breathtaking determination to balance internal contradictions and view it from a wiser, altogether sadder perspective.

And perhaps something similar could be said of the Third Symphony in relation to the Second. Here Elgar throws his embrace wider than in either of the two previous symphonies. We hear familiar Elgarian heroism and love music in the first movement, enhanced and transformed in the historically aware 'chivalric' music (partly derived from a theatre score for a play about the legendary British King Arthur) in the finale. The slow movement – the central gemstone of the Third Symphony – is perhaps Elgar's greatest tragic statement, Anthony Payne's own brilliant creative contribution notwithstanding. As a confrontation with imminent mortality, its poignantly incomplete ending (it's definitely the ending, Elgar said so!), and still more the silence that follows, compare in effect with the devastating silences at the start of the finale of Mahler's 10th Symphony – another incomplete masterpiece that cries out to be heard.

Yet before that soul-scouring slow movement comes something that is just as much Elgar as

General Charles Gordon ('Gordon of Khartoum'), whom Elgar initially considered celebrating in his First Symphony, before deciding against any external narrative or influence

anything else in this score: a delicate, soft-voiced second movement that Elgar labelled 'in place of scherzo'. This is the lighter Elgar, creator of what he called 'woodland magic', the weaver of childhood dreams. We have never heard his voice in a symphony before – or at least not so clearly or extensively. His strange little parting gesture, a kind of vanishing on the instant into 'airy nothing', may not be as devastating as the slow movement's ending, yet it seems like another take on the same notion, another kind of farewell: wistful rather than tragic. To go back to that Beethoven quotation, both opposites are true, authentic Elgar.

He remains paradoxical even to his last breath – or, in this case, breaths.

The Third Symphony's actual ending is pure Anthony Payne: Elgar left no clue as to how the finale was to finish. For a long time Payne felt that this was the effective end point, beyond which even as a composer he couldn't go. But I remember meeting Payne while he was near to completing his 'performing version' of the Third Symphony. It was the mischievous look that came into his eyes when he told me, 'I've got an idea …'. I felt then that this was the kind of thing Elgar himself might have said when something stupendous occurred to him at the very last minute. Payne's hushed final bars subtly recall both the second and third movements' gestures of farewell before allowing the march-rhythms that provide the impetus for so much of Elgar's music to fade into silence. For complicated, tormented souls like Elgar, death can also be the 'consummation devoutly to be wished'. If Elgar proved incapable of penning that ultimate resolution in music, Anthony Payne has done it for him with a tender, magisterial empathy for which we, as listeners, can be profoundly grateful. ●

Stephen Johnson is the author of books on Bruckner, Mahler and Wagner, and a regular contributor to *BBC Music Magazine*. For 14 years he was a presenter of BBC Radio 3's *Discovering Music*.

Symphony No. 1
PROM 2 • 15 JULY

Symphony No. 2
PROM 4 • 16 JULY

Symphony No. 3 (sketches elaborated and completed by Anthony Payne)
PROM 51 • 22 AUGUST

NATURAL
REFLECTION

Should the classical music world do more to represent the rich ethnic mix of the wider population, and how organic should the process be? Classical music programmer **Toks Dada** surveys the situation

I magine a country devoid of everything that makes each of us unique. A country devoid of different racial backgrounds, sexual orientation, religions or beliefs. For most people, this is impossible to conceive, because it couldn't be further from reality. In fact, an examination of census data between 1991 and 2011 reveals the country is becoming increasingly diverse – already in the city of Leicester, no single ethnic group accounts for more than 50% of the population, and a number of other towns and cities are well on the way to becoming similarly 'super-diverse'. However, despite the UK population being on a road to greater diversity, its classical music industry continues to struggle to reflect this.

In a recent article for *Classical Music* magazine, I talked about how tokenism solves nothing, and how reflecting the country's ethnic variety should be business as usual. In an industry lacking diversity, it is all too easy to get excited when a musician, artist or producer from an under-represented ethnic minority emerges onto the scene. However, unless this is underpinned by talent, the perception is that individuals are progressing for the wrong reasons. The classical music world is built on excellence and, in the quest for diversity, it is important never to lose sight of that. Yet that's easier said than done. So how can the industry get to a point where diversity is not sporadic but commonplace, while still maintaining artistic standards?

The answer begins with actively seeking out talented performers and ensuring access to opportunity. One person accepting this challenge head-on is Chi-chi Nwanoku, founder and Artistic Director of Chineke! – Europe's first orchestra of BME (Black and

Chineke!, a new orchestra formed entirely of Black and Minority Ethnic players, makes its Proms debut this summer

Minority Ethnic) musicians, which performs in the Late Night Prom on 30 August – but, as she has found out, this is by no means an easy task. When establishing Chineke!, Nwanoku faced resistance from a small handful of BME musicians who felt that the orchestra was 'too exclusive' and that favouring individuals from minority ethnic backgrounds was not the best approach to encouraging diversity. In a recent conversation with Nwanoku, we talked about whether more needed to be done to communicate what Chineke! was trying to achieve. 'The purpose of Chineke!,' she explained, 'is to change perception about who can and who can't play at a world-class level in classical music. In our concerts so far, the players have represented no fewer than 35 different nationalities.' Furthermore, she openly acknowledges that, when Chineke! has truly achieved its mission, there will no longer be a need for it to exist.

This declaration of Chineke!'s purpose reminded me of the contrasting views I witnessed in interviews given by a (white)

classical musician and a (black) rap artist. They were the same age, from the same city, yet the contrast between their experience of their city's major concert hall was stark. 'To me, it's just … for the rich. I know it sounds bad, but … it's something that's never really stuck out to me as my kind of music,' the rap artist revealed. As a non-white person with no personal experience of my ethnicity being a barrier to my progression in the classical music industry, these words stuck with me, but it took a while for me to understand what was really meant here: there is a lack of role models. If people feel they can't relate to the artists on stage, this explains why it's so difficult to create ethnically diverse audiences.

As Nwanoku observes, for years orchestras have been producing education programmes (in schools with a high ethnic mix) in order to tackle this. However, in her experience, the orchestral members being asked to front such initiatives are drawn from the same palette. 'We live in such a visual world,' she says, 'and people of certain nationalities and

certain colours don't see themselves in the classical music world. You can't underestimate the power of a role model!' One rising role model of note is the cellist Sheku Kanneh-Mason, winner of the 2016 BBC Young Musician competition and a member of the Chineke! orchestra; he also appears as soloist with Chineke! at this year's Proms.

The decision to feature Chineke! as part of this internationally renowned festival is exactly the kind of thinking that is needed in order to provide a platform for 'specialist groups' of under-represented musicians. As David Pickard, Director of the BBC Proms, explains, the decision to include Chineke! – which he made following the BBC Diversity and Inclusion Conference in Manchester last year – was not altogether straightforward. 'They need to be viewed as an orchestra that has earned its place and is not here because of tokenism. I invited Chineke! because of the quality of the music that it makes. We wouldn't be doing anybody a service by bringing in anything other than a first-rate orchestra.' As a member of the Steering Committee for the Conference, I was adamant that positive outcomes be produced rather than an 'all-talk, no-action' result, which can too easily be the case with such conferences. So the announcement at the conference that BBC Radio 3 – reflecting diversity goals across the BBC – would not only reappraise its commissioning process but also commission a new work for Chineke! from a talented BAME (Black, Asian and Minority Ethnic) composer not previously commissioned by the station was welcomed by many. This new commission – by Hannah Kendall, a composer with British and Caribbean roots – will receive its premiere at Chineke!'s Late Night Prom, but what is perhaps even more

Excellence
in Education & Music

- Excellent, diverse music programme
- Outstanding chamber music, ensembles and choirs
- Consistently high academic results
- Generous music scholarships
- Academic scholarships and bursaries
- Choice of A Level or IB Diploma

An independent school for girls aged 4-18

Jazz vocalist Dianne Reeves, who appears alongside trumpeter James Morrison in a tribute marking the centenaries of Ella Fitzgerald and Dizzy Gillespie

important is that the programme will see Chineke! playing the same kind of repertoire performed by other orchestras – as opposed, for instance, to repertoire specifically referencing black history. Complementing this new work, baritone and composer Roderick Williams (of Welsh and Jamaican parentage) will write a new work to be performed by the vocal group I Fagiolini at the first concert in the 'Proms at …' Cadogan Hall series.

While ensuring that groups of under-represented musicians performing or composing Western classical music are featured on a level playing field with other professional ensembles, it is also important for the Proms to reflect a range of musical traditions outside of the Western classical canon. This year, the festival includes a Late Night Prom referencing three key Indian classical music traditions: the Hindustani tradition from North India, the Carnatic tradition from South India and Sufi classical

music from Pakistan. The Prom reflects on the 70th anniversary of India's independence from British rule and the partition of India. Elsewhere, the music label Stax Records and the 50th anniversary of the Stax Volt European Revue Tour is celebrated with a Late Night Prom, featuring Jools Holland and his Rhythm and Blues Orchestra, showcasing the Southern Soul that grew out of Memphis in the 1960s and 1970s. Also referencing this period is a concert celebrating composer, bandleader and bass player Charles Mingus, who combined the deep traditions of jazz with the radical spirit of black music in the 1950s, 1960s and 1970s. There will also be a Prom marking the centenaries of both Ella Fitzgerald and Dizzy Gillespie, featuring a host of jazz musicians performing with the BBC Concert Orchestra. David Pickard rightly believes that 'the Proms needs to be representative as well as a pinnacle of excellence' and, while the Proms can't do it all – as Chineke! and a number of like-minded organisations and initiatives are proving – important steps forward are being taken.

The emergence of specialist groups is often seen as a boon to diversity in the sector. However, even if there have been clear achievements in establishing a specialist group, what can result is not diversity across the sector as a whole, but a concentration of diversity in just one part of it. A true representation of society exists when you have a mix of individuals from a variety of backgrounds all coexisting on the same stage. To that end, this year sees the formation of the BBC Proms Youth Choir Academy, an ongoing project that will annually bring together 50 children from very different musical backgrounds. The Academy members will receive intensive tuition before performing as part of the BBC Proms Youth

Choir in John Adams's *Harmonium* at the First Night.

This type of integrated performance is not new to the Proms, as was demonstrated by last year's appearance of the Able Orchestra as part of the Ten Pieces II Prom. This orchestral project enabled young people with a variety of physical disabilities to perform on equal terms alongside their more able-bodied counterparts, and is another example of how the industry can change perception of what a modern-day orchestra looks like. In addition it is important for young people to see that opportunities exist for them at all levels of the industry. A case in point, in February 2017 the British Paraorchestra – the world's first professional ensemble for disabled musicians – performed at Symphony Hall in Birmingham combined with members of the City of Birmingham Symphony Orchestra.

The challenge moving forwards is to cultivate as much integration of this kind as possible, but this requires a cross-industry effort that includes venues, producing companies, funding bodies, performers, academic institutions and policy-makers, working in partnership to create pathways for the most talented artists. Then, as an industry, we'll all be on the same road towards diversity becoming commonplace. This road is unlikely to be free of obstacles, but it will be a journey taken together. Imagine, if you will, a thriving classical music industry with a dynamic mix of racial backgrounds, gender, age, sexual orientation, religions and beliefs. This simply reflects the country we live in and so, surely, our industry can look like this too. ●

Toks Dada is a Classical Music Programmer and Creative Producer. He is the Programme Co-ordinator for Classical Music at Town Hall and Symphony Hall in Birmingham and a Board Director of Welsh National Opera.

Jerris Madison

LAUREL B. LAWSHAE

violinist and teacher

I live in Texas in the USA but I've been a Proms regular since 2013. I first came to the UK with my husband on summer holiday that year – initially to visit Cornwall, as a fan of the TV show *Doc Martin* – but I knew about the Proms and wanted to go to some concerts in London. I have made it to the Royal Albert Hall every year since then. I have to be up at 3.00am local time in Texas to buy tickets online when booking opens, but it's worth it – the Proms is the highlight of my summer in the UK. The high level of music-making and the variety of concerts every year is fantastic.

AT THE MOMENT I'M ENJOYING ...

Music by the Norwegian composer Ola Gjeilo. I have performed some of his pieces with choirs and I find his compositional style at times serene and other times highly energetic. His harmonies are rich and often gently dissonant and I think his music is simply beautiful.

MY MOST RECENT MUSICAL 'DISCOVERY'

Benjamin Britten's *Gloriana*. I was not familiar with this opera but I had the opportunity to perform in it last summer. I love the variety of musical styles, from Elizabethan dances to contemporary tunes, and I learnt more about British history too!

MY PROMS HIGHLIGHTS

I had heard many stories about the West–Eastern Divan Orchestra from a Syrian colleague who has played with the group, so I was excited to hear the orchestra at the Proms last year. There was such chemistry between Daniel Barenboim and the musicians, and Martha Argerich also played splendidly. You could have heard a pin drop during the four-hands piano encore from Argerich and Barenboim – it was mesmerising.

THOMAS NETTLE

music student

I study cello at Wells Cathedral School and I've always been a big fan of the Proms – I can't remember it not being part of my life! For the past five years I've bought the BBC Proms Guide on the day it comes out – I go through the listings with great excitement. In 2015 I went to about 13 concerts but last year I really beat that with 40 Proms! I had a Gallery season ticket and my parents (who are both musicians) came to some with me, but mostly I was on my own. I love the variety that's available at the Proms, not just different genres but so many different types of classical music too.

AT THE MOMENT I'M ENJOYING ...

Berg's opera *Lulu*, which I recently went to see in London. It's the first serial composition I've got to know well. I'm really enjoying exploring a vast array of contemporary music, composers such as John Adams, Philip Glass, Nico Muhly, Steve Reich and Max Richter, and I've been lucky enough to see recent productions of Philip Glass's *Akhnaten* and John Adams's *The Gospel According to the Other Mary*.

MY MOST RECENT MUSICAL 'DISCOVERY'

Stravinsky's *Pulcinella*. Despite people telling me how great this piece was, I had never actually listened to it until it was performed at the Proms last year. I thought it was wonderful and I've now persuaded my teacher to let me learn Stravinsky's *Suite Italienne*, which is an arrangement of movements from *Pulcinella*.

MY PROMS HIGHLIGHTS

There are so many concerts to choose from: my dad loved the Quincy Jones Prom and my mum enjoyed Bartók's *Duke Bluebeard's Castle*, but my highlight was last year's performance of *Boris Godunov*. It was my first opera at the Proms and I think it's really great that you can go and see an opera for just £6, in London, with such an amazing cast and orchestra.

Dare to believe.

BIRMINGHAM CONSERVATOIRE

THE FUTURE OF MUSIC EDUCATION

We're investing £57 million into a world-class teaching and performance facility, the first of its kind in the digital age.

Take a virtual tour of our new building, opening in September 2017.

bcu.ac.uk/new-conservatoire-tour

Birmingham Conservatoire will have facilities unrivalled in the UK

Our new jazz club will be Birmingham's only dedicated jazz venue

New 500 seat concert hall, one of five performance spaces

Birmingham City University

LSO

2017/18 Concert Season
This is Rattle
Bernstein Centenary
New Music Britain
The Essential Debussy
Choral Masterworks
lso.co.uk/alwaysmoving

ALWAYS
MOVING

CITY
LONDON

Supported using public funding by
**ARTS COUNCIL
ENGLAND**

barbican

Resident
Orchestra

London Symphony Orchestra

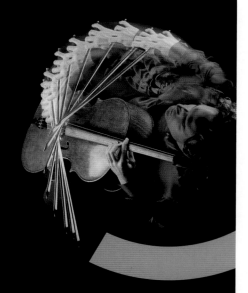

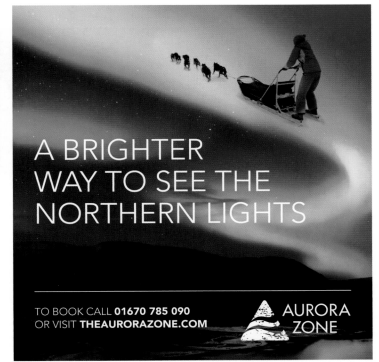

NEW MUSIC

Proms founder-conductor Henry Wood's passion for new music has remained at the heart of the Prom s over its 122-year history and the festival continues to bring new musical discoveries. **Tim Rutherford-Johnson** introduces this year's world, European, UK and London premieres from the British composers continuing that tradition in the 21st century

The name Charles Kenningham may not be on the tip of every music-lover's tongue, but he holds a unique place in the history of British music. When, partway through the first First Night of the Proms on 10 August 1895, Iver McKay stood up to sing Kenningham's song 'Since thou hast come', a tradition began of showcasing contemporary British music that has become one of the hallmark features of the BBC Proms.

Kenningham – better-known in his time as a singer with the D'Oyly Carte Opera Company – may have made only a modest contribution to that tradition, but the roll-call of world premieres of British music at the Proms since then is impressive and includes, for example, Benjamin Britten's Piano Concerto (1938), Ralph Vaughan Williams's Symphony No. 5 (given a moving wartime performance in 1943 by the London Philharmonic Orchestra, under the composer), Peter Maxwell Davies's *Worldes Blis* (1969), a work whose expressionistic intensity is perhaps unmatched in all British music, and John Tavener's *The Protecting Veil* (1989), whose enormous success (both at its premiere and on a subsequent recording) would establish its composer as one of the most popular of the late 20th century.

This year's Proms festival features world, European, UK or London premieres by British composers including Julian Anderson, Kerry Andrew, Sir Harrison Birtwistle, Tom Coult, Jonathan Dove, Brian Elias, Cheryl Frances-Hoad, Hannah Kendall, Sir James MacMillan, Mark Simpson, Mark-Anthony Turnage, Judith Weir and Roderick Williams. I spoke to them – some while their pieces were still in a very early stage of realisation – about what the Proms has meant to them personally and to British musical life in general. Sir James MacMillan's exclamation was typical: 'The Proms represents a jewel in the British musical crown! It is universally admired and it is always a thrill for a composer to have his or her work featured in this festival.'

The special pleasure of a Proms performance comes down to two things in particular. The first is the venue itself. 'In some ways the Royal Albert Hall is tricky,' says Julian Anderson, referring to its cavernous size and awkward acoustic – much improved today on how it used to be. 'But I adore the sound all the same – it's perhaps my favourite concert venue in the UK – and there's no doubt that this kind of festival belongs in that kind of

building. Even on the radio, as soon as you hear the audience hubbub you know you're in a very particular place indeed.' Anderson's Proms commission this year, a piano concerto for Steven Osborne, is a sequence of movements taking the piano on an imaginary journey into a series of different resonant spaces, such as a cave, a rainforest, a cathedral and even the Royal Albert Hall itself. These locations are reflected in the changing textures for both soloist and orchestra.

The Hall, in all its Victorian strangeness and grandeur, makes an appropriate setting in another way for Mark Simpson's *The Immortal*, receiving its London premiere this season, following its first performance at the Manchester International Festival in 2015. Simpson describes his oratorio as a 'kind of musical seance', based on the life and death of the 19th-century occultist Frederic Myers. A founder of the (still active) Society for Psychical Research, Myers was thought to have communicated from the grave through a number of mediums situated throughout the world and their incoherent transcriptions of his supposed post-mortem communications form the basis of Simpson's libretto, co-compiled with the author Melanie Challenger.

Another new oratorio coming to the Proms is *In the Land of Uz*, by Master of the Queen's Music, Judith Weir. The work takes its title from the opening phrase of the Book of Job – 'perhaps the strangest and most beautiful book of the Bible', according to the composer – and follows its story over the course of 30-plus minutes. The whereabouts of Uz itself is somewhat mysterious: it is mentioned several times in the Bible, yet historians have long debated, but never agreed on, what modern-day land it may correspond to. In contrast to Simpson's swirling, feverous maelstrom of sound and text, however, Weir applies the lightest of touches. Besides the BBC Singers, she uses just six instruments (organ, viola, double bass, soprano saxophone, trumpet and tuba), introducing them only occasionally and usually as soloists in their own right.

Voices feature in two more major works, both receiving their first European performances. MacMillan's *A European Requiem* is not a political work (it was completed a year before the referendum), but a reference to the 'spiritual, moral and artistic patrimony' that defines Europe for him – what Pope John Paul II called 'a Europe of the spirit'. Written for baritone and counter-tenor soloists, chorus and orchestra, it draws inspiration from the symphonic *Requiem* style of the 19th century, exemplified by Brahms's *A German Requiem*, as well as the conflicts between revolutionary violence, God and secular tyranny expressed in Beethoven's *Missa solemnis* and Poulenc's *Dialogues of the Carmelites*. In so far as MacMillan has chosen the text of the Requiem Mass to voice his feelings about Europe, 'there may indeed be a case that European civilisation now requires a *Requiem* and maybe that which made Europe "Europe" in its fullest spiritual sense can be reborn.'

Sir Harrison Birtwistle at work at his home in Wiltshire

Mark-Anthony Turnage's *Hibiki* also addresses themes of consolation, loss and recovery, but from a very different cultural standpoint. The work was commissioned by the Suntory Hall in Tokyo and first performed there in November last year. Its title comes from the Japanese word for 'beautiful sound', and the work makes reference to the earthquake and devastating tsunami that struck north-east Japan in 2011 (three of the movements are named after areas particularly affected by the tsunami: Iwate, Miyagi and Fukushima). A children's chorus and settings of Japanese poetry for soprano and mezzo-soprano soloists add to what will surely be an emotionally charged evening.

Not all new works are written on such a large scale: one of the strengths of the BBC Proms's programming is its variety. Jonathan Dove and Cheryl Frances-Hoad are both contributing miniatures to what promises to be one of the more unusual and intriguing events of the season. Prom 47 on 20 August celebrates the music of J. S. Bach and once more the Hall will take centre-stage, in the form of its famous organ. As well as organ music by Bach himself, the concert will feature excerpts from the Orgelbüchlein Project, a 21st-century 'completion' of his intended compendium of chorale preludes for the church year, which Bach is believed to have begun in 1713. In the event, Bach only wrote 46 of the 164 pieces he set out to include: the Orgelbüchlein Project, curated by organist William Whitehead, has spent the past few years commissioning an international roster of composers to finish the missing 118. Those by Dove and Frances-

Betty Freeman/Lebrecht Music & Arts

Hoad will be receiving their first performances here, alongside a handful of others from the project and Bach's originals.

The music of three British composers – Tom Coult, Hannah Kendall and Roderick Williams – is appearing in the Proms for the very first time. 'It's completely thrilling,' says Coult, whose piece *St John's Dance* will open the First Night of the Proms. 'It's a very nice thing to tell people outside the classical world. Also, my mum's been wanting me to be in the Proms for ages, so she's very excited!' Kendall, whose piece for Chineke! was untitled when we spoke, shares that sense of excitement: 'Many of my earliest experiences of being exposed to classical music were through attending the Proms. It feels particularly special to now be having my music performed on such an incredible platform.' As a performer, baritone Roderick Williams is a little more familiar with the Royal Albert Hall, having sung in 16 previous Proms. Although his new piece for I Fagiolini will be performed at Cadogan Hall, the challenge of the RAH he tells me, shared by performers and composers alike, is 'simply to make an impression on that vast space'. Coult is preparing for his moment by reviewing old Proms broadcasts, 'watching as the conductor comes on, the lights go down on this amazing space, hearing the silence, then pausing the video and thinking, "What would I do to puncture that silence?"'

The second special quality of the Proms that was mentioned by every composer to whom I spoke is its audience – distinct from that at almost any contemporary music event in the world. 'Like a rare bird that comes in the summer but you don't know where it goes in the winter' is Sir Harrison Birtwistle's

characterisation. Birtwistle himself – whose *Deep Time*, receiving its UK premiere in Prom 4, returns to the subject of geological timescales explored previously in *The Triumph of Time* and *Earth Dances* – claims to write only the pieces he wants to write, not pieces to order for specific occasions. 'I wouldn't know how to do it,' he laughs. Brian Elias shares the same view. His Cello Concerto, intricately constructed but lyrical in tone, will join a list of others by British composers to have featured at the Proms in recent years, including Graham Fitkin and Huw Watkins. Yet, despite the special privilege of writing for the Proms, which Elias calls 'a cause for celebration and hope', when it comes to composing itself, 'of course one puts all that aside'.

Other composers find their efforts enlivened by the prospect of such a large, attentive and generous listenership. Dove refers to the great fortune of having a new piece appear within a mainstream concert programme. 'It's the largest audience that you can have at a live classical music event – that in itself is enormously gratifying, to be listened to attentively by so many people. I think they come with high hopes,' he adds. 'The Prommers in particular have invested a lot of time in queuing to get in and so several hours before the concert they are already gearing up for it!' Frances-Hoad and Simpson, among the younger composers featured in this year's Proms, both credit performances in previous Proms seasons with greatly increasing their exposure and prospects.

Part of this affection for the audience comes from the fact that most British composers have grown up with the Proms; they have been members of the audience themselves, often for many years. Everyone has a story about their first encounter. 'I started going

Hannah Kendall, leading a Proms Extra Inspire Session for young composers at last year's BBC Proms

around the age of 9 with my mother,' Turnage tells me. 'She was obsessed with Beethoven, so it would always be an all-Beethoven Prom.' Weir remembers a formative hearing of Boulez's *Le marteau san maître*, conducted by the composer – a remarkable 1968 concert that also featured Proms premieres of works by Berg, Messiaen and Stockhausen.

After speaking to so many British composers about their love of the Proms, I feel that it is Anderson who gets closest to what it means to write for this remarkable festival: 'I feel that I know the Proms very, very well. I feel very close to the best aspects of the Proms audience,' he tells me. 'It's the kind of audience that I feel I can take anywhere. They've always been prepared to follow whatever I've thrown at them or wherever I've taken them. And with my new piece I'm going to take them some pretty strange places, I should think.' •

Tim Rutherford-Johnson is the author of *Music after the Fall: Modern Composition and Culture since 1989*, and editor of the *Oxford Dictionary of Music*.

THREE DEBUT COMPOSERS AT THE PROMS

LAURENT DURUPT (born 1978)

Like many composers of his generation who grew up around the turn from analogue to digital media, French composer and pianist Laurent Durupt is fascinated by the sounds and expressive capabilities of mechanical recording technologies. Occasionally this is reflected in his titles, such as the 2013 string octet *Super8* (named after a film format developed in the 1960s); at other times it is more implicit, as in the hour-long *Hip Hop Algorithm* (2015) for percussion, viola, trumpet, keyboard, turntables and electronics. *Audioportraits,* a radiophonic self-portrait, uses the studio itself as an instrument, foregrounding its processes and technologies: microphone technique, editing and mixing. It ends with a 'report from the recording studio' that features a range of heavily treated sound-sources, from footsteps to a mobile-phone ringtone. When acoustic instruments are present – as they are in many works, including his new piece for the Van Kuijk Quartet – they are also rethought from first principles, highlighting often hidden sonic qualities over melodic or harmonic potential.

Although Durupt has a taste for dry, percussive sounds, his music draws vigour and warmth from its high-tempo rhythms and many pieces recruit his percussionist brother Rémi. One such is *Studi sulla notte* for prepared piano, percussion and electronics, presented at a festival at the Villa Medici, where its mechanical poetics drew a hip Roman crowd to dance outside the Renaissance palace as the skies darkened overhead.

MISSY MAZZOLI (born 1980)

Appropriately for a resident of New York City, Missy Mazzoli frequently writes robust music that is on the edge of falling apart. In her own words, *Magic with Everyday Objects* (2007) is 'a piece about finding rapture and beauty in the midst of chaos'; *Still Life with Avalanche* (2008) is 'essentially a pile of melodies collapsing in a chaotic freefall'; and the 2013 work *Sinfonia (for Orbiting Spheres)* (to be heard in its orchestral version at this year's Proms) 'churns and rolls … transforming the ensemble into a makeshift hurdy-gurdy flung recklessly into space'. Like the crossing tides of traffic and pedestrians at a Manhattan intersection, it's not always clear how it all holds together: the key is the music's sturdy rhythmic and harmonic underpinning, a legacy of her teachers Louis Andriessen and David Lang.

Like those composers, and indeed New York itself, Mazzoli also moves easily between classical and vernacular worlds. Her output is split between commissions for the concert hall and opera house (her second opera, *Breaking the Waves*, based on Lars von Trier's film, was premiered at Opera Philadelphia last September) and music for her all-female art-pop band Victoire. Interested in bringing together opposites rather than highlighting differences, she fills her work with contrasts of all kinds. Nowhere is this better seen than in an early sketch for her *Violent, Violent Sea* (2011), which simply reads in part: 'Loud but slow. Light but dark … How to do this?'

LOTTA WENNÄKOSKI (born 1970)

'My music does not concretely describe anything; it is more about topics and moods,' says Finnish composer Lotta Wennäkoski. Yet it can encompass a wide range of atmospheres, from the airy abstractions of her flute concerto *Soie* (2009), inspired by the textures of different types of material, to the operatic monodrama *Lelele* (2010), which broaches the topic of forced prostitution.

Wennäkoski studied at the Béla Bartók Conservatory in Hungary; the Sibelius Academy in Helsinki, where Kaija Saariaho was among her teachers; and in the Netherlands with Louis Andriessen. Although an instinctively lyrical composer, her compositional palette stretches to vocal screams and whispers and a range of instrumental noise when the work's expressive demands require it. 'I enjoy mixing timbral thinking (noise sounds and string harmonics) with quick, sometimes even lightly pulsing music,' she claims. The dramatic song-cycle *N! Naisen rakkauta ja elemaa* ('N! A Woman's Love and Life', 2002–3), an earthily unsentimental counterpart to Schumann's *Frauenliebe und -Leben*, offers a perfect example, matching soaring vocals to an Expressionistic, often anguished instrumental accompaniment. Her music is featured at the Proms for the first time this year as part of the Last Night celebrations. Although she is excited by the prospect – 'It is perhaps the biggest audience ever for my music' – she is not anxious. 'In general as a composer the orchestra is my favourite instrument.'

PREMIERES AT THE PROMS

Tom Coult St John's Dance
BBC commission: world premiere
PROM 1 • 14 JULY

Sir Harrison Birtwistle Deep Time
BBC co-commission with the Staatskapelle Berlin: UK premiere
PROM 4 • 16 JULY

Roderick Williams Là ci darem da mano
BBC commission: world premiere
PROMS AT ... CADOGAN HALL,
PCM 1 • 17 JULY

Pascal Dusapin Outscape
BBC co-commission with the Casa da Música Foundation (Porto), Chicago Symphony Orchestra, Opéra de Paris and Stuttgart Opera: UK premiere
PROM 7 • 19 JULY

Kerry Andrew No Place Like
BBC commission: world premiere
PROMS 11 & 12 • 23 JULY

Laurent Durupt Grids for Greed
BBC commission: world premiere
PROMS AT ... CADOGAN HALL,
PCM 2 • 24 JULY

Julian Anderson Piano Concerto
BBC co-commission with the Bergen Philharmonic Orchestra and Sydney Symphony Orchestra: world premiere
PROM 16 • 26 JULY

Mark Simpson The Immortal
London premiere
PROM 17 • 27 JULY

Anders Hillborg Sirens
UK premiere
PROM 18 • 28 JULY

Sir James MacMillan
A European Requiem
European premiere
PROM 21 • 30 JULY

Francisco Coll Mural
London premiere
PROM 28 • 5 AUGUST

Brian Elias Cello Concerto
BBC commission: world premiere
PROM 32 • 9 AUGUST

Judith Weir In the Land of Uz
BBC commission: world premiere
PROMS AT ... SOUTHWARK CATHEDRAL • 12 AUGUST

Mark-Anthony Turnage Hibiki
European premiere
PROM 39 • 14 AUGUST

Thomas Larcher Nocturne – Insomnia
UK premiere
PROM 40 • 15 AUGUST

Michael Gordon Big Space
BBC commission: world premiere
PROM 44 • 17 AUGUST

Jonathan Dove Chorale Prelude 'Christ unser Herr zum Jordan kam'
BBC commission: world premiere
PROM 47 • 20 AUGUST

Cheryl Frances-Hoad Chorale Prelude 'Ein feste Burg ist unser Gott'
BBC commission: world premiere
PROM 47 • 20 AUGUST

Gerald Barry Canada
BBC commission: world premiere
PROM 50 • 21 AUGUST

Andrea Tarrodi Liguria
UK premiere
PROM 61 • 30 AUGUST

Hannah Kendall The Spark Catchers
BBC commission: world premiere
PROM 62 • 30 AUGUST

Missy Mazzoli Sinfonia (for Orbiting Spheres)
European premiere of orchestral version
PROM 70 • 5 SEPTEMBER

John Adams Lola Montez Does the Spider Dance
London premiere
PROM 75 • 9 SEPTEMBER

Lotta Wennäkoski Flounce
BBC commission: world premiere
PROM 75 • 9 SEPTEMBER

PROMS EXTRA

With lively introductions, readings, films and a series of Proms Sing workshops, **Amanda Holloway** outlines the range of free daily events that run alongside the Proms concerts

Anyone who has been to one of the series of free talks, workshops and music-making sessions running throughout the BBC Proms season – Proms Extra – knows how much they add to the Proms experience. They're not 'extra', they're an essential part of the Proms offering. Promoting a public appetite for music has been at the heart of the Proms since Henry Wood first raised his baton to launch the festival at the Queen's Hall in 1895. He would surely approve of this year's wealth of free pre-concert events, workshops, editions of BBC Radio 3 programmes, readings and films designed to appeal to families, students, newcomers and enthusiasts alike.

For those who want to learn more about the music they're about to hear, Proms Extra Talks precede around 45 of the concerts (all at Imperial College Union's concert hall, a minute's walk from the Royal Albert Hall). If you prefer to roll your sleeves up and take part, there are participation events led by professional musicians (members of the BBC's Orchestras and Choirs), in which you and your family can play and sing through a selection of highlights from the Proms programmes *(see pages 76–78)*. Edited versions of most of the events can be heard during the interval of the daily Proms broadcasts on Radio 3.

Favourite BBC Radio 3 programmes and presenters are a key part of Proms Extra. *In Tune* decamps to Imperial College Union just before the First Night of the Proms, when Sean Rafferty interviews some of the artists appearing during the season; Tom Service presents a special edition of *The Listening Service* on the subject of Revolution, one of this year's recurring themes; and there's a live broadcast of *The Choir* introduced by Sara Mohr-Pietsch ahead of the Last Night.

Guest speakers for the talks include poets, historians, scientists and musicians, while BBC Radio 3 New Generation Thinkers bring new research and ideas to the mix. There are three events on the subject of 'mood and emotion': New Generation Thinker and academic Sean Williams looks at Schiller's essay on naive and sentimental poetry before a performance of John Adams's *Naive and Sentimental Music*; Elgar's First Symphony is preceded by Professor Thomas Dixon, Director of the Queen Mary Centre for the History of the Emotions, exploring how composers have engaged with the themes of sentimentality, happiness and sorrow; and novelist Charlotte Mendelson tackles the question: why do novelists prefer to write about unhappy people?

Elgar's Third Symphony, realised by Anthony Payne, throws up the subject of 'unfinished works', giving author Meg Rosoff the chance to consider the ramifications of finishing off a friend's novel months after he died. Unfinished works are also explored by pianist and broadcaster David Owen Norris in a mini-series exploring topics suggested by the evening's concert.

New commissions are a vital part of the BBC's musical offering and composers such as Gerald Barry, Mark Simpson and Mark-Anthony Turnage will join Radio 3 presenters to talk about their works receiving premieres at the 2017 Proms.

This year's Proms Extra sees a boost to the series in which actors read passages from novels and poetry, while a series of four documentaries from the BBC archives includes a 1967 programme about Monteverdi's *Vespers*, featuring musicologist H. C. Robbins Landon.

The popular Proms Family Workshops return for five sessions: adults and children over 7 can bring an instrument and join in, but it's not obligatory – there will be percussion instruments on hand. The same is true of the two Family Orchestra and Chorus events (though here you can opt to sing instead of play): sessions in which adults and children have the rare chance to rehearse and perform on stage at the Royal Albert Hall with professional musicians. For the first time, this year there's also a similar event (at Imperial College Union) aimed specifically at adults, the Proms Scratch Orchestra and Chorus.

Singers can join the queen of vocal technique, Mary King, to read through parts of Beethoven's 'Choral' Symphony (No. 9) before performing them with the BBC National Orchestra of Wales. Most choral singers will never have the privilege of performing Schoenberg's *Gurrelieder*, so seize the chance on 19 August to learn from one of the world's best-known chorus directors, Simon Halsey, as you explore this complex, beautiful score.

The BBC Proms Inspire scheme has offered a platform for over 900 young composers aged 12 to 18 from across the UK to develop their skills, share their ideas and get their music heard. Sign up early for Inspire Day on 5 August, a day packed with workshops at Imperial College Union led by composers and artists sharing the fundamentals of composing and arranging. On 14 August the Aurora Orchestra performs the winning pieces of the BBC Proms Inspire Young Composers' Competition. Winners of the Proms Poetry Competition are announced and read from their winning work, at a special Poetry event on 7 September. This year's judges are Ian McMillan (of Radio 3's *The Verb*), Judith Palmer (Director of the Poetry Society) and Jacob Polley (winner of the 2016 T. S. Eliot Prize).

Sadly there's no room to give details of every event in the season. Lenin and Lincoln, Byron and Ella Fitzgerald, Beating Insomnia and Translating Cuneiform – the breadth and variety of subjects add up to a veritable University of the Proms: a fantastic opportunity to dip into culture and science as an introduction to the concerts – or as education and entertainment in their own right. ●

Amanda Holloway is a classical music journalist and former editor of the Royal Opera House magazine. She has contributed features and reviews to specialist magazines such as *Gramophone*, *Opera* and *Opera Now*, reviews to the Critics' Circle website and music stories to national newspapers.

Proms Scratch Orchestra and Chorus
SATURDAY 22 JULY, 1.30pm–3.30pm

Proms Extra Sing
Beethoven Symphony No. 9, 'Choral'
SUNDAY 30 JULY, 10.00am–12.45pm

Songs made popular by **Ella Fitzgerald**
FRIDAY 4 AUGUST, 5.30pm–6.30pm

Schoenberg Gurrelieder
SATURDAY 19 AUGUST, 2.00pm–4.00pm

Mozart La clemenza di Tito
MONDAY 28 AUGUST, 12.30pm–3.30pm

Suitable for ages 16-plus. Places must be booked in advance. Booking opens at 9.00am on 9 June. Visit bbc.co.uk/proms, call 020 7765 0557 or email getinvolved@bbc.co.uk. For more details of Family Workshop and Proms Family Orchestra and Chorus events, see pages 76–78.

PROMS POTENTIAL

Three young musicians describe how opportunities offered by Proms Learning initiatives to nurture young talent have enriched their musical experiences

Bringing classical music to new audiences is a vital part of the Proms mission. While the BBC Proms Learning programme has introduced children to classical music through Family Proms and by inviting creative responses to classical repertoire through the nationwide Ten Pieces project, a key part of its commitment to nurturing emerging talent from across the UK is through participation, particularly in schemes such as the BBC Proms Youth Choir, BBC Proms Youth Ensemble and BBC Proms Inspire for young composers.

One of its longest-running projects is BBC Proms Inspire, which offers year-round events to support the development of the composers of the future. Central to the programme is the BBC Proms Inspire Competition, with prizes including a BBC Radio 3 commission and broadcast, for composers aged 12 to 18. Previous winners have included the BBC Philharmonic's Composer in Association, Mark Simpson, and Tansy Davies, a recent recipient of a British Composer Award, but it's not only winners who benefit from the scheme.

For Sofia Swenson-Wright, who was highly commended in the competition in 2015 and is now an Inspire Ambassador, the access to other composers has helped to open her mind to new ways of composing. 'I've been to a number of workshops as part of Inspire, including one last year with Anna Meredith for International Women's Day. It was great to learn about her way of working, how she structures a piece and also compare that to the other young composers who were there.'

Although the BBC Proms Youth Ensemble is one of the Learning programme's most recent initiatives – founded in 2015, to perform a specially commissioned piece with Aurora Orchestra under Nicholas Collon – it has already made an impact on young tuba player Adam Jibran Collins for similar reasons. He credits the chance to work closely with professional musicians, a core aspect of all of the Proms Learning schemes, as something he couldn't have experienced anywhere else. 'I spent a whole morning one-on-one with the Principal Tuba of the Aurora Orchestra, which meant I got to learn so much more than I would at a side-by-side rehearsal. You also learn an immense amount working with experienced conductors like Nicholas Collon and Sakari Oramo [who directed the Proms Youth Ensemble at last year's Last Night of the Proms].'

For both Sofia and Adam, taking part in projects has furthered their musical education. One particular Inspire workshop, on song-writing, recalls Sofia, 'has made me listen to songs quite differently. I now think about the creative process and having contact with professionals has really changed my approach to composition.' Adam found that the Proms Youth Ensemble (which this year premieres a new BBC commission by Michael Gordon, to be performed alongside the Bang on a Can All-Stars) highlighted the challenges of playing contemporary repertoire, particularly from memory, something of which Aurora has made a speciality and which Adam had never encountered before. 'It helped me tune in to what was happening around me and it was great for my musicianship. I've used those skills in projects I've done since.'

Developing the musicianship of undiscovered voices from all musical backgrounds is a fundamental aim of the newly launched BBC Proms Youth Choir Academy, which will feed in to the BBC Proms Youth Choir, whose performances have included concerts with the Vienna Philharmonic under Sir Simon Rattle at both the BBC Proms and Lucerne festivals. The chance to explore choral technique through workshop sessions with members of the BBC Singers is, for one of the Academy's young recruits, Kylie Wong, 'a precious opportunity that I would not get anywhere else', but she also emphasises the importance of being part of a group. 'Singing in a choir is different to solo singing. Each person needs to use his or her ears to listen and to feel the music together: it's teamwork.' In particular for Kylie, who moved to London from Hong Kong three years ago, 'I like the fact that music has no language barrier, which makes singing a very good way to make friends with people from all over the world.'

The advantages of sharing experiences with other like-minded young musicians is a common feature for all of the young participants: 'Everyone is at different stages of musical training in the Youth Ensemble,' says Adam, 'so we all learn from each other as well'; while Sofia, who has met other young composers through Inspire, adds, 'It's really nice to have a community of people who are out there doing the same thing as you.' •

BBC Proms Youth Choir
PROM 1 • 14 JULY

National Youth Orchestra of Great Britain
PROM 28 • 5 AUGUST

National Youth Choir of Great Britain
PROM 30 • 7 AUGUST

BBC Proms Youth Ensemble
PROM 44 • 17 AUGUST

OPPORTUNITIES FOR YOUNG MUSICIANS AT THE PROMS

The **Proms Inspire Young Composers' Competition** is open to 12- to 18-year-olds (closing date for entries 25 May) and winners will have their piece performed at the BBC Proms and broadcast on BBC Radio 3, as well as receive a BBC commission. All members of the Inspire scheme will be invited to an Inspire Day on 14 August, featuring workshops and talks with leading composers. To join the scheme or find the terms and conditions of the competition, visit bbc.co.uk/promsinspire.

The **Proms Sessions** run in partnership with Royal Albert Hall Education & Outreach, continue in 2017, offering young people aged 16 to 25 the chance to work with high-profile artists appearing at the Proms in the intimate setting of the Royal Albert Hall's Elgar Room. Booking opens at 9.00am on 9 June at bbc.co.uk/proms.

The **BBC Proms Youth Ensemble** offers talented young musicians the chance to participate in innovative performances, while developing their skills alongside some of the UK's top professional musicians. This year the BBC Proms brings together young musicians aged 16 to 25 with the Bang on a Can All-Stars to perform the world premiere of a work by Michael Gordon on 17 August. To find out more and apply, email getinvolved@bbc.co.uk or phone 020 7765 0557.

The **BBC Proms Youth Choir**, established in 2012, offers talented members of youth choirs the opportunity to perform at the BBC Proms, while developing their choral skills during a week-long residency in Birmingham led by Chorus Master Simon Halsey. This year the BBC Proms Youth Choir Academy offers young singers the chance to explore choral singing and technique, while working alongside professional classical singers. To find out more about future Proms Youth Choir Academy opportunities, email getinvolved@bbc.co.uk or phone 020 7765 0557.

SUMMER ADVENTURES

Sing, play, get involved! **Rick Jones** discovers the array of events running alongside the Proms concerts that offer the chance to play or sing together with other families

Education remains a core BBC value and, if the Proms were to take place in term time, there would surely be a healthy number of children in school uniform among the audience. But, while the regulation skirts and blazers have been stuffed at the back of the wardrobe for the summer, the Proms becomes a crucible for countless realisations and discoveries. Generations of music-lovers have described how the Proms has effectively provided their musical education, but for over a decade the Proms Learning team has also planned a whole series of complementary events for all the family.

School music departments and educators all over the UK are familiar with the BBC's award-winnng Ten Pieces project, which has reached over 4 million young people since its launch in 2014. Performances of 10 specially selected pieces are presented to schoolchildren through an innovative BBC film, and supported in schools by a range of resources, concerts and workshops that encourage students to produce their own creative responses to the music.

> 66 Generations of music-lovers have described how the Proms has effectively provided their musical education. 99

The Ten Pieces Presents … Prom this year (subtitled 'Sir Henry's Magnificent Musical Inspirations') takes the concept and applies it to pieces specially selected for this

Sound skills: members of the Able Orchestra, formed of students with a range of physical disabilities, perform via digital devices at the Ten Pieces II Prom, 2016

performance. Composers across the ages have been inspired by nature, dreams, love and literature among many other subjects, and Henry Wood, founder-conductor of the Proms, magically appears on stage to explain how, with the help of the entire Royal Philharmonic Orchestra as well as the 450-strong Ten Pieces Choir.

Alongside the live orchestra, you can expect the spectacle of drama, films, dance, comedy and storytelling. Audiences will discover how a group of paintings led Mussorgsky to write his *Pictures at an Exhibition* and hear how Shakespeare's *Henry V* inspired Walton's battle music for Laurence Olivier's film. We will find out how the young Lili Boulanger drew on nature to evoke a spring morning

in her symphonic poem *D'un matin de printemps* and how Ravi Shankar brought together East and West in his exhilarating *Symphony*, featuring the exotic sounds of the sitar.

As well as singing in Elgar's *The Music Makers* and Vivaldi's *Gloria*, the vast Ten Pieces choir will also perform a brand-new new *a cappella* work, *No Place Like*, by Kerry Andrew, founder of the vocal ensemble Juice.

A new concert format joins the schedule this year in the Relaxed Prom on 29 July. Proms Senior Learning Manager Ellara Wakely explains that 'relaxed' applies not to the audience or the programme but to the rules and conventions of concert-going. Suitable

On their mettle: young participants in a 2016 Proms Family Orchestra and Chorus event

for children and adults with autism, sensory and communication impairments and learning disabilities, as well as people who are Deaf, hard of hearing, blind or partially sighted, the result is an exciting family concert which encourages spontaneous reactions to the music.

Don't forget that, aside from the concerts especially aimed at younger audiences, children aged 7 and upwards are encouraged to go to any of the Proms. The series of Sunday matinee concerts might prove convenient as well as stimulating, among them Mozart and Schumann conducted by Bernard Haitink on 16 July. Clare Teal returns with dual big bands led by Guy Barker and Winston Rollins to set the Royal Albert Hall swinging on 27 August; and there's an all-Mendelssohn Prom on 3 September, celebrating the composer's gift for melody and pictorial display.

There are also opportunities for everyone – regardless of age or ability – to get involved, through the series of introductory Family Workshops. Five of these precede Proms concerts at the Royal Albert Hall, starting with a session before Bernard Haitink's Mozart/Schumann programme. 'Bring your instruments!' the cry goes out. Musicians, often from the orchestras playing in the concert, explore the themes and create music with workshop participants. The concert on 17 August, with Saint-Saëns's 'Organ' Symphony, will surely capture young imaginations, while the music of Korngold and Anders Hillborg on 28 July may be less familiar but should be equally exciting.

There are further chances to play or sing as part of an extra-large orchestra at the two Proms Family Orchestra and Chorus events. In the first of these on 6 August, family members aged 7-plus are introduced to and then play themes from across the Proms season – on-stage at the Royal Albert Hall, no less – and on 12 August music from Rodgers and Hammerstein's *Oklahoma!* is on the bill. There's also a huge array of percussion instruments on hand waiting to be played, so no-one will be without a job. School may be out, but that doesn't mean the learning – or the fun – should stop. ●

Rick Jones writes for *The Tablet* and *BBC Music Magazine*. He is Secretary of the Critics' Circle and a council member of the Lute Society.

Ten Pieces Presents … Sir Henry's Magnificent Musical Inspirations
PROMS 11 & 12 • SUNDAY 23 JULY
2.00pm & 6.00pm

Relaxed Prom
PROM 19 • SATURDAY 29 JULY, 12.00pm
See also pages 40–41

See also pages 40–41

Family Workshops
Family-friendly introductions to the music of the following Prom. Bring an instrument or just sit back and take it all in. (Suitable for ages 7-plus.)

SUNDAY 16 JULY, 2.00pm–2.45pm

FRIDAY 28 JULY, 5.45pm–6.30pm

THURSDAY 17 AUGUST, 4.45pm–5.30pm

SUNDAY 27 AUGUST, 1.15pm–2.00pm

SUNDAY 3 SEPTEMBER, 11.15am–12.00pm

Family Orchestra and Chorus
Play or sing alongside professional musicians, whatever your age or ability. (Suitable for ages 7-plus.)

SUNDAY 6 AUGUST
10.00am–12.30pm
Music inspired by highlights from the 2017 Proms season

SATURDAY 12 AUGUST
10.00am–12.15pm
Music inspired by 'Oklahoma!'

All family events are free but tickets must be bought for the related concerts. Places must be booked in advance for Proms Family Orchestra and Chorus events.

Sign up from 9.00am on 9 June at bbc.co.uk/proms, call 020 7765 0557 or email getinvolved@bbc.co.uk.

PAUL WALLIS

account manager

I've been coming to the Proms every year since 1992. I wanted to experience classical music live, so where better than at the BBC Proms? I go online as soon as booking opens and there's always a sense of excitement when my tickets are confirmed. Throughout my years of Proms-going I've sat in the Circle, in a box and in the Stalls, but my favourite is the Choir seats – having a bird's-eye view of the conductor and being so close to the orchestra is really special. My first Prom was with my dad and since then we try to go to at least a couple of concerts every summer. There's a real energy and excitement about the Proms that nothing else matches.

AT THE MOMENT I'M ENJOYING ...

Music by Nils Frahm – I heard of him in an interview with Gilles Peterson on BBC 6 Music, although I missed his performance at the Proms in 2015. I'm intrigued by artists like Frahm who make incredible music by fusing other styles. I love how musical genres can be melded together.

MY MOST RECENT MUSICAL 'DISCOVERY'

Pekka Kuusisto. I was at the Prom last year when he delivered a hilarious encore after performing Tchaikovsky's Violin Concerto. I loved his style, and playing with a smile on his face was so refreshing and engaging. I also make lots of musical discoveries listening to the radio: just recently on Cerys Matthews's show on BBC Radio 6 Music I discovered the rich, ambient sounds of Bonobo – it would make a great Late Night Prom!

MY PROMS HIGHLIGHTS

My favourite Prom last year was the Late Night with Jamie Cullum. I love that the Proms isn't just about classical music and I've followed Jamie Cullum since he started out. I think he's a fantastic showman and he seems to live and breathe music. He's also so generous in the way that he engages with other performers. My stand-out moment, though, is Maxim Vengerov playing Shostakovich's First Violin Concerto in 1997. I've never seen an artist connect with their instrument and the music so completely as in that performance – it was electrifying.

STAFF SARGENT

Malcolm Sargent epitomised the Proms from 1947 until his death in 1967, 50 years ago. Was he a shameless entertainer or a compelling leader, destined to reinvent the Last Night for the television age? **Leanne Langley** traces his career and highlights his achievements

Malcolm Sargent was never happier than when directing a big public concert. Showmanship, driving energy and careful preparation were his stock-in-trade – as were stratagems.

In early 1921, years before adopting his signature look of Brylcreemed hair, dapper dress and white carnation, the young musician set out to pique the interest of Henry Wood – founder-conductor of the Proms – with an original composition. His wily plan was to hold back his score, written for a Leicester visit of Wood's New Queen's Hall Orchestra, until the last minute. As expected, the elder conductor then required Sargent to rehearse his own piece, enabling him to show what he could do. Wood was so taken with Sargent's performance that he asked the young musician to repeat his work, *An Impression on a Windy Day* (which can be heard at this year's Last Night), in London at the 1921 Promenade season.

Wood's chosen date was not just any Prom, but the Last Night of 1921 – a signal honour for the 26-year-old from Stamford, Lincolnshire. Although Wood would programme two further Sargent works at later Proms and would schedule the evocative *Windy Day* twice more (in 1923 and 1924), he had already spotted Sargent's true gift. He advised the young composer to focus wholly on conducting. Sargent never looked back.

It was an auspicious start for the man who would one day take Henry Wood's place. In the intervening years Sargent developed a frenetic freelance career. From private music teacher, local Gilbert & Sullivan director and conductor of the amateur Leicester Symphony Orchestra – created for him – he rose quickly. In 1924 he moved to London. Besides teaching at the Royal College of Music, where Michael Tippett was among his pupils, he made early recordings of Vaughan Williams's *Hugh the Drover*, then Holst's *At the Boar's Head*. He even took over the Robert Mayer Children's Concerts from Adrian Boult. Never in short supply, Sargent's self-belief now mushroomed.

By the late 1920s the young maestro was pushing further, bullishly overhauling Rupert D'Oyly Carte's G&S productions by cleaning up old parts and insisting on Sullivan's faster original tempos. Work for Diaghilev's Ballets Russes and the Royal Choral Society followed, the latter featuring costumed versions of Coleridge-Taylor's *Hiawatha* at the Royal Albert Hall. More important was his adroit handling of the premiere, at Leeds in 1931, of Walton's *Belshazzar's Feast*. Sargent turned what might have been a disaster, with a chorus liable to falter in complex rhythms, into a victory. He emerged as the most sought-after choral conductor in Britain, directing the Huddersfield Choral Society from 1932.

Having devised a scheme mixing modern and canonic works – the Courtauld–Sargent Concerts – Sargent was well placed to assist when, in 1932, Samuel Courtauld and Thomas Beecham started a new orchestra, the London Philharmonic Orchestra. Then in 1936 he caused a rift with rank-and-file players, callously advocating their job insecurity ('As soon as a man thinks he is in an orchestral job for life … he tends to lose something of his supreme fire'). In the war years Sargent directed the Hallé and Liverpool orchestras as well as the LPO, touring nationwide to great effect despite black-outs. He also made cultural visits to neutral European countries for the British Council, and became a sparkling regular on

Malcolm Sargent with his wife Eileen; they married in 1923 after meeting at the house of Harold Furness, Sargent's golfing partner, where Eileen worked as a maid

Any Questions? (later *The Brains Trust*). Millions of radio listeners admired his spontaneous answers. Spirits were lifted.

Sargent was knighted in summer 1947. His concerts and recordings garnered praise for vivid performances of Elgar, Delius, Walton, Vaughan Williams, Holst, Britten, Sibelius and Shostakovich. Yet the key role in his last two decades was as Proms conductor. Starting out as co-conductor with Boult and Basil Cameron in 1947, he soon became accepted as conductor-in-chief of the Proms, a role in which he was officially confirmed after relinquishing his appointment as Chief Conductor of the BBC SO (1950–57), and

one which he retained right up until his death, working for his last few years in collaboration with the BBC's Music Controller, William Glock. The trajectory reflects Sargent's changing status within the BBC. For there's no hiding the difficulties BBC administrators encountered: calculating, unpredictable and averse to studio work and much contemporary music, Sargent proved maddening to deal with. But the Corporation needed him. His unrivalled popularity with audiences revitalised a revered series that had lost some of its cachet in the wake of Wood's death in 1944.

Sargent's particular contributions seem visionary now, though they built on Wood's precedents. If they tended to boost the conductor's celebrity, that too was after Wood's image – no bad thing: an infectious atmosphere and public rapport don't preclude serious music-making. What had changed radically since Wood's day was the Proms' function in national life. Before 1915 the series was the engine-room of the Queen's Hall operation, giving several world premieres a week to avid listeners. By 1947, an efflorescence of year-round concerts in London and elsewhere had greatly lowered the Proms' relative importance, though not the public's affection. Sargent built on that esteem, opening up serious musical pleasure by means unavailable to Wood – television, world-class British music and choral works.

In 1947 many musicians were wary of the televisual medium. Sargent seized upon it. When the first televised relay of a UK orchestral concert took place, of parts of the Last Night in 1947, he eagerly appeared, directing Mendelssohn's First Piano Concerto. The programme drew positive responses. For

PC8/Lebrecht Music & Arts

THE

MUSIC BOX

UNION STREET SE1

WORKING WITH SARGENT

Sylvia Darley, Sargent's personal assistant and manager for the last two decades of his life, recalls working with the conductor

I remember from my interview with Sir Malcolm in 1947 that you were expected not to make any mistakes and he counted on reliability and punctuality. In those days he would do three Proms a week; and on the non-concert days there were often choir rehearsals in the evenings. A concert day for me would start at 9am at his flat and you finished around 11pm by the time everything was tidied up, so it was quite heavy going. I used to try and put on a bit of weight beforehand, because I knew I was going to lose several pounds by the end.

There was one Prom in the late 1950s when I ended up sitting in a gangway seat by the stage, where the ushers would normally sit. To my consternation a photographer appeared from behind the curtains and started to creep stealthily down the gangway, behind the first violins. I was caught like a rabbit in the headlights. Should I stop him and risk creating a disturbance or should I sit tight? Lo and behold, the photographer got almost to the bottom. Sir Malcolm spotted him and stopped the whole orchestra and the slow movement of Beethoven's Ninth had to be started again. I got a rocket afterwards from Lady Wood, Henry Wood's widow, for not stopping him.

Sir Malcolm was a good conversationalist – if you got a word in edgeways – and much-loved by his friends. He used to come out with silly Edward Lear-type rhymes: he enjoyed life to the full.

operational reasons TV returned to the Proms only in 1953, when Sargent dominated all segments of the First and Last Nights. Despite power struggles between BBC Radio and Television, both Nights were regularly televised thereafter. In the meantime, Sargent gave lively radio interviews. His Last Night speeches were cordial and assured.

In fact the Last Night as we know it, an annual event in the nation's calendar, was almost entirely Sargent's creation. Wood's *Fantasia on British Sea-Songs* (1905) had been a fixture since the 1920s, and he had given the original Last Night speech in 1941. But these were isolated elements, not a formula: the typical Last Night before 1950 was simply a glorifed 'Popular Night'. From 1948 Sargent sought a more deliberate pattern, focusing on British music and encouraging celebration.

With TV in mind and keen to place himself at the centre of a thrilling evening, he particularly favoured the new Benjamin Britten score he had premiered at Liverpool in 1946, *The Young Person's Guide to the Orchestra*. It was perfect for visually highlighting sections of the orchestra, with the bonus of an exciting ending. Although the *Young Person's Guide* could never permanently supplant the *Sea-Songs* (as it did in 1953), it may have represented Sargent's idea of a modern parallel, a newer kind of British fantasia. He would eventually position the piece on six Last Nights and five First Nights, while the familiar patriotic sequence of Elgar (*Pomp and Circumstance* March No. 1), Wood (*Sea-Songs*), Arne (*Rule, Britannia!*) and Parry (*Jerusalem*) was in place by 1954. Far from displaying jingoism, couldn't Sargent have been expressing joy at the great distance British classical music had travelled in the

previous half-century? When Henry Wood programmed all-British sequences in the early 1900s, they emptied the hall.

Finally, Sargent's introduction of substantial choral works, old and new, reflected real expertise and set a path for new partnerships. Owing to practical limits, Wood had been unable to incorporate much choral music in what was, after all, an orchestral series. From 1949, Sargent began stretching the Proms tradition, introducing a Bach motet. With a range of choral groups, and latterly Glock's advice, he built an impressive list of Proms choral premieres, including Walton's *Coronation Te Deum* (1953), Fauré's *Requiem* (1955), Honegger's *Le roi David* (1959), Mozart's *Requiem* (1961), Berlioz's *Te Deum* (1962), Vaughan Williams's *Dona nobis pacem* and Holst's *Hymn of Jesus* (1964), Brahms's *A German Requiem* (1965) and Delius's *A Mass of Life* (1966).

Animating the Proms by widening audiences, celebrating British music and expanding the traditional repertory was more than a Sargent stratagem. It was an artful, lasting achievement. ●

Leanne Langley is a social historian of music. A Lifetime Fellow of London University and Council member of the Royal Philharmonic Society, she contributed a chapter to *The Proms: A New History* (Thames & Hudson, 2007).

Malcolm Sargent's 500th Prom
PROM 13 • 24 JULY

Works premiered by Sargent
Vaughan Williams Symphony No. 9
PROM 14 • 25 JULY

Walton Belshazzar's Feast
PROM 30 • 7 AUGUST

WATER MUSIC

Anna Picard wades into the background of Handel's celebrated ceremonial music, written for a river party on the Thames thrown by George I, as the Proms marks the work's 300th anniversary with waterside performances in Hull, UK City of Culture 2017

When George Frideric Handel arrived in London in 1711, having hastily absconded from his appointment as Kapellmeister to Georg Ludwig, the Elector of Hanover, the city was changing. A strip of buildings along the Strand, on the north shore of the river, had recently closed the gap between the old conurbations of Westminster and London. To the east of this double metropolis there were silk and dye factories, trade ships, spice warehouses and the naval dockyards. To the west there were genteel villas that provided sweet-scented respite from the bustle and stink of the fastest-growing capital in Europe.

The spheres of court, church, coffee house, commerce, science, industry, art and politics moved in ever closer orbit in the last years of the reign of Queen Anne. A Commission for Building Fifty New Churches had been established to serve the growing population, many of them immigrants. There were taverns, gallows, markets and theatres but the greatest performance space in London was its river. The Thames was thoroughfare, sewer and stage; a place of trade, travel and the conspicuous display of wealth. It was here that London – or as much of it as could fit into hired barges, wherries, skiffs and lighters – heard the first bristling, brilliant trills of Handel's *Water Music* on the balmy evening of 17 July 1717. Now soft, now loud, now bucolic, now urbane, scored here for strings, there for flute or brass, this music – which Handel composed to tickle the ears of his former employer, Georg Ludwig, now King George – would prove critical to the reputations of both men.

To be a Londoner in the early 18th century was to be international. 'Sometimes I am justled [*sic*] among a body of Armenians,' wrote the essayist and politician Joseph Addison; 'sometimes I am lost in a crowd of Jews; and sometimes make one in a group of Dutchmen. I am a Dane, Swede, or Frenchman at different times; or rather fancy myself like the old philosopher, who upon being asked what countryman he was, replied that he was a citizen of the world.'

Dedicated to Queen Anne, *Rinaldo*, the first Italian opera that Handel wrote for London, was an instant hit in 1711. As he had done in Italy, at the start of his career, the young composer retained his financial and artistic independence in London, worked hard, and

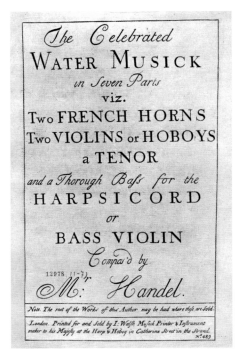

Title-page from an early edition of Handel's *Water Music*, c1733

paid attention to local tastes. But, for every favourable notice of his settings of English texts, from the *Ode for the Birthday of Queen Anne* to the *Utrecht Te Deum and Jubilate*, there was a reference to the continuing pre-eminence of the native 'English Orpheus', Henry Purcell, who had died in 1695. As yet, Handel was still seen as a visitor.

When Anne died in 1714, the crown passed to her nearest Protestant relative, Georg Ludwig. Fifty-four years old, stocky, plain, fluent in French but with only rudimentary English, King George was no-one's dream come true. He was messily divorced, and father to three illegitimate daughters by a woman unflatteringly known as the 'Maypole', Melusine von der Schulenburg. In the months after his coronation, the obstinate, shy 'Turnip King' was mocked as a bumpkin and slandered as a libertine who 'rejects no woman, so long as she is very willing, very fat and has great breasts'. Xenophobia was fanned at street level. While his son and daughter-in-law enjoyed popularity at public banquets, George preferred to dine in private with the Maypole and other confidantes, including the 'Elephant', his ambitious half-sister Sophia Charlotte von Kielmansegg. Gossip spread about the imagined depravity of the insular Hanoverians, exacerbated by George's 28-week absence from Britain in 1716.

By the summer of 1717, criticism of the king could no longer be ignored. According to the Prussian diplomat, Friedrich Bonet, George expressed to Baron Kielmansegg (Sophia Charlotte's husband) a desire to have 'a concert on the river'. Unable to persuade the theatre producer John James Heidegger to invest in a subscription scheme, Kielmansegg

SEVENTEEN · PENCE

WATER · MUSIC
George Frideric Handel

UK postage stamp issued as part of a 1985 collection celebrating British composers in European Music Year

agreed to fund it himself at 'a cost of £150 for the musicians alone'. This event was to be the launch of a public-relations campaign that would see a sequence of balls, receptions, hunting parties, dinners, a royal progress to Cambridge, visits to the country estates of Whig politicians, and the redecoration of Kensington Palace and Hampton Court.

Handel, whose departure from Hanover had been finessed by Kielmansegg, was engaged to compose the music. He created three flexible suites, in F, G and D major, that synthesised English traditions with Continental novelties, including the use of hunting horns as orchestral instruments. There were bourrées, minuets, rigaudons, graceful airs, meaty hornpipes and boisterous country dances, and an unparalleled variety of sonorities across an hour of music that was scored to be audible on a busy waterway. Written with a deliberately Purcellian stamp, the *Water Music* would, together with the anthems that a newly naturalised Handel would write for

TURNING TALENT INTO SUCCESS

"MY CONSERVATOIRE TAUGHT ME TO MAKE MUSIC – CMF IS TEACHING ME TO MAKE A LIVING"

Andrey Lebedev, classical guitarist

Support CMF and the artists we work with:

Donate at citymusicfoundation.org

Email info@citymusicfoundation.org

Registered Charity Number: 1148641

Join us at future events:

Thursday 6 July 2017, City Beerfest at Guildhall Yard

Monday 24th – Friday 29th July 2017, Wallace Collection Residency

Find us on Twitter @CityMusicF

the 1727 coronation of George's son, and his 1749 *Music for the Royal Fireworks*, come to define the sound of Georgian England.

According to Bonet, the weather was 'all that could be desired' when George embarked from Whitehall Steps at 8.00pm on 17 July. Sophia Charlotte was among the guests in his barge, as were the Duchess of Bolton and the Countess of Godolphin. Their destination was the fragrant district of Chelsea, where the late Lord Ranelagh had built the villa at which the King would eat 'a choice supper' arranged by Sophia Charlotte. Anne Boleyn and Anne of Cleves had been serenaded by 'trumpets, shawms and other divers instruments' on the Thames on their wedding days but London had heard nothing like this. Three royal barges of 6, 8 and 12 oars were used, and 36 royal watermen and 50 musicians employed, the musicians playing from a barge that moved in parallel with the royal party.

Bonet's report details 'trumpets, horns, hautboys [oboes], bassoons, German flutes [recorders], French flutes, violins and basses' and notes with evident surprise that there were 'no singers'. Regardless of the absence of voices, the *Water Music* was a work of theatre, with the barge as its stage, the city as its scenery, and the King as its leading man. A report in the *Daily Courant* noted 'so great a Number of Boats, that the whole River in a manner was cover'd' with spectators and courtiers. It spoke approvingly of the 'finest Symphonies, compos'd express for this Occasion, by Mr Hendel; which his Majesty liked so well, that he caus'd it to be plaid over three times in going and returning'.

The evening had been a public and private success. 'At Eleven his Majesty went a-shore at Chelsea, where a Supper was prepar'd, and

George I, for whose party on the River Thames in 1717 Handel wrote his *Water Music*

then there was another very fine Consort of Music, which lasted till 2; after which, his Majesty came again into his Barge, and return'd the same Way, the Musick continuing to play till he landed,' concluded the *Courant*. The invisible king had made himself visible, even likeable, and the 'Celebrated Water Musick' marked not only a softening of attitudes to George but also a significant step in Handel's adoption as Purcell's heir. ●

Anna Picard studied voice and harpsichord, and worked in the field of early music for a decade before moving into journalism. From 2000 to 2013 she was Classical Music Critic of *The Independent on Sunday*; she now writes for *The Times* and *BBC Music Magazine* among other publications.

Handel's Water Music at the Proms

PROMS AT ... STAGE@THEDOCK, HULL • 22 JULY
Royal Northern Sinfonia/ Nicholas McGegan

Overlooking the River Hull and the Humber Estuary, Stage@TheDock is a new, 350-seater outdoor amphitheatre built on Hull's disused Central Dry Dock. As well as being home to arts performances, it provides a setting for local events and exhibitions; it also acts as a rehearsal space. Stage@TheDock is a permanent venue, built as part of the city's status as City of Culture 2017.

Other 'Proms at ...' events

PROMS AT ... SOUTHWARK CATHEDRAL • 12 AUGUST
Works by Palestrina and Judith Weir
BBC Singers/David Hill

PROMS AT ... BOLD TENDENCIES MULTI-STOREY CAR PARK, PECKHAM • 26 AUGUST
Works by J. S. Bach (arr. Bantock), Kate Whitley and John Adams
The Multi-Story Orchestra/ Christopher Stark

PROMS AT ... WILTON'S MUSIC HALL, LONDON • 2 SEPTEMBER
Works by John Luther Adams and Peter Maxwell Davies
Birmingham Contemporary Music Group/Sian Edwards

PROMS AT ... THE TANKS AT TATE MODERN • 6 SEPTEMBER
Cutting-edge new work exploring the borders of music, performance art and electronics
London Contemporary Orchestra, Exaudi/Hugh Brunt

De Agostini Picture Library/akg-images

BROADWAY'S GIFT TO OPERA

Set among the pioneer settlers of the American West and spotlighting the rivalries of farmers and cowboys, *Oklahoma!* drew together Rodgers and Hammerstein in a first collaboration that altered the course of the American musical, as **Tim Carter** reveals

No-one expected great things of *Oklahoma!* when it opened on Broadway on 31 March 1943. Composer Richard Rodgers was still committed to his longtime partnership with Lorenz Hart, although the latter was increasingly incapacitated by illness. Librettist Oscar Hammerstein II had been brought in as a placeholder, with a strong track record from his collaborations with Jerome Kern on works such as *Show Boat* (1927) but also a more recent string of flops. The Theatre Guild, which produced the show, was in serious financial difficulties. The show's director Rouben Mamoulian and choreographer Agnes de Mille spent most of the rehearsals arguing over who was responsible for what. Act 2 was rewritten several times during the try-outs in New Haven and Boston, and rescued by turning a tap-dance solo into a grand choral number arranged at the last minute by orchestrator Robert Russell Bennett. Even the title came late: the show opened in New Haven as *Away We Go!*.

This was not the first 'musical play' produced by the Theatre Guild: in 1935 they had scored some success by taking a work they had staged in 1927, DuBose and Dorothy Heyward's *Porgy*, and having George and Ira Gershwin turn it into a 'folk opera', *Porgy and Bess*. Now the idea was to do the same with another Guild play, Lynn Riggs's *Green Grow the Lilacs* (1931). Riggs claimed that his was a gritty account of real life in the rural community of Claremore in the Indian Territory of Oklahoma around 1900. Aunt Eller and her niece, Laurey Williams, work the hardscrabble land, aided by the rough farmhand Jeeter Fry (Jud Fry in the musical) who lives in the smokehouse surrounded by lurid pin-up postcards on its walls. Cowboy Curly McClain falls for Laurey and realises that times are changing: he decides to settle down as a farmer, though a jealous Jeeter fights him for Laurey's hand and dies in the brawl. The other colourful characters include Laurey's scatterbrained friend, Ado Annie, who takes a fancy to a 'Syrian' pedlar (Ali Hakim in the musical).

Hammerstein did not need to add much to Riggs's play: just a competing love-interest for Ado Annie – the rather dumb cowboy Will Parker – creating a second, more comic triangle to match the main Laurey–Curly–Jud one. But a Broadway musical clearly needed more than just the folk songs that Riggs had used to link his scenes. And, while *Green Grow the Lilacs* was perfectly in tune with the Great Depression, the world was different in 1943. Now the country was at war, and Hammerstein saw the potential for farmers and cowmen becoming friends in a morale-boosting celebration of Americana, with Oklahoma on the verge of becoming a 'brand-new state' ('gonna treat you great!' – we hear in that revised title-song). The Theatre Guild offered cheap tickets and special matinees for the troops shipping out to Europe. What most felt was headed for a short run suddenly became a hit.

Oklahoma! soon gained landmark status as the first 'integrated' musical, in which songs and dances help develop a serious dramatic plot rather than being irrelevant interpolations. Critics at the time were in full agreement on the high quality of the show, although they were confused about what to call it: a 'musical comedy', 'folk opera' or 'musical play' (as the Theatre Guild styled it). Its successful fusion of the arts also

figured prominently in the reviews: one commentator even went so far as to say that it came close to a Wagnerian *Gesamtkunstwerk* (total work of art), which was a tricky assertion to make during the Second World War.

Such claims were clearly overstated: there were plenty of precedents for what *Oklahoma!* tried to achieve. But opening the show with Curly's 'Oh, What a Beautiful Mornin'' certainly captured the ear and eye in new ways. Agnes de Mille's 'Dream Ballet' at the end of Act 1 – where Laurey imagines her wedding to Curly disrupted by Jud and his burlesque 'postcard girls', leading to a fight to the death – brought modern American dance to the Broadway stage: it was seeing de Mille's choreography for Aaron Copland's *Rodeo* (1942) that had encouraged Rodgers and Hammerstein to bring her on board. And, even though many thought that Jud's death at the end of the show would kill its box-office prospects, Hammerstein resisted sparing him – he called him the 'bass fiddle', giving depth to an otherwise anodyne plot – and he and Rodgers provided the character with a song ('Lonely Room') that managed to humanise him in powerful ways.

Jud's violent tendencies make him an outsider to the Claremore community. Ali Hakim, on the other hand, is assimilated into it, if at a distance (by marrying Gertie Cummings and managing her father's general store in Bushyhead). The point was not lost on wartime audiences, especially given that the role of the pedlar (now 'Persian') was played by Joseph Buloff, a prominent actor in New York's Yiddish theatre. There were other timely messages in *Oklahoma!* as well. The distinguished music critic of *The New*

Barbara Lawrence (Gertie Cummings) and Eddie Albert (Ali Hakim) in the 1955 movie of *Oklahoma!*

York Times, Olin Downes, claimed that it was 'Broadway's gift to opera', showing 'one of the ways to an integrated and indigenous form of American lyric theatre'. As the USA fought Germany and Italy on the battlefields of Europe, the cultural propaganda was clear: a 'brand-new state' also opened up a brave new world. ●

Tim Carter is David G. Frey Distinguished Professor of Music at the University of North Carolina at Chapel Hill and the author of *Oklahoma!: The Making of an American Musical* (Yale University Press, 2007).

Oklahoma! at the Proms
John Wilson conducts the
John Wilson Orchestra
PROMS 34 & 35 • 11 AUGUST

MAESTRO MUSINGS

A single figure on a podium in front of a large orchestra is a familiar sight to classical music audiences, but how does a conductor prepare for a performance? Photographer **Andrew Hayes-Watkins** gets a glimpse of four Proms conductors' individual approaches to bringing a score to life

Getting a sense of her surroundings is important for the City of Birmingham Symphony Orchestra's new Music Director Mirga Gražinytė-Tyla, seen here at the orchestra's home, Symphony Hall in Birmingham.

Andrew Hayes-Watkins

Andrew Hayes-Watkins

Thomas Dausgaard, Chief Conductor of the BBC Scottish Symphony Orchestra, likes to feel that his senses are 'open to the possibility of experiencing the music as though for the first time' during a concert, so it's important to have some time before a performance to reset his mind in quiet contemplation, as pictured here at City Halls, Glasgow.

Rehearsing at Maida Vale Studios in London, Edward Gardner says: 'I always make sure I have a good amount of time before the rehearsal to gulp down coffee and think about what I want to get out of the music we're working on. In this space I've learnt to think foremost about the warmth and passion of the music we're rehearsing.'

For Sian Edwards, who is Head of Conducting at the Royal Academy of Music, learning scores at home (with her cat Amsie) is 'about developing an understanding of what the composer means through the notes they write; looking at the lines and dots and trying to imagine them as sound.'

Andrew Hayes-Watkins

LIGHTS! CAMERA! ACTION!

Presenter **Clemency Burton-Hill** goes behind the scenes at the Royal Albert Hall in the run-up to the First Night of the Proms, as various teams converge in an intricate operation to install the broadcasting infrastructure for the BBC's radio and TV broadcasts

It's the greatest musical show on earth. From intimate solo recitals to epic choral masterpieces, from chamber ensembles to magnificent symphonies, every year the Proms delights and dazzles audiences – whether in the Royal Albert Hall and other venues, on TV, radio or online. But how does it all come together? It may be the starry international artists and intriguing programming that grab the headlines, but behind the scenes scores of people work in the run-up to the First Night to ensure that every aspect of the festival will run without a hitch, right down to the tiniest detail. From catering to carpentry, lighting to LCD screens, organ tuning to computer networking, these are the people who, often invisibly and without fanfare, set the stage for the Proms in what is known as 'rig week'.

The sheer scale of the operation is breathtaking. The fun begins on the Monday morning before the First Night, when Helen Heslop, Live Events Manager for the Proms and Radio 3, arrives at the Royal Albert Hall at 7.00am, armed with spreadsheets, security passes and copies of the formidable Proms Health and Safety Handbook. Over the next five days, at least 15 technical teams will be working around the Hall, from the highest point of the roof (over 40m high) to the depths of the sub-basement, all jostling for their own space on stage, in the lifts and in loading bays. Radio 3 will be rigging extensive microphone slings from the balcony; the TV department will be establishing 20-plus camera positions; cables will be run from broadcasting trucks nestled in front of the Hall and live circuits will be set up via microwave link on the roof to transmit back to BBC Broadcasting House. There are complex production offices to be set up; high-tech editing suites to be established; front-of-house screens, marketing and exhibitions to be put up – to say nothing of the bust of dear old Henry Wood being placed on a plinth in front of the organ loft. It's a gigantic jigsaw puzzle – not to mention a health and safety headache – and Helen, along with the Hall's lead Event Manager for the Proms, must co-ordinate the show with military precision. Her epic master spreadsheet breaks down each day of rig week into detailed 15-minute segments. Every location – including the outside broadcast compound, the stage, backstage, auditorium, Stalls, Arena and Gallery – has its own timeline so that everyone, in theory at least, knows exactly where they need to be at any given point on a given day.

Deadlines loom large. The Radio 3 technical team, for example, will have to wait their turn to access the stage until lighting designer Bernie Davis and the team at his production services company ELP have raised their magnificent lighting truss or canopy, which is usually in place by Tuesday lunchtime. From 6.00pm that evening, nobody is allowed onto the stage until the following morning, in order for it to be coated in a special high-gloss paint that will keep it looking camera-worthy for the duration of the season. By Thursday, the backstage area will start to come alive with musicians unpacking their instruments and warming up, for 2.00pm marks the start of the first of many General Rehearsals for the BBC Symphony Orchestra. And of course the clock is ticking on the biggest deadline of them all: Friday night's First Night.

So does rig week always run smoothly? 'There are occasional moments when there'll be a squabble for space in a lift,' Helen laughs, 'and of course there are huge challenges – like identifying the pinch points where everyone

Truss-worthiness: checking the lighting rig before it is raised into position high over the Royal Albert Hall stage

needs to be in the same place at the same time. Or scheduling how, practically, to get such a mammoth amount of gear into the Hall. Or fencing off the outside broadcast compound. All the trucks have to be parked in a certain configuration, so you've got these 18-ton vehicles reversing into a specific spot and meanwhile the Hall is in such a public space: busloads of schoolchildren might be being dropped off to go to a museum or something at exactly the same time. But in general the crews work together brilliantly. There are so many stakeholders, all working towards the same goal, and that creates a real buzz around the place, with everyone in their hard hats and high-vis jackets. There's great camaraderie.'

Helen has been working on the Proms for more than two decades and says it still feels like the best job in the world. 'I joined for a week, and 21 years later I'm still here! I just love it. That moment at the beginning of rig week, when the auditorium is stacked with flight cases and huge boxes; seeing the whole construction being built; the lighting canopy going up; how it all goes from nothing to the magic of the First Night. It's very exciting.'

Neil Pemberton also got hooked on the Proms early. The Senior Studio Manager of the Classical Music Team for BBC Radio Resources fondly recalls queuing up on the South Steps of the Hall in 1972 'to see the

'GENIUS, PURE AND SIMPLE'

GUARDIAN

ROALD DAHL's

Matilda

THE MUSICAL

MatildaTheMusical.com

CAMBRIDGE THEATRE, London, WC2H 9HU

#MatildaPose

London Symphony Orchestra and André Previn doing Walton's *Belshazzar's Feast*, and the composer coming onto the stage at the end. Unforgettable.' By 1980 he found himself working on the Proms radio team and, 37 years later, he still enjoys every moment. 'Rig week is a race against the clock – as all broadcasting is, not least because of the pressures on the venue during the season,' he says. 'On any given day of the Proms you might have three different rehearsals and two live concerts; that's essentially five live events which have to be rigged for. And the Proms is often used as a test bed for new technology, so as well as our standard microphone slings – which might involve 100 or so microphones to serve all those different possible listening experiences – we might put in an extra array of eight mics on a separate sling for an experiment, say, in binaural sound. These things are worth exploring every year, but it's complicated. You're putting in a rig that's got to work very hard in a lot of different ways.'

'The Proms has one of the biggest microphone rigs in the world,' adds Neil's colleague Robert Winter, Senior Studio Manager for Classical, Radio and Music Operations. 'Every mic we think we might possibly want or need has to be rigged in before we start, so that we're covered for every eventuality – from a solo violin to something as full-on as last year's Quincy Jones Prom – and all with very limited rehearsal time.' He tells me about the Radio 3 rig week 'bible' that has been built up over the years, containing heights, angles, measurements, distances between the floor and mic points, and other critical technical information. But it's not merely a case of replicating what happened last year. 'As the technology evolves, the rig evolves,' he points out. 'At the end of every season there's a

wash-up meeting, a debrief in which we go through what worked – and what didn't.'

Rig week, Robert jokes, often feels like an exercise in unrolling 'miles and miles of cable' and indeed the Proms requires more than a kilometre's worth of sound cable and a further kilometre of fibre-optic cable, which is used for specific set-ups, including the presenters' monitors. Radio 3's vast cable runs are planned by Simon Tindall, Senior Sound Supervisor for BBC Radio's Outside Broadcasts, who puts together the crucial 'plugging sheet'. 'Imagine a great big knitting pattern,' he chuckles. 'It's all in the detail. People go off to their own separate areas and start plugging bits into other bits and, in theory, partway through rig week, we find it all joins together. That's the miraculous bit!'

Television goes somewhat further, requiring a whopping 4.5 kilometres of cable. 'Say we have 20 camera positions throughout the season, we'll install maybe 28 cables as spares in case something fails,' reveals Mike McGaw, Engineering Manager for NEP Visions (TV Outside Broadcasts). 'Imagine: if you're partway through a performance and something goes wrong, you want to be in the best possible position to rectify it there and then without too much fuss.' Like changing a tyre in a Grand Prix, or a violinist replacing a broken string mid-concerto. A significant part of Mike's preparations during rig week involves trying to prevent this scenario by testing, testing, testing. 'We have to check every facility is working: radio talkback, pictures in the truck, the live circuits that go back to Broadcasting House,' he says. 'It's usually at the moment when the On-Air light comes on that the faults start, after things have been working perfectly all day.

Lifting bronze: the bust of Henry Wood being carried to the Royal Albert Hall, to take its place on stage

Your heart definitely races in that situation, but you learn to react as calmly as possible, get on with the job and make sure there's limited disruption to the concert.' Robert Winter agrees. 'Above all,' he says, 'the thing we're all working towards is to do justice to the amazing musicians of the Proms.'

Rig week requires meticulous planning and attention to detail, combined with tremendous respect and co-operation between disparate teams. In that way, it is analogous to any act of harmonious music-making. 'It's humbling,' as Simon Tindall notes. 'For all the work I have done before rig week, when we get into that Hall, I am completely reliant on my colleagues. You have to trust that people are going to do what they need to do – and somehow, they always do.' ●

Broadcaster Clemency Burton-Hill has been a presenter for the BBC Proms on television and radio since 2008. An author, journalist and violinist, she hosts numerous arts and music programmes, including Radio 3's *Breakfast*, *New Generation Artists* and *BBC Young Musician*.

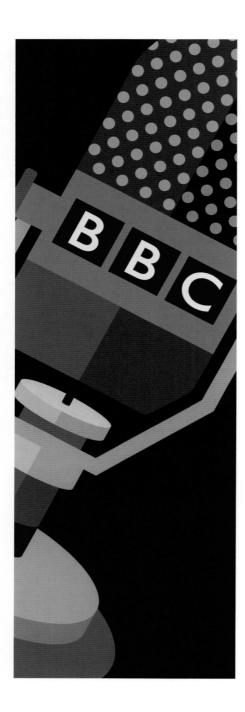

BRINGING THE PROMS TO YOU

In the 90 years since the BBC took over the Proms and broadcast the first concerts on radio, it has become easier to access the Proms wherever and whenever you want. Every Prom is broadcast live on Radio 3 and in HD Sound online, so music-lovers in the UK and all over the world can listen from 'the best seat in the house'. Take the Proms with you on your mobile, catch up for 30 days via the Proms website, or feel part of the festival atmosphere with TV broadcasts on BBC Two and BBC Four throughout the summer

THE PROMS ON BBC RADIO 3

Every Prom broadcast live (available on digital radio, via TV, mobile, laptop and tablet and on 90–93FM)

—

Proms-related programmes throughout the season, including *In Tune, Record Review* and *Composer of the Week*

—

Twenty Minutes – related interval features exploring themes of the concert

—

Coverage of Proms Extra pre-Prom talks and events given by Radio 3 presenters and other experts

THE PROMS ONLINE AND ON MOBILE

Discover the whole season with multimedia articles on bbc.co.uk/proms

—

Download every Prom, keep it for 30 days and listen wherever and whenever you want via the BBC iPlayer Radio app

—

Download the *Proms Unplucked* podcast, presented by Vikki Stone, for a unique backstage view of the festival

—

Discover playlists on the BBC Music app or build your own to play on your favourite music-streaming service

—

Listen to every Prom in HD Sound live and on demand for 30 days at bbc.co.uk/proms

THE PROMS ON TV

Watch full concerts throughout the season, including regular broadcasts on Fridays and Sundays on BBC Four

—

Watch and catch up for 30 days on BBC iPlayer and at bbc.co.uk/proms

—

Proms Extra, hosted by Katie Derham, on BBC Two every Saturday night during the season

FOR PROMS NEWS…

facebook.com/theproms
@bbcproms (#bbcproms) or sign up for our newsletter: bbc.co.uk/proms

Proms followers across the UK*

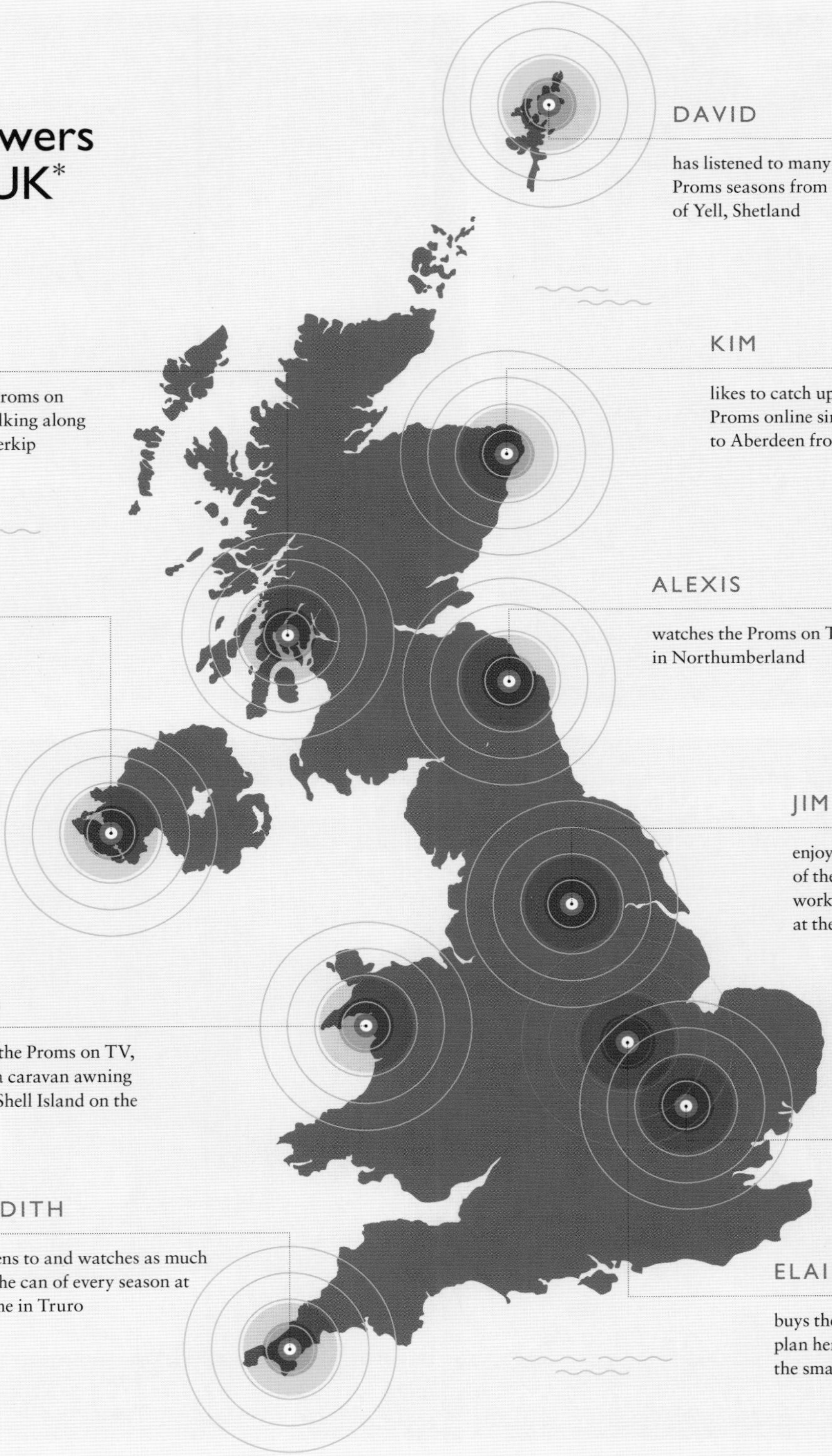

DAVID

has listened to many complete Proms seasons from the island of Yell, Shetland

CLARA

listens to the Proms on her mobile walking along a beach in Inverkip

KIM

likes to catch up with the Proms online since moving to Aberdeen from the USA

SELENE

in Fermanagh has been a Proms fan since her daughter performed at the Ten Pieces Prom in 2015

ALEXIS

watches the Proms on TV in Northumberland

JIM

enjoys the calming influence of the Proms on Radio 3 while working on a merchandise stall at the Leeds Festival

ADRIAN

has watched the Proms on TV, while under a caravan awning overlooking Shell Island on the Welsh coast

JUDITH

listens to and watches as much as she can of every season at home in Truro

THOMAS

in Hertfordshire has the Proms for company in his tractor during harvest

ELAINE

buys the BBC Proms Guide to plan her listening in Rutland, the smallest county in the UK

*Contributions taken from comments on BBC Proms social media pages

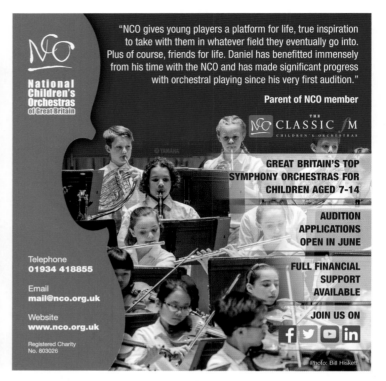

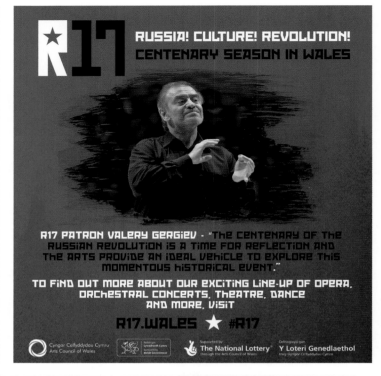

CLAIM YOUR FREE* COPY OF 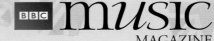 BBC music MAGAZINE

Here's an opportunity to sample an issue of the fantastic and informative *BBC Music Magazine* – **absolutely free*!** There are no obligations or catches.

WHAT YOU CAN EXPECT FROM YOUR FREE* ISSUE:

- **THE LATEST NEWS** The finest talent, the biggest events – read about it all in every issue

- **FEATURES** With fascinating features and interviews with great artists, our writers never fail to stimulate and entertain

- **REVIEWS** Unbeatable reviews from the No. 1 classical music magazine

- **COMPOSERS** From Bach to Vaughan Williams, we bring the music of the great composers to life

Claim your FREE* copy now! ☎ 0844 776 035†

English National Ballet

NUREYEV'S BLAZING BALLET

ROMEO & JULIET

SOUTHBANK CENTRE
TICKETS 020 7960 4200
SOUTHBANKCENTRE.CO.UK

1 – 5 AUGUST 2017
ballet.org.uk/romeo

Dancers: Alina Cojocaru and James Forbat. Photo © Jason Bell. Art Direction and Design: Charlotte Wilkinson Studio

LOTTERY FUNDED

Supported using public funding by ARTS COUNCIL ENGLAND

UNIVERSITY OF
WEST LONDON
London College of Music

Realise your potential

London College of Music is an internationally recognised music institution with a long tradition of providing innovative and creative courses. Many courses are specifically designed to fit around personal and professional commitments and are offered on a full or part time basis.

Our well established industry links and professional partnerships in London, the UK and abroad ensure that your studies are real and relevant to your musical interests.

UNDERGRADUATE PORTFOLIO
- Performance
- Film Composition
- Composition
- Music Management
- Music Technology
- Musical Theatre
- Musical Theatre with Foundation
- Acting
- Theatre Production
- Actor Musicianship
- Text and Performance
- Voice in Performance

POSTGRADUATE PORTFOLIO
- Composition
- Music Management
- Music Technology
- Musical Theatre
- Performance

London College of Music Examinations offer a wide range of external graded exams and diplomas.

 uwl.ac.uk/lcmexams

LONDON
COLLEGE
OF MUSIC

PERSEVERE
1887-2017

130
YEARS

LOVE SUPREME

JAZZ FESTIVAL

LIVE 2017

LINE UP

THE JACKSONS · **GEORGE BENSON** · **GREGORY PORTER**
50TH ANNIVERSARY CONCERTS

HERBIE HANCOCK · **LAURA MVULA** · **BADBADNOTGOOD**

NAO · **ROBERT GLASPER EXPERIMENT**

ST PAUL & THE BROKEN BONES

CHRISTIAN SCOTT · HOT 8 BRASS BAND · JORDAN RAKEI · COMET IS COMING

SONS OF KEMET · YUSSEF KAMAAL · LEE FIELDS & THE EXPRESSIONS

MICHAEL WOLLNY TRIO · CLARE TEAL & MINI BIG BAND · MAMMAL HANDS

MAKAYA MCCRAVEN · SHABAKA & THE ANCESTORS · CHARENEE WADE

MICHAEL JANISCH PARADIGM SHIFT · ASHLEY HENRY TRIO

MANY MORE ARTISTS, DJS AND AFTERSHOW PARTIES TO BE ANNOUNCED.
PLUS KIDS AREA, FOOD VILLAGE, WELLNESS AREA, THE VERVE JAZZ LOUNGE & THE VERDICT BANDSTAND.

30 JUNE — 02 JULY 2017

CAMPING, LOVE SUPREMIUM, JUNIOR, FAMILY,
GLAMPING AND DAY TICKET OPTIONS AVAILABLE

LOVESUPREMEFESTIVAL.COM
LOVESUPREMEFEST

JAZZ FUNK SOUL

GLYNDE (PLACE) SUSSEX

LOVE SUPREME IS 5

TICKETS ARE ON SALE NOW

Jazz FM · Verve 60 · Neapolitan · Clear Channel · jazzwise · YAMAHA

The Haberdashers' Aske's Boys' School

Nurturing Excellence

The Independent School of the Year 2017

Music at Habs – scholarships available

THE SUNDAY TIMES
Independent School of the Year 2017

www.habsboys.org.uk
Headmaster Peter Hamilton MA

Butterfly Lane, Elstree, Hertfordshire WD6 3AF   020 8266 1700
admissions@habsboys.org.uk   registered charity no: 313996

PIERINO

37 Thurloe Place, London SW7 2HP
Tel:0207 581 3770

Monday to Saturday
12 noon – 11.30pm

Sunday
12 noon – 11pm

Prompt service guarenteed for you to be in time for the performance

We are within walking distance of the Royal Albert Hall, near South Kensington tube station.

You are welcome before and after the performance.

41 YEARS

EXPERIENCE OF SERVING GENUINE ITALAN FOOD AND FOR HOME-MADE PASTA AND THE BEST PIZZA IN LONDON

Concerts 2017–18

Enjoy an exhilarating season of glorious choral music from across the centuries with the BBC Singers and superb guest performers, in the intimate setting of Milton Court Concert Hall.

BBC SINGERS

Saturday 23 September

This is Rattle: Birtwistle

From Byrd to Birtwistle via Varèse in an intriguing programme curated by Sir Harrison Birtwistle as a musical greeting to Sir Simon Rattle.

Martyn Brabbins conductor

Sunday 11 February

Bach St Matthew Passion

A rare chance to hear Bach's Baroque masterpiece of great power and passion in Mendelssohn's 1829 version.

Peter Dijkstra conductor
Nicholas Mulroy Evangelist
Brindley Sherratt Christus
St James' Baroque

Friday 4 May

Handel Coronation Anthems

Three of Handel's much-loved Coronation Anthems and his thrilling Dixit Dominus.

Sofi Jeannin conductor
Stephen Farr organ
St James' Baroque

Saturday 23 June

Captain Noah and His Floating Zoo

Joseph Horowitz's delightful piece tells the story of Noah and his Ark, in a concert for audiences of all ages.

John Wilson conductor

Singers at Six

Short concerts in St Giles' Cripplegate complementing the BBC Symphony Orchestra's Barbican Hall concerts.

St Paul's Knightsbridge

Free concerts in the Victorian splendour of St Paul's Knightsbridge, featuring a wide range of glorious choral music.

Come & Sing

Lively and informative workshops with vocal coach Mary King, exploring music by Elgar, Handel and Joseph Horowitz.

Total Immersion

Concerts in the BBC Symphony Orchestra's Total Immersion days, celebrating the music of Julian Anderson, Leonard Bernstein and Esa-Pekka Salonen.

Book Tickets
Visit **bbc.co.uk/singers** for full details of all events including our exciting learning projects.

BBC RADIO 3

@bbcsingers
facebook.com/bbcsingers

BBC *Concert* ORCHESTRA

Bringing Inspiring Music to Everyone

Music from Film Noir
Friday 8 December 2017

A dramatic evening of music from the Film Noir greats, including a radio production of the 1940s masterpiece *Double Indemnity*, performed live alongside Miklós Rózsa's original score.

Sondheim on Sondheim
Thursday 15 March 2018

The newly orchestrated musical revue *Sondheim on Sondheim* makes its sparkling European premiere, accompanied by film of Stephen Sondheim himself.

With a Little Bit of Lerner
Wednesday 23 May 2018

Delight in an evening of glitz, glamour and charm celebrating the 100th birthday of Alan J. Lerner under the baton of Broadway maestro Larry Blank.

David Bedford at 80
Tuesday 12 June 2018

A celebration of the music of David Bedford, who would have turned 80 in 2017. The orchestral version of Mike Oldfield's *Tubular Bells* and Bedford's mesmerising Symphony No. 1 meet a new commission by musician Scanner.

@bbcco
facebook.com/bbcconcertorchestra

bbc.co.uk/concertorchestra

ASSOCIATE AT
SOUTHBANK CENTRE
southbankcentre.co.uk
020 7960 4200

The Bridgewater Hall
Manchester

The 2017/18 Season

On Sale Now

Book now: 0161 907 9000
bbc.co.uk/philharmonic

BBC SCOTTISH SYMPHONY ORCHESTRA

Thomas Dausgaard Chief Conductor	**Matthias Pintscher** Artist-in-Association	**Donald Runnicles** Conductor Emeritus
Ilan Volkov Principal Guest Conductor	**John Wilson** Associate Guest Conductor	**Laura Samuel** Leader

Season 2017/18

Thomas Dausgaard Conducts Composer Roots...

A series of major concerts exploring musical influences on **Beethoven, Rachmaninov, Nielsen, Sibelius** and **Bartók**. With the **Danish String Quartet, Simon Trpčeski, Henning Kraggerud, Behzod Abduraimov,** the **BBC Singers,** folk musicians from across Europe, and many more.

Plus: **Tippett Symphony Cycle Concludes, Scottish Inspirations II, The Jussen Brothers Play Mozart, Tectonics Festival 2018.** As well as appearances at the 2017 **Edinburgh International Festival** and our regular concert series in Aberdeen, Ayr, Edinburgh, Inverness and Perth.

bbc.co.uk/ bbcsso

BBC MUSIC

 BBC Scotland

 BBC RADIO 3

BBC Symphony Chorus

The BBC Symphony Chorus is one of the country's finest and most distinctive amateur choirs, enjoying the highest broadcast profile of any non-professional choir in the UK. It performs a wide range of exciting and challenging works in its appearances with the BBC Symphony Orchestra at the Barbican and the BBC Proms.

Performances during this year's Proms include John Adams's *Harmonium*, Kodály's *Te Deum*, and Mahler's Symphony No. 2, while forthcoming Barbican appearances include Vaughan Williams's *A Sea Symphony*, Esa-Pekka Salonen's *Karawane* and Elgar's *The Dream of Gerontius*.

Would you like to join us?

If you are an experienced choral singer who would like to sing new and challenging music, as well as key choral works, in a fun and friendly chorus - with leading conductors in world-class venues - then the BBC Symphony Chorus could be for you!

Membership is free, and auditions for new members are held throughout the year. To find out more, visit bbc.co.uk/symphonychorus or contact the Chorus Manager at bbcsc@bbc.co.uk.

bbc.co.uk/symphonychorus   @bbcso #bbcsc

Photo © Chris Christodoulou

BBC Symphony Orchestra & Chorus

CONCERTS
2017–18

SAKARI ORAMO | CHIEF CONDUCTOR

THRILLING CONCERTS FROM SAKARI ORAMO AND THE BBC SYMPHONY ORCHESTRA
World-class artists join us for a season filled with true originality, imaginative repertoire and firm favourites.

CELEBRATING THE MUSIC OF FINLAND

Sakari Oramo conducts the complete Sibelius Symphonies and music by his compatriots Aarre Merikanto and Esa-Pekka Salonen.

COMPOSER 'TOTAL IMMERSION' DAYS

Full days of concerts, films and discovery exploring the life and works of Julian Anderson, Esa-Pekka Salonen and Leonard Bernstein.

OPERA & THE VOICE

Don't miss Granados's opera *Goyescas* under the baton of Josep Pons, Joyce DiDonato in a concert staging of Jake Heggie's dramatic opera *Dead Man Walking* and Elgar's greatest oratorio, *The Dream of Gerontius*.

NEW MUSIC

Experience 11 UK premieres by composers including Thomas Larcher and Betsy Jolas, plus recent works by Sir Harrison Birtwistle, Poul Ruders and Raymond Yiu.

barbican
Associate
Orchestra

BOOK NOW 020 7638 8891
barbican.org.uk

BBC RADIO 3

CONCERT
LISTINGS

Full details of all the 2017 BBC Proms concerts are in this section *(pages 118–155)*. Please note: concert start-times vary – check before you book.

EVERY PROM IS BROADCAST LIVE ON BBC RADIO 3

BOOKING

Online: bbc.co.uk/proms
Telephone: 0845 401 5040[†]

General booking opens at 9.00am on Saturday 13 May. For full booking and access information, see pages 158–168.

[†]*see page 159 for call-cost information*

PROMS ON TV

For broadcasts on TV, look out for this symbol

PROMS EXTRA

Look out for the complementary series of free Proms Extra events: find out more about the music through lively introductions, or join in with workshops for all the family *(see also pages 72–73 and 76–78)*.

... Berlin bring
...tion of Elgar's
...oncert of the
...modernity and
...e even now.
...eter Maxwell Davies,
...son Birtwistle's *Deep*
...long fascination with
...tion in a sweeping new
...that swaps the relentless tick-tock
...yday for something more powerful and
...alien. See 'Darkness and Light', pages 46–49;
'New Music', pages 66–71.

📺 *Broadcast on BBC Four tonight*

PROMS EXTRA FAMILY
2.00pm–2.45pm • **Imperial College Union** Join professional musicians for a family-friendly introduction to this afternoon's Prom. Bring your instrument and join in! *Suitable for all the family (ages 7-plus). See pages 76–78 for details.*

PROMS EXTRA TALK
6.00pm–6.45pm • **Imperial College Union** Geologist Iain Stewart and geographer and broadcaster Nicholas Crane consider the concept of 'deep time' in geological and scientific terms.
Edited version broadcast on BBC Radio 3 during tonight's interval

FRIDAY 14 JULY

PROM 1

7.30pm–c9.45pm • Royal Albert Hall

PRICE BAND **B**

WEEKEND PROMMING PASS *see page 159*

EDWARD GARDNER

FIRST NIGHT OF THE PROMS 2017

Tom Coult St John's Dance   c5'
BBC commission: world premiere

Beethoven
Piano Concerto No. 3 in C minor   36'

INTERVAL

John Adams Harmonium   33'

Igor Levit *piano*

BBC Proms Youth Choir
BBC Symphony Chorus
BBC Symphony Orchestra
Edward Gardner *conductor*

John Adams's *Harmonium* is an intricate tapestry of sound, with bright vocal threads and driving brass and percussion rhythms. Marking the composer's 70th birthday this year, it features the BBC Proms Youth Choir. Award-winning pianist Igor Levit is the soloist in Beethoven's groundbreaking Third Piano Concerto, and this year's First Night opens with the world premiere of *St John's Dance* by rising British composer Tom Coult. See *'Maximal Minimalists'*, pages 32–35; *'New Music'*, pages 66–71.

📺 *First half on BBC Four, second half on BBC Two*

PROMS EXTRA IN TUNE
4.30pm–6.30pm • Imperial College Union A live Proms edition of BBC Radio 3's *In Tune*, presented by Sean Rafferty and Suzy Klein. *Tickets available from BBC Studio Audiences: bbc.co.uk/showsandtours. Broadcast live on BBC Radio 3*

SPOTLIGHT ON ...

Igor Levit • Prom 1

When Igor Levit sits down at the piano at the First Night of the Proms, he'll be playing his beloved Beethoven: 'This is the composer I feel closest to. It has always been the case. His music is incredibly humane and it breathes life,' says the 30-year-old Russian-German pianist. His two brilliant solo Beethoven recordings have earned him a clutch of awards, so it's no surprise that an artist who made his Proms debut just five years ago is now opening the season.

For this special Prom, Levit has chosen the turbulent Piano Concerto No. 3. 'Of all the Beethoven concertos, of which every single one is my favourite, this one is my favourite,' he laughs. 'I love this piece. It's a whole miracle, and one of the great pinnacles of the repertoire.' Premiered in 1803, this characterful work owes a debt to Mozart but could only be by Beethoven, representing a turning point in his musical language. 'It's very intense and very dark but, having said that, it's incredibly funny in parts,' remarks Levit. 'It's a piece of great freedom and it's very improvisational. The way Beethoven builds up the dialogue between the piano and orchestra is fantastic.'

That dialogue will be with the BBC Symphony Orchestra and Edward Gardner, a conductor with whom Levit will be working for the first time. 'I absolutely can't wait,' he says.

SATURDAY 15 JULY

PROM 2

7.30pm–c9.40pm • Royal Albert Hall

PRICE BAND **D**

WEEKEND PROMMING PASS *see page 159*

DANIEL BARENBOIM

Sibelius
Violin Concerto in D minor   33'

INTERVAL

Elgar Symphony No. 1 in A flat major   52'

Lisa Batiashvili *violin*

Staatskapelle Berlin
Daniel Barenboim *conductor*

Fresh from two remarkable Elgar recordings with his Staatskapelle Berlin, Daniel Barenboim launches this year's cycle of Elgar symphonies with a performance of the First – a work of thrilling emotional contrasts and a slow movement of Mahlerian richness and beauty. He pairs it with one of the great Romantic violin concertos, once described by musicologist Donald Francis Tovey as 'more original, more masterly and more exhilarating' than any of its rivals, in which former BBC Radio 3 New Generation Artist Lisa Batiashvili is the soloist. See *'Darkness and Light'*, pages 46–49.

PROMS EXTRA TALK
5.45pm–6.30pm • Imperial College Union Thomas Dixon, Director of the Queen Mary Centre for the History of the Emotions, and musicologist Wiebke Thormählen look at sentimentality, happiness and sorrow, and how composers have engaged with these themes in their work. *Edited version broadcast on BBC Radio 3 during tonight's interval*

Benjamin Ealovega (Gardner) Robbie Lawrence (Levit) Monika Rittershaus (Barenboim)

SPOTLIGHT ON ...
Lisa Batiashvili • Prom 2

Sibelius's Violin Concerto has become something of a calling card for Lisa Batiashvili. It brought her to international attention as second prize-winner at the Sibelius Competition in 1995 and she has since toured with it around the world, as well as recording it not once but twice. The Georgian violinist plays it at this year's Proms, making her seventh appearance here since her Proms debut back in 2000. 'I recently recorded this concerto with the Staatskapelle Berlin and Daniel Barenboim and it was a completely new experience,' she says. 'Barenboim has absolutely his own conception of the concerto, and it was energising to have this view.' So has her interpretation changed much? 'There are a lot of things I used to do intuitively, but you need a balance between that and analysis,' she says. 'It was very interesting to work with Barenboim on the whole structure and how it connects from the first note to the last.'

'I am such a fan of Barenboim, not only as a musician but as an entire personality,' she adds. 'It isn't just about music but everything around it as well – the thinking and the understanding.' Add to that the Staatskapelle Berlin and it's an unbeatable trio. 'I just love playing with them,' says Batiashvili. 'It's one of the most friendly, welcoming orchestras and their playing is very alive. You don't experience two similar concerts with them. Something new happens every time.'

SUNDAY 16 JULY

PROM 3
3.45pm–c5.50pm • Royal Albert Hall

PRICE BAND D
WEEKEND PROMMING PASS *see page 159*

BERNARD HAITINK

Mozart
Symphony No. 38 in D major, 'Prague' 29'
Violin Concerto No. 3 in G major 24'

INTERVAL

Schumann
Symphony No. 2 in C major 38'

Isabelle Faust *violin*

Chamber Orchestra of Europe
Bernard Haitink *conductor*

The two symphonies that frame this Prom each offer a defiant, optimistic challenge to the status quo. Mozart's pioneering 'Prague' Symphony rewrites the rule book for the genre, while in Schumann's Second Symphony the composer overcomes the demons of his own mental health to produce a work of invigorating, captivating extremes. Conductor Bernard Haitink – a Proms regular for over half a century – returns with frequent collaborators, the Chamber Orchestra of Europe. They are joined by award-winning German violinist Isabelle Faust, the soloist in Mozart's graceful Violin Concerto No. 3.

Broadcast on BBC Four on 23 July

PROMS EXTRA FAMILY
2.00pm–2.45pm • Imperial College Union Join professional musicians for a family-friendly introduction to this afternoon's Prom. Bring your instrument and join in! *Suitable for all the family (ages 7-plus). See pages 76–78 for details.*

SUNDAY 16 JULY

PROM 4
7.45pm–c9.50pm • Royal Albert Hall

PRICE BAND D
WEEKEND PROMMING PASS *see page 159*

DANIEL BARENBOIM

Sir Harrison Birtwistle
Deep Time 25'
BBC co-commission with the Staatskapelle Berlin: UK premiere

INTERVAL

Elgar
Symphony No. 2 in E flat major 56'

Staatskapelle Berlin
Daniel Barenboim *conductor*

Daniel Barenboim and the Staatskapelle Berlin bring the generous scope of their interpretation of Elgar's Second Symphony to their second concert of the season, celebrating a work whose modernity and astonishing textural effects startle even now. Dedicated to the memory of Peter Maxwell Davies, who died last year, Sir Harrison Birtwistle's *Deep Time* continues his career-long fascination with time and its manipulation in a sweeping new orchestral work that swaps the relentless tick-tock of the everyday for something more powerful and more alien. *See 'Darkness and Light', pages 46–49; 'New Music', pages 66–71.*

Broadcast on BBC Four tonight

PROMS EXTRA TALK
6.00pm–6.45pm • Imperial College Union Geologist Iain Stewart and geographer and broadcaster Nicholas Crane consider the concept of 'deep time' in geological and scientific terms.
Edited version broadcast on BBC Radio 3 during tonight's interval

MONDAY 17 JULY

PROMS AT... CADOGAN HALL, PCM 1
1.00pm–c2.00pm • Cadogan Hall

For ticket prices, see page 159

Monteverdi
Cruda Amarilli	3'
Sfogava con le stelle	4'
Longe da te, cor mio	3'
Orfeo – 'Possente spirto'	9'
Chiome d'oro	3'
Vorrei baciarti, o Filli	5'

Roderick Williams
Là ci darem la mano	c6'

BBC commission: world premiere

Monteverdi
Laudate pueri Dominum a 5 (concertato)	7'
Volgendo il ciel per l'immortal sentiero	11'

I Fagiolini
Robert Hollingworth *director*

There will be no interval

Who better to celebrate the 450th anniversary of Monteverdi's birth than I Fagiolini, who have spent a career unpicking the knotty conflicts and emotional truths of the composer's music. The vocal ensemble is joined by strings, cornetts and continuo to explore love, lust, anger, jealousy and despair in a concert that spans the gamut of Monteverdi's music, both sacred and secular. This season's first Monday-lunchtime Prom at Cadogan Hall also includes the world premiere of a new commission from composer, baritone and Proms regular Roderick Williams, inspired by the text of a well-known aria from Mozart's *Don Giovanni*. *See 'New Music', pages 66–71.*

> **Every Prom broadcast**
> **live on BBC Radio 3**

SPOTLIGHT ON ...

Robert Hollingworth • PCM 1

Theatricality, wit, drama and fun, side by side with serious scholarship – these are the two distinctive hallmarks of English vocal ensemble I Fagiolini, currently celebrating its 30th anniversary. Founding director Robert Hollingworth finds nothing unusual in this apparently stark contrast. 'I don't see that one gets in the way of the other. I use academic research as a way of trying to get closer to what composers might have meant by their music – but there's no reason why we shouldn't present things in a completely different way.'

His group returns to Monteverdi for its lunchtime Prom and Hollingworth has a simple aim: 'I wanted listeners who have never been to a Monteverdi concert before, as well as audiences that love the composer, to get a little bit of everything.' Which even includes a vocal dance suite – 'I think that's a lost genre of Monteverdi's,' Hollingworth adds. They also unveil a brand-new work by Roderick Williams. 'Contrary to popular belief,' Hollingworth says, 'we're not an early music group. We've always sung a great deal of contemporary music and we've commissioned about 40 works over our lifetime.'

But what is it about Monteverdi's music that keeps Hollingworth returning to it? 'It's so powerfully emotional. And he keeps reinventing things as though nobody had ever written for these forces before. It's really quite alarming!'

MONDAY 17 JULY

PROM 5
7.30pm–c10.05pm • Royal Albert Hall

PRICE BAND Ⓐ

BEHZOD ABDURAIMOV

Sibelius
Symphony No. 7 in C major	21'

Rachmaninov
Piano Concerto No. 2 in C minor	33'

INTERVAL

Shostakovich
Symphony No. 10 in E minor	57'

Behzod Abduraimov *piano*

BBC National Orchestra of Wales
Thomas Søndergård *conductor*

The BBC National Orchestra of Wales makes its first Proms appearance of the season, with Principal Conductor Thomas Søndergård, in a programme of big themes and even bigger melodies. Sibelius's single-movement Seventh Symphony compresses all the intensity of a conventional symphony into around 20 minutes. That intensity only builds with the tempestuous extremes of Rachmaninov's Second Piano Concerto, the first in our cycle of the composer's complete piano concertos, and the visceral rage of Shostakovich's Symphony No. 10, a horrifying portrait of life in Stalin's Russia. Brilliant young Uzbek pianist Behzod Abduraimov, who made an exciting Proms debut in Rachmaninov's Third Piano Concerto last year, returns as soloist. *See 'Russian Revolutions', pages 20–25.*

PROMS EXTRA TALK
5.45pm–6.30pm • Imperial College Union Musicologist Marina Frolova-Walker introduces Shostakovich's 10th Symphony.
Edited version broadcast on BBC Radio 3 during tonight's interval

TUESDAY 18 JULY

PROM 6
7.00pm–c9.20pm • Royal Albert Hall

PRICE BAND **A**

NICOLA BENEDETTI

Shostakovich
October   *12'*
Violin Concerto No. 1 in A minor   *39'*

INTERVAL

Sibelius
Symphony No. 2 in D major   *44'*

Nicola Benedetti *violin*

BBC National Orchestra of Wales
Thomas Søndergård *conductor*

Violinist Nicola Benedetti joins Thomas Søndergård and the BBC National Orchestra of Wales as they continue their exploration of music by Shostakovich and Sibelius. Here they pair the latter's stirring Second Symphony – adopted as a potent symbol of nationalism and resistance by the people of Finland – with Shostakovich's symphonic poem *October*, a work whose subversive musical message sees the composer at his most pointedly political. Shostakovich dedicated his First Violin Concerto to the celebrated violinist David Oistrakh, who praised its solo part as 'Shakespearean', and the concerto's demonic Scherzo gives its soloist plenty of opportunity for virtuosity. *See 'Russian Revolutions', pages 20–25.*

See 'Russian Revolutions', pages 20–25.

PROMS EXTRA TALK
5.15pm–6.00pm • Imperial College Union Writer and broadcaster Stephen Johnson introduces Sibelius's Symphony No. 2.
Edited version broadcast on BBC Radio 3 during tonight's interval

WEDNESDAY 19 JULY

PROM 7
7.30pm–c9.45pm • Royal Albert Hall

PRICE BAND **A**

JOSHUA WEILERSTEIN

Rebel Les élémens – Le cahos   *7'*
Pascal Dusapin Outscape   *28'*
BBC co-commission with the Casa da Música Foundation (Porto), Chicago Symphony Orchestra, Opéra de Paris and Stuttgart Opera: UK premiere

INTERVAL

Berlioz Symphonie fantastique   *50'*

Alisa Weilerstein *cello*

BBC Symphony Orchestra
Joshua Weilerstein *conductor*

Visions of chaos give way to a diabolical scene in a musical thrill-ride that takes us from creation itself to the wild dances of a Witches' Sabbath. Jean-Féry Rebel's suite *The Elements* is one of Baroque music's most unusual works, opening with a vivid portrait of Chaos. The same audacity surfaces a century later in Berlioz's quasi-autobiographical *Symphonie fantastique*, whose large orchestral forces and colourful textures make it a perfect fit for the Royal Albert Hall. Star cellist Alisa Weilerstein is soloist for the UK premiere of Pascal Dusapin's nature-inspired concerto *Outscape* – a work written for her – while her brother, rising young star Joshua Weilerstein, conducts. *See 'From Seed to Fruition', pages 42–45; 'New Music', pages 66–71.*

See 'From Seed to Fruition', pages 42–45; 'New Music', pages 66–71.

PROMS EXTRA TALK
5.45pm–6.30pm • Imperial College Union Author Richard Davenport-Hines and BBC Radio 3 New Generation Thinker Daisy Hay consider how opium became a stimulus to creativity in 19th-century Paris.
Edited version broadcast on BBC Radio 3 during tonight's interval

THURSDAY 20 JULY

PROM 8   📺
7.30pm–c10.00pm • Royal Albert Hall

PRICE BAND **B**

KEITH LOCKHART

CELEBRATING JOHN WILLIAMS

BBC Concert Orchestra
Keith Lockhart *conductor*

Winner of five Academy Awards, 22 Grammy Awards and seven BAFTAs, John Williams is among the greatest of film composers. His scores for *Star Wars*, *Schindler's List*, *Harry Potter*, *E. T. The Extra-Terrestrial*, *Jurassic Park* and the *Indiana Jones* films have made him a household name. The BBC Proms celebrates his extraordinary achievements in a concert to mark Williams's 85th birthday. Keith Lockhart – a long-time colleague of Williams at the Boston Pops Orchestra – conducts the BBC Concert Orchestra in an evening featuring excerpts from the composer's best-loved scores, as well as some lesser-known gems.

📺 *Broadcast on BBC Four on 21 July*

PROMS EXTRA TALK
5.45pm–6.30pm • Imperial College Union Ahead of tonight's celebration of the music of John Williams, BBC Radio 3 presenter Matthew Sweet discusses the career of the Academy Award-winning film composer.
Edited version broadcast on BBC Radio 3 during tonight's interval

FRIDAY 21 JULY

PROM 9
7.30pm–c10.00pm • Royal Albert Hall

PRICE BAND B
WEEKEND PROMMING PASS *see page 159*

RICARDA MERBETH

Beethoven Fidelio   108'
(concert performance; sung in German)

Stuart Skelton *Florestan*
Ricarda Merbeth *Leonore*
Brindley Sherratt *Rocco*
Louise Alder *Marzelline*
Benjamin Hulett *Jaquino*
Detlef Roth *Don Pizarro*
David Soar *Don Fernando*

Orfeón Donostiarra
BBC Philharmonic
Juanjo Mena *conductor*

There will be one interval

The first of three politically charged stage works
this season is Beethoven's only opera, *Fidelio* –
a passionate musical protest against political
oppression, first performed in the wake of the
French Revolution. At its heart is the stirring
'Prisoners' Chorus', a poignant hymn to freedom
and the power of the human spirit. Australian tenor
Stuart Skelton stars as the imprisoned Florestan,
with soprano Ricarda Merbeth as his faithful and
resourceful wife Leonore.

Broadcast on BBC Four on 30 July

PROMS EXTRA TALK
5.45pm–6.30pm • Imperial College Union Musicologist
Flora Willson introduces Beethoven's opera, *Fidelio*.
Edited version broadcast on BBC Radio 3 during tonight's interval

---

SPOTLIGHT ON ...

Stuart Skelton • Prom 9

How does Stuart Skelton feel when he has the
role of Florestan in Beethoven's *Fidelio* in the
diary? 'I think the first thought is that it's not
Wagner!' laughs the Australian Heldentenor,
who is one of today's most in-demand Wagnerians.
'It's nice to have something that doesn't mean
husbanding one's resources. Wagner has this way
of leaving the really demanding stuff for the last
act, so it's welcome to have something that
doesn't really pose any stamina issues.'

Fidelio is Beethoven's only opera – as well as
the best-known example of the 'rescue opera'
genre that became popular after the French
Revolution – and it turns a spotlight on the themes
of liberty, justice and love. Florestan is a political
prisoner who has been put behind bars by Don
Pizarro; his wife, Leonore, is trying to free him.
'Florestan is not an easy role. It is short, but it
does place some demands on the singer because
the tessitura is so fiendishly high, particularly in
the aria that opens Act 2,' says Skelton. 'But I
really love singing Florestan and it is fun to sing
with the sort of abandon you can't really do in
lengthy Wagner. You can let your hair down a
little bit more with this.'

And, says Skelton, there's a certain freedom
that comes from a concert performance:
'It's nice to concentrate only on the musical
values. All the great operas have the drama
written into the music.'

SATURDAY 22 JULY

PROMS AT... STAGE@THEDOCK, HULL
12.30pm–c2.00pm
3.00pm–c4.30pm • 5.30pm–c7.00pm

For ticket prices, see page 159

ROYAL NORTHERN SINFONIA

Telemann Water Music – overture   8'
Delius Summer Night on the River   5'
Handel
Water Music – Suite No. 3 in G major   11'
Mendelssohn
Calm Sea and Prosperous Voyage   12'
Rameau Naïs – overture   5'
Grace Williams Sea Sketches –
High Wind; Calm Sea in Summer   10'
Handel
Water Music – Suite No. 2 in D major   12'

Royal Northern Sinfonia
Nicholas McGegan *conductor*

There will be no interval

The BBC Proms travels out of London, to Hull –
UK City of Culture 2017 – for a site-specific
performance of music inspired by water, centring
on Handel's *Water Music* suites, first performed
300 years ago at a river party for George I on the
Thames. Pioneering early music expert Nicholas
McGegan directs the Royal Northern Sinfonia at
Stage@TheDock – Hull's outdoor amphitheatre –
in a programme featuring everything from storms
and shipwrecks to calm seas and seductive sirens.
See 'Water Music', pages 84–87.

Broadcast live on BBC Radio 3 (3.00pm performance)

SPOTLIGHT ON ...

Nicholas McGegan
Proms at ... Stage@TheDock

By now, we're used to the Proms spreading its varied activities outside its iconic home base at London's Royal Albert Hall – just think of Proms Chamber Music at nearby Cadogan Hall. But this year the festival travels much further afield than Sloane Square – to Hull, UK City of Culture 2017. 'And where better to do Handel's *Water Music* than by the Humber?' enthuses the event's conductor, period performance specialist Nicholas McGegan.

It might be a long way north of the River Thames, location of the piece's celebrated premiere in 1717 and where Handel's dance suites famously serenaded King George I on his river excursion from Whitehall to Chelsea and back. But McGegan's three performances, outdoors at Hull's historic dock, celebrate not only the 300th anniversary of the piece itself, but also the city's own maritime achievements.

McGegan conducts the Royal Northern Sinfonia in the concerts. 'I've worked with them for more than a decade,' he explains. 'Over the years we've done quite a lot of Handel together, including three oratorios, as well as lots of Beethoven and even some Mahler. The RNS has a great feeling for musical style – whether it's of the 18th century, or something more recent. They always play with such joy and elan. I'm really looking forward to an exciting trip!'

Randy Beach (McGegan); Darren Gillam (Gillam)

SATURDAY 22 JULY

PROM 10 📺
7.30pm–c9.40pm • Royal Albert Hall

PRICE BAND Ⓐ

WEEKEND PROMMING PASS *see page 159*

R. Strauss Metamorphosen   24'

Tom Service and Nicholas Collon introduce Beethoven's Symphony No. 3, with live excerpts 25'

INTERVAL

Beethoven
Symphony No. 3 in E flat major, 'Eroica'   47'

Tom Service *presenter*

Aurora Orchestra
Nicholas Collon *conductor*

No symphony pulses more vigorously with the rhythms of political protest than Beethoven's 'Eroica', whose defiant opening chords mark the arrival of the Romantic symphony. In their novel introduction, BBC Radio 3's Tom Service and conductor Nicholas Collon dismantle and reassemble this groundbreaking work, with the help of live excerpts, before the Aurora Orchestra gets under the skin of the work by performing the complete symphony – from memory. The concert opens with Richard Strauss's 1945 *Metamorphosen*. Scored for 23 solo strings, this ecstatic, elegiac work closes with an 'Eroica' quotation that mourns the devastation brought about by another, even darker, political regime.

📺 *Broadcast on BBC Four on 18 August (Beethoven)*

PROMS EXTRA
SCRATCH ORCHESTRA AND CHORUS
1.30pm–3.30pm • Imperial College Union Join professional musicians for the first Proms Scratch Orchestra and Chorus and create a piece of music inspired by tonight's Prom. You don't need to be able to read music, and all abilities are welcome. *Open to ages 16-plus. See pages 72–73 for details.*

PROMS EXTRA READING
5.45pm–6.30pm • Imperial College Union Readings inspired by Napoleon Bonaparte, to whom Beethoven originally dedicated his 'Eroica' Symphony.
Edited version broadcast on BBC Radio 3 during tonight's interval

---

SUNDAY 23 JULY

PROMS 11 & 12 📷
Prom 11 2.00pm–c4.00pm • Royal Albert Hall
Prom 12 6.00pm–c8.00pm • Royal Albert Hall

PRICE BAND Ⓗ

JESS GILLAM

TEN PIECES PRESENTS ...
SIR HENRY'S MAGNIFICENT MUSICAL INSPIRATIONS!

Programme to include music by Beethoven, Copland, Elgar, Mozart, Respighi and Ravi Shankar

Kathryn Lewek *soprano* • **Jess Gillam** *saxophone*

Ten Pieces Children's Choir
Royal Philharmonic Orchestra
Jessica Cottis *conductor*
There will be one interval

Join rollicking ringmaster Sir Henry Wood (founder-conductor of the Proms) on an exciting adventure for all the family. Together with young performers, the Ten Pieces Children's Choir and guests, he discovers how nature, history, dreams, love, magic and lots more have inspired composers to create musical masterpieces. See 'New Music', pages 66–71; 'Summer Adventures', pages 76–78.

British Sign Language-interpreted performance (Prom 11)

📷 *Broadcast live on BBC Radio 3; recorded for future broadcast on BBC Radio 2 (Prom 12)*

PROMS EXTRA FILM
12.00pm–1.00pm • Imperial College Union *Ten Pieces I:* An inspiring and immersive cinematic film that introduces children to 10 pieces of classical music. With performances by the BBC National Orchestra of Wales.

PROMS EXTRA FILM
4.00pm–5.00pm • Imperial College Union *Ten Pieces II:* Celebrities introduce performances by the BBC Philharmonic of the second selection of Ten Pieces.

MONDAY 24 JULY

PROMS AT... CADOGAN HALL, PCM 2
1.00pm–c2.00pm • Cadogan Hall

For ticket prices, see page 159

ANNELIEN VAN WAUWE

Webern Langsamer Satz 11'

Laurent Durupt
Grids for Greed c10'
BBC commission: world premiere

Mozart Clarinet Quintet in A major 32'

Van Kuijk Quartet
Annelien Van Wauwe *clarinet*

There will be no interval

Two of BBC Radio 3's current New Generation Artists come together for a programme of chamber music spanning over 200 years. The Van Kuijk Quartet joins forces with clarinettist Annelien Van Wauwe for Mozart's lyrical Clarinet Quintet, whose expansive melodies and sunny A major key belie the struggles and sadnesses of his personal life. Webern's *Langsamer Satz* (Slow Movement) is, by contrast, the ecstatic outpouring of a young man in love, happier than ever before and writing music once described as '*Tristan and Isolde* compressed into 11 minutes'. In his first string quartet, which today receives its world premiere, French composer and pianist Laurent Durupt explores contrasts both of musical material and musical time, and asks whether the differences are conflicting or complementary. *See 'New Music', pages 66–71.*

SPOTLIGHT ON ...
Van Kuijk Quartet • PCM 2

It's been a remarkably swift ascent to success for the Paris-based Van Kuijk Quartet. Formed in 2012, the foursome swept to victory with three awards – including First Prize – at the 2015 Wigmore Hall International String Quartet Competition, and the group has been a BBC Radio 3 New Generation Artist since 2015. How has their musical personality developed over such a short space of time? 'We're more mature, following more and more stage experience,' explains second violinist Sylvain Favre-Bulle. 'Our connection together and our identity have grown stronger and we feel freer now in our choices and artistic direction.'

That freedom in terms of artistic choices extends to their Proms debut, for which they contrast an iconic chamber classic with a brand-new piece by their compatriot Laurent Durupt. 'He's an extremely talented composer, of our own generation,' continues Favre-Bulle, 'and we feel it's very important to play the music of our time.' And for Mozart's glorious Clarinet Quintet, they're joined by Belgian clarinettist and fellow New Generation Artist Annelien Van Wauwe. 'It's one of the most beautiful chamber works,' says Favre-Bulle, 'and we particularly love it because the clarinet connects so completely with the instruments of the string quartet. We've already played with Annelien and we're really looking forward to reuniting for this project.'

MONDAY 24 JULY

PROM 13
7.30pm–c10.00pm • Royal Albert Hall

PRICE BAND **A**

MALCOLM SARGENT'S 500th PROM

Trad., arr. Henry Wood
The National Anthem 3'

Berlioz
Overture 'Le carnaval romain' 9'

Schumann
Piano Concerto in A minor 34'

INTERVAL

Elgar
Overture 'Cockaigne (In London Town)' 14'

Walton Façade Suite No. 1;
Suite No. 2 – Popular Song 14'

Holst The Perfect Fool – ballet music 11'

Delius
On Hearing the First Cuckoo in Spring 6'

Britten The Young Person's Guide to the Orchestra 18'

Beatrice Rana *piano*

BBC Symphony Orchestra
Sir Andrew Davis *conductor*

To mark the 50th anniversary of the death of Malcolm Sargent, chief conductor of the Proms from 1947 until his death in 1967, Sir Andrew Davis recreates Sargent's 500th Prom from 1966, highlighting his work as a champion of English music. *See 'Staff Sargent', pages 80–83.*

Broadcast on BBC Four on 28 July

PROMS EXTRA TALK
5.45pm–6.30pm • Imperial College Union Broadcaster Humphrey Burton discusses the career of Malcolm Sargent, who was closely connected with the Proms for the last 20 years of his life.
Edited version broadcast on BBC Radio 3 during tonight's interval

Christian Ruvolo (Wauwe); Andreas H. Vega (Van Kuijk Quartet)

SPOTLIGHT ON ...

Beatrice Rana • Prom 13

Beatrice Rana first fell in love with Schumann's fiendishly challenging Piano Concerto when she was a teenager and she badgered her teacher to let her play it. 'But he said it was too early and I had to wait,' the Italian pianist recalls. 'I was so frustrated but now I thank him, as it's a very special and delicate concerto that requires maturity.'

Fast-forward a few years, factor in a silver medal at the Van Cliburn Competition, a recording contract and a place on the BBC Radio 3 New Generation Artists scheme, and 24-year-old Rana is now ready. She'll be playing the Schumann for her Proms debut. 'On the one hand, it's very Classical, with a solid structure; on the other hand, it has this incredible Romantic inspiration,' says Rana. 'There's a balance between the two.' Completed in 1845, Schumann's only piano concerto became one of his most popular works, and has remained a favourite among pianists and listeners alike. 'This concerto is like enlarged chamber music,' says Rana. 'That's what I find really amazing.'

'I have an incredibly special relationship with this composer,' she adds. 'I've actually played more Schumann than Chopin, which is strange for a pianist. Yet I have always liked composers with a contrapuntal approach, and I'm also a very passionate Bach player. There's a strong connection between Bach and Schumann.'

Nicolas Bets (Rana); Sim Canetty-Clarke (Wilson); Sean Purser (Buckley)

TUESDAY 25 JULY

PROM 14
6.30pm–c8.30pm • Royal Albert Hall

PRICE BAND Ⓐ

JOHN WILSON

Vaughan Williams
Symphony No. 9 in E minor   *34'*

INTERVAL

Holst The Planets   *50'*

CBSO Youth Chorus (female voices)
BBC Scottish Symphony Orchestra
John Wilson conductor

Proms favourite John Wilson – who returns later this season with his John Wilson Orchestra (Proms 34 & 35) – tonight makes his first appearance at the Proms as the BBC Scottish Symphony Orchestra's new Associate Guest Conductor. Here he swaps Hollywood and Broadway classics for another of his personal passions: the great British symphonic classics. Holst's galactic suite conjures up the epic scope of a movie blockbuster in luminous music of infinite vistas, while Vaughan Williams's enigmatic final symphony also revels in an augmented sound-world: it's a piece Wilson sees as a suitably radical counterpart to *The Planets*.

PROMS EXTRA TALK
4.45pm–5.30pm • Imperial College Union Musicologist Kate Kennedy introduces Vaughan Williams's Symphony No. 9. *Edited version broadcast on BBC Radio 3 during tonight's interval*

TUESDAY 25 JULY

PROM 15 • LATE NIGHT   🌙 📻 📺
10.15pm–c11.30pm • Royal Albert Hall

PRICE BAND Ⓒ

JULES BUCKLEY

THE 'GODLIKE GENIUS' OF SCOTT WALKER

Jarvis Cocker
John Grant

Heritage Orchestra
Jules Buckley conductor

There will be no interval

An icon of the 1960s, Scott Walker has travelled from Walker Brothers teen idol to avant-garde contemporary musician, influencing artists from David Bowie and Leonard Cohen to Goldfrapp along the way. Tonight's Late Night Prom tribute presents tracks from his four self-titled albums with live orchestral backing for the very first time. Among the special guests are Jarvis Cocker and John Grant.

📻 *Broadcast live on BBC Radio 3 and BBC Radio 6 Music*

📺 *Broadcast on BBC Four on 28 July*

> **Every Prom broadcast live on BBC Radio 3**

WEDNESDAY 26 JULY

PROM 16
7.30pm–c9.40pm • Royal Albert Hall

PRICE BAND Ⓐ

ILAN VOLKOV

Liszt Hamlet   10'

Julian Anderson Piano Concerto   c25'
BBC co-commission with the Bergen Philharmonic Orchestra and Sydney Symphony Orchestra: world premiere

INTERVAL

Liszt
From the Cradle to the Grave   14'

Mussorgsky, orch. Ravel
Pictures at an Exhibition   34'

Steven Osborne *piano*

BBC Scottish Symphony Orchestra
Ilan Volkov *conductor*

In his 13 symphonic poems Liszt transformed the concert overture into something urgently new. The BBC Scottish Symphony Orchestra and its Principal Guest Conductor Ilan Volkov here perform two of the last in the series – the mercurial *Hamlet*, a study of Shakespeare's tragic hero, and *From the Cradle to the Grave*, one of Liszt's most experimental works. They sit alongside Mussorgsky's much-loved *Pictures at an Exhibition* and the world premiere of a new piano concerto by Julian Anderson, which offers a tour around 'an imaginary museum' of contrasting worlds and sensations. *See 'New Music', pages 66–71.*

PROMS EXTRA TALK
5.45pm–6.30pm • Imperial College Union The first in a three-part series in which pianist and broadcaster David Owen Norris explores a musical theme connected with the following Prom: today's subject is orchestration.
Edited version broadcast on BBC Radio 3 during tonight's interval

---

THURSDAY 27 JULY

PROM 17
7.30pm–c9.25pm • Royal Albert Hall

PRICE BAND Ⓐ

JUANJO MENA

Mark Simpson The Immortal   34'
London premiere

INTERVAL

Tchaikovsky
Symphony No. 6 in B minor, 'Pathétique' 46'

Christopher Purves *baritone*

London Voices
Crouch End Festival Chorus
BBC Philharmonic
Juanjo Mena *conductor*

Life and death collide in a concert that explores what lies beyond the limits of human existence. In his passionate Sixth Symphony, which the composer described as 'the best thing I ever composed or shall compose', Tchaikovsky reimagined what the symphony could be, daring to face death with uncertainty. The BBC Philharmonic's Composer in Association and a former BBC Young Musician winner and BBC Radio 3 New Generation Artist, Mark Simpson, also looks to the afterlife in his critically acclaimed oratorio *The Immortal*. Inspired by Victorian seances, he conjures up eerie visions of a world beyond. *See 'New Music', pages 66–71.*

PROMS EXTRA TALK
5.45pm–6.30pm • Imperial College Union Ahead of the London premiere of his oratorio *The Immortal*, composer Mark Simpson talks to presenter Kate Molleson.
Edited version broadcast on BBC Radio 3 during tonight's interval

---

FRIDAY 28 JULY

PROM 18
7.30pm–c9.35pm • Royal Albert Hall

PRICE BAND Ⓐ
WEEKEND PROMMING PASS *see page 159*

IDA FALK WINLAND

Korngold The Sea Hawk – overture   6'

Anders Hillborg Sirens   33'
UK premiere

INTERVAL

Rimsky-Korsakov
Scheherazade   45'

Hannah Holgersson *soprano*
Ida Falk Winland *soprano*

BBC Symphony Chorus
BBC Symphony Orchestra
James Gaffigan *conductor*

Rimsky-Korsakov's *Scheherazade* tells magical tales from the *Thousand and One Nights* in music suffused with oriental colour and seafaring drama. Swashbuckling battles are played out on the high seas in Korngold's stirring score to the 1940 film *The Sea Hawk*, while danger also lurks in the waters of Anders Hillborg's *Sirens*, inspired by the mythical seductresses of Homer's *Odyssey*. See 'New Music', pages 66–71.

PROMS EXTRA FAMILY
5.45pm–6.30pm • Imperial College Union (Dining Hall)
Join professional musicians for a family-friendly introduction to tonight's Prom. Bring your instrument and join in!
Suitable for all the family (ages 7-plus). See pages 76–78 for details.

PROMS EXTRA TALK
5.45pm–6.30pm • Imperial College Union (Concert Hall)
Emeritus Professor of European Archaeology at the University of Oxford, Sir Barry Cunliffe, considers the role of the sea in Greek myth with journalist and classicist Charlotte Higgins.
Edited version broadcast on BBC Radio 3 during tonight's interval

SATURDAY 29 JULY
PROM 19
12.00pm–c1.00pm • Royal Albert Hall

For ticket prices, see page 158

GRANT LLEWELLYN AND ANDY PIDCOCK

RELAXED PROM

Programme to include music by Rimsky-Korsakov, Rossini and Johann Strauss II, as well as Pharrell Williams's 'Happy' and the 'Doctor Who' theme

Andy Pidcock *presenter/musician*

BBC National Orchestra of Wales
Grant Llewellyn *conductor/presenter*

There will be no interval

A concert suitable for children and adults with autism, sensory and communication impairments and learning disabilities as well as individuals who are Deaf, hard of hearing, blind and partially sighted. Presented by conductor Grant Llewellyn and musician Andy Pidcock, the first ever Relaxed Prom is a fun and interactive musical experience in a welcoming environment, with plenty of opportunities for participation. During the concert there is a relaxed attitude to movement and noise in the auditorium. (There are over 80 musicians in the orchestra alone, so it will be loud!) You can move about, dance, sing or just listen. 'Chill-out' spaces outside the auditorium are available. Produced in collaboration with the BBC National Orchestra of Wales and Royal Albert Hall Education & Outreach, the Relaxed Prom also features picture communication systems projected onto large screens, as well as audio description and British Sign Language interpretation. See 'Open to All', pages 40–41.

SATURDAY 29 JULY
PROM 20
7.30pm–c9.40pm • Royal Albert Hall

PRICE BAND (A)
WEEKEND PROMMING PASS *see page 159*

STEPHEN HOUGH

Brahms
Piano Concerto No. 1 in D minor   49'

INTERVAL

David Sawer
The Greatest Happiness Principle   14'

Haydn
Symphony No. 99 in E flat major   25'

Stephen Hough *piano*

BBC Philharmonic
Mark Wigglesworth *conductor*

Though booed at its premiere in 1859, Brahms's First Piano Concerto has gone on to become one of the most-beloved of piano concertos. A giant of a piece with an emotional scope to match, it is at its most tender in the slow movement – a 'gentle portrait' of Clara Schumann. Tempering this intensity is Haydn's graceful Symphony No. 99 and David Sawer's The Greatest Happiness Principle, with its dancing, rhythmically charged textures. Inspired by Jeremy Bentham's Utopian philosophies, it is performed tonight as part of the PRS for Music Foundation's Resonate scheme, promoting British music of the past 25 years, in partnership with the Association of British Orchestras and BBC Radio 3.

PROMS EXTRA TALK
5.45pm–6.30pm • Imperial College Union Novelist Charlotte Mendelson asks why writers seem reluctant to engage with happiness and why so much literature depicts unhappy people. With psychologist and broadcaster Claudia Hammond.
Edited version broadcast on BBC Radio 3 during tonight's interval

SUNDAY 30 JULY
PROM 21
7.00pm–c9.25pm • Royal Albert Hall

PRICE BAND (A)
WEEKEND PROMMING PASS *see page 159*

XIAN ZHANG

Sir James MacMillan
A European Requiem   43'
European premiere

INTERVAL

Beethoven
Symphony No. 9 in D minor, 'Choral'   65'

Erin Wall *soprano*
Sonia Prina *mezzo-soprano*
Iestyn Davies *counter-tenor*
Simon O'Neill *tenor*
Jacques Imbrailo *baritone*
Alexander Vinogradov *bass*

CBSO Chorus
BBC National Chorus of Wales
BBC National Orchestra of Wales
Xian Zhang *conductor*

Beethoven's great hymn to humanity joins Sir James MacMillan's *European Requiem*, which also makes a plea for unity. See 'New Music', pages 66–71.

Broadcast on BBC Four this evening

PROMS EXTRA SING
10.00am–12.45pm • Royal Albert Hall Join Mary King and members of the BBC Singers and BBC National Orchestra of Wales to sing excerpts from Beethoven's Symphony No. 9. Experience in sight-reading or a knowledge of the piece is an advantage but not essential. *Suitable for ages 16-plus. See pages 72–73 for details.*

PROMS EXTRA TALK
5.15pm–6.00pm • Imperial College Union Novelist Lawrence Norfolk selects writers who have considered the idea of 'Europe', with readings performed by an actor.
Edited version broadcast on BBC Radio 3 during tonight's interval

MONDAY 31 JULY

PROMS AT… CADOGAN HALL, PCM 3
1.00pm–c2.00pm • Cadogan Hall

For ticket prices, see page 159

ANU KOMSI

FROM THE KALEVALA TO KAUSTINEN: FINNISH FOLK AND BAROQUE MUSIC

Anu Komsi *soprano*
Kreeta-Maria Kentala *violin*
Andrew Lawrence-King *harp/kantele/psaltery*
Eero Palviainen *theorbo/guitar*
Milla Viljamaa *harmonium*

There will be no interval

Finnish folk music meets familiar Baroque textures in a programme exploring two genres with a shared love of song and dance. Soprano Anu Komsi and violinist Kreeta-Maria Kentala both have family roots in the folk-rich municipality of Kaustinen, Western Finland. They are joined by fellow boundary-crossing musicians for a whistle-stop journey through Finnish musical history encompassing the 16th-century *Piae cantiones* (the earliest printed book of Finnish music) and the 19th-century national folk epic, the *Kalevala*, which so inspired Sibelius. The concert also features favourites by Corelli and other Baroque composers, as well as folk songs from Kaustinen and music by Kreeta Haapasalo (1813–93), who was born in the region.

> **Every Prom broadcast live on BBC Radio 3**

MONDAY 31 JULY

PROM 22
7.30pm–c9.20pm • Royal Albert Hall

PRICE BAND **B**

RAPHAËL PICHON

Monteverdi Vespers of 1610   100'

Giuseppina Bridelli *soprano*
Eva Zaïcik *mezzo-soprano*
Emiliano Gonzalez Toro *tenor*
Magnus Staveland *tenor*
Virgile Ancely *bass*
Renaud Bres *bass*
Geoffroy Buffière *bass*

Pygmalion
Raphaël Pichon *director*

There will be no interval

Before there was Bach's Mass in B minor or Beethoven's *Missa solemnis* there was Monteverdi's *Vespers*, a choral masterpiece of unprecedented musical scope and audacious beauty. The work's textural extremes, multiple choirs and sonic effects are brought to life in a performance marking the 450th anniversary of the composer's birth. Award-winning French Baroque ensemble Pygmalion makes its Proms debut under its director Raphaël Pichon, together with an exciting line-up of young soloists.

PROMS EXTRA FILM
5.30pm–6.30pm • Imperial College Union Musicologist H. C. Robbins Landon and composer Nadia Boulanger explore the life and music of Monteverdi in this film, made in 1967 to mark the 400th anniversary of the composer's birth.

TUESDAY I AUGUST

PROM 23
7.30pm–c10.15pm • Royal Albert Hall

PRICE BAND **B**

WILLIAM CHRISTIE

Handel
Israel in Egypt (original 1739 version)   129'

Anna Devin *soprano*
Rowan Pierce *soprano*
Christopher Lowrey *counter-tenor*
Jeremy Budd *tenor*
Dingle Yandell *bass-baritone*
Callum Thorpe *bass*

Choir of the Age of Enlightenment
Orchestra of the Age of Enlightenment
William Christie *conductor*

There will be one interval

Filled with frogs, locusts, hailstones and rivers of blood, *Israel in Egypt* is one of Handel's most extravagantly dramatic oratorios. Placing the chorus in the spotlight, Handel uses the collective voices to tell the story of an entire people, demanding greater virtuosity than ever before in some thrilling choral writing. William Christie conducts the period ensemble the Orchestra of the Age of Enlightenment, joined by the group's own choir, in the launch of a series of Handel oratorios to be performed over the coming seasons at the Proms.

PROMS EXTRA TALK
5.45pm–6.30pm • Imperial College Union Musicologist Suzanne Aspden introduces Handel's *Israel in Egypt*.
Edited version broadcast on BBC Radio 3 during tonight's interval

Maart Kytöharju (Komsi); Piergab (Pichon); Denis Rouvre (Christie)

WEDNESDAY 2 AUGUST

PROM 24
7.00pm–c8.55pm • Royal Albert Hall

PRICE BAND **B**

MARIANNE CREBASSA

J. S. Bach, arr. Stravinsky
Canonic Variations on 'Vom Himmel
hoch, da komm' ich her', BWV 769   *11'*
Ravel Shéhérazade   *17'*

INTERVAL

John Adams
Naive and Sentimental Music   *49'*

Marianne Crebassa *mezzo-soprano*

Philharmonia Voices
Philharmonia Orchestra
Esa-Pekka Salonen *conductor*

The celebrations of John Adams's 70th birthday continue with his *Naive and Sentimental Music*, conducted by its dedicatee, Esa-Pekka Salonen. A symphony in all but name, the work glows with multi-layered textures. From meditative Minimalism to intricate counterpoint in Stravinsky's *Canonic Variations on 'Vom Himmel hoch, da komm' ich her'* – a colourful 'recomposition' of Bach's own chorale variations on the Lutheran hymn. Rising French mezzo-soprano Marianne Crebassa is the soloist in Ravel's heady song-cycle *Shéhérazade*, an exotic musical fantasy of distant lands and forbidden love. See 'To Sing a New Tune', pages 26–31; 'Maximal Minimalists', pages 32–35.

PROMS EXTRA TALK
5.15pm–6.00pm • Imperial College Union BBC Radio 3 New Generation Thinker Seán Williams considers Friedrich Schiller's essay *On Naive and Sentimental Poetry*, with writer Rachel Hewitt.
Edited version broadcast on BBC Radio 3 during tonight's interval

SPOTLIGHT ON …
Esa-Pekka Salonen • Prom 24

Conductor Esa-Pekka Salonen feels a strong personal connection to the centrepiece of his Prom with the Philharmonia Orchestra. 'John Adams's *Naive and Sentimental Music* was actually my commission, when I was Music Director at the Los Angeles Philharmonic. I premiered it too – and John even dedicated it to me.' Salonen is keen to stress Adams's impact on his career, both as a conductor and a composer. 'He's a good friend of mine and he was one of the most important influences on me as a composer when I was in my thirties. He's found something that feels very free, very undogmatic and he can move very easily between idioms and materials – I still really admire that today.'

Naive and Sentimental Music is a symphony in all but name, and full of challenges for any orchestra and conductor – but how does Salonen view it now, 18 years after he conducted its premiere? 'It's still a technically demanding piece, but I think I have a better grasp of its overall shape now. It'll be like meeting an old friend again – even if it's in a wrestling match that I have to win!'

Also in his Proms concert are pieces by two composers Salonen especially loves. 'Stravinsky's *Vom Himmel hoch* is a piece I hardly knew before, but it's always fun to learn something new. And Ravel's *Shéhérazade* – well, it's just perfection in its balance, its contrasts, its colours. I don't know anybody who doesn't love it!'

WEDNESDAY 2 AUGUST

PROM 25 • LATE NIGHT
10.15pm–c11.30pm • Royal Albert Hall

PRICE BAND **F**

SIR JOHN ELIOT GARDINER

Schütz
Nun lob, mein Seel, den Herren,
SWV 41   *8'*
Nicht uns, Herr, sondern deinem
Namen, SWV 43   *6'*
Danket dem Herren, denn er
ist freundlich, SWV 45   *7'*

J. S. Bach
Cantata No. 79 'Gott der Herr ist
Sonn und Schild'   *15'*
Cantata No. 80 'Ein feste Burg ist
unser Gott'   *25'*

Monteverdi Choir
English Baroque Soloists
Sir John Eliot Gardiner *conductor*

There will be no interval

In 2000 Sir John Eliot Gardiner, the Monteverdi Choir and the English Baroque Soloists performed all of Bach's surviving church cantatas in an unprecedented year-long musical pilgrimage. They return to these astonishing musical statements of faith, continuing our series of concerts marking the 500th anniversary of the Protestant Reformation. Hear two of Bach's Lutheran cantatas – including *Ein feste Burg ist unser Gott*, itself composed for a Reformation-anniversary celebration – alongside psalm-settings by his German musical forebear Heinrich Schütz, alive with dance rhythms and vivid instrumental textures. See 'To Sing a New Tune', pages 26–31.

Simon Fowler/Erato–Warner Classics (Crebassa); Katja Tähjä (Salonen); Sim Canetty-Clarke (Gardiner)

THURSDAY 3 AUGUST

PROM 26
7.30pm–c9.50pm • Royal Albert Hall

PRICE BAND **B**

PAAVO JÄRVI

Erkki-Sven Tüür Flamma 16'
UK premiere

Mozart
Sinfonia concertante in E flat major 30'

INTERVAL

Brahms
Symphony No. 2 in D major 45'

Vilde Frang *violin*
Lawrence Power *viola*

Deutsche Kammerphilharmonie Bremen
Paavo Järvi *conductor*

The Deutsche Kammerphilharmonie Bremen and its Artistic Director Paavo Järvi return to the Proms, joined by British violist Lawrence Power and Norwegian violinist Vilde Frang for Mozart's genial *Sinfonia concertante*. Sitting somewhere between a concerto and a symphony, it's a perfect showcase for the virtuosity of this ensemble and its sunny good humour offers a striking contrast to Erkki-Sven Tüür's arresting *Flamma* – a vivid musical portrait of fire as both purifying force and agent of destruction. Smoke clears and sunshine returns in Brahms's optimistic Second Symphony, with its free-flowing melodies and irrepressible closing dance. *See 'New Music', pages 66–71.*

PROMS EXTRA TALK
5.45pm–6.30pm • Imperial College Union Musicians from the Deutsche Kammerphilharmonie Bremen talk about the life of the orchestra and its innovative education collaboration with Bremen East School.
Edited version broadcast on BBC Radio 3 during tonight's interval

---

SPOTLIGHT ON ...
Vilde Frang • Prom 26

'This is Mozart at his most glorious,' says Norwegian violinist Vilde Frang, who this year makes her second Proms concerto appearance. 'It is like an opera for two instruments.' The piece? Mozart's *Sinfonia concertante* in E flat major for violin and viola, which the Norwegian violinist performs at this year's Proms with Lawrence Power, who is, in her words, 'an aristocrat of the viola – this is a dream scenario!'

Mozart wrote this miraculous work in 1779, perhaps inspired by the fashion in Paris and Mannheim for hybrid symphony-concertos. 'The interaction between the two solo instruments is the essence of the piece,' says Frang. 'The whole structure is so involved. It outshines that of Mozart's five violin concertos: it's simply on another level.'

For as long as she can remember, Mozart's music has been part of Frang's life. 'It has been with me since before I was aware. I grew up with Mozart and he belongs to some of my earliest impressions,' she says. 'He was like a sort of oxygen.' But that doesn't mean his music has been any simpler to play. 'I have gone through different stages with Mozart. It's like love: it means something different from when you are 2 to 19 to 48 to 73. You discover new aspects,' she says. 'But I think I can say that the *Sinfonia concertante* has always meant a lot to me – and I play it as often as I can.'

FRIDAY 4 AUGUST

PROM 27 📺
7.30pm–c10.00pm • Royal Albert Hall

PRICE BAND **B**
WEEKEND PROMMING PASS *see page 159*

DIANNE REEVES

ELLA AND DIZZY: A CENTENARY TRIBUTE

Dianne Reeves *singer*
James Morrison *trumpet*

BBC Concert Orchestra
John Mauceri *conductor*

There will be one interval

Described by *The New York Times* as 'the most admired jazz diva since the heyday of Sarah Vaughan, Ella Fitzgerald and Billie Holiday', Dianne Reeves is joined by virtuoso trumpeter James Morrison to pay a double tribute to Ella Fitzgerald and Dizzy Gillespie in the centenary year of their births. Conducted by Broadway musical and Hollywood movie-score legend John Mauceri, the celebrations contrast the Great American Songbook, which played a key role in Fitzgerald's live and recording career, with the bebop and Afro-Latin sounds in which Gillespie excelled. *See 'The First Lady of Song', pages 36–39.*

📺 *Broadcast on BBC Four this evening*

PROMS EXTRA SING
5.30pm–6.30pm • Imperial College Union (Metric Bar) Join Ken Burton to sing standards associated with Ella Fitzgerald in a fun session. No experience of singing is required. *Suitable for ages 16-plus. See pages 72–73 for details.*

PROMS EXTRA TALK
5.45pm–6.30pm • Imperial College Union (Concert Hall) Writers Jackie Kay and Ali Smith talk to Kevin Le Gendre about how Ella Fitzgerald's voice has inspired them. *Edited version broadcast on BBC Radio 3 during tonight's interval*

Kaupo Kikkas (Järvi), Marco Borggreve (Frang), Jerris Madison (Reeves)

SATURDAY 5 AUGUST

PROM 28
7.30pm–c9.20pm • Royal Albert Hall

PRICE BAND **A**

WEEKEND PROMMING PASS *see page 159*

THOMAS ADÈS

Francisco Coll Mural   24'
London premiere

Thomas Adès Polaris   14'

INTERVAL

Stravinsky The Rite of Spring   34'

National Youth Orchestra of Great Britain
Thomas Adès *conductor*

Hear some of the UK's finest young musical talent, directed by composer and conductor Thomas Adès, in a bold programme of works that push the orchestra to its technical and sonic limits. Adès's own *Polaris*, subtitled 'A Voyage for Orchestra', takes inspiration from the North Star, conjuring a vast interstellar landscape that unfolds from a simple piano theme into a massive sonic spiral. Francisco Coll's *Mural*, tonight receiving its London premiere, is another richly textured, large-scale work – a 'grotesque symphony, in which Dionysus meets Apollo'. The concert's climax is Stravinsky's ballet score *The Rite of Spring*, whose frenzied rhythms and provocative harmonies prompted a legendary riot at its Paris premiere. *See 'Russian Revolutions', pages 20–25; 'New Music', pages 66–71.*

Broadcast on BBC Four on 6 August

PROMS EXTRA NYO YOUNG PROMOTERS
5.30pm–6.30pm • Imperial College Union Join musicians from the NYOGB at this unique and friendly event for teenagers hosted by the NYO's Young Promoters – a great chance to find out about the music in this evening's Prom. *Book tickets at bbc.co.uk/proms from 9 June.*

SUNDAY 6 AUGUST

PROM 29
6.00pm–c10.15pm • Royal Albert Hall

PRICE BAND **B**

WEEKEND PROMMING PASS *see page 159*

Mussorgsky, orch. Shostakovich
Khovanshchina   190'
(concert performance; sung in Russian)

Ante Jerkunica *Ivan Khovansky*
Christopher Ventris *Andrey Khovansky*
Vsevolod Grivnov *Golitsin*
Elena Maximova *Marfa*
Ain Anger *Dosifey*
George Gagnidze *Shaklovity*
Jennifer Rhys-Davies *Susanna*
Norbert Ernst *Scribe*
Vlada Borovko *Emma*
Colin Judson *Kuzka*

Schola Cantorum of The Cardinal Vaughan Memorial School
Tiffin Boys' Choir
BBC Singers
Slovak Philharmonic Choir

BBC Symphony Orchestra
Semyon Bychkov *conductor*
Paul Curran *stage director*

There will be two intervals

Shot through with noble melodies, Mussorgsky's 'national music drama' weaves a darkly tangled political web in which Russia herself is the casualty. Caught between reformists and continuity, the nation struggles to find peace, and the conflict leads only to death in the opera's shattering climax. Semyon Bychkov conducts the BBC Symphony Orchestra and an international cast, including mezzo-soprano Elena Maximova as the enigmatic Marfa. *See 'Russian Revolutions', pages 20–25.*

PROMS EXTRA FAMILY
10.00am–12.30pm • Royal Albert Hall Perform onstage at the Royal Albert Hall and create music inspired by highlights of this year's Proms season. Led by the BBC Concert Orchestra's Sarah Freestone. *Suitable for all the family (ages 7-plus). See pages 76–78 for details.*

PROMS EXTRA TALK
4.15pm–5.00pm • Imperial College Union Rosamund Bartlett discusses Mussorgsky's *Khovanshchina*. *Edited version broadcast on BBC Radio 3 during tonight's interval*

SPOTLIGHT ON ...

Semyon Bychkov • Prom 29

'*Khovanshchina* is the drama of Russia,' says conductor Semyon Bychkov, who brings Mussorgsky's five-act opera (left unfinished at his death in 1881) to the Proms this summer. '*Boris Godunov* is about an individual, but in *Khovanshchina* you have the tragedy of an entire nation.' It's an epic work that heads back in history to the Russia of 1682. Peter the Great was advocating reform and the Westernisation of society, but another group wanted Russia to honour its traditions. 'This conflict has always resided in Russian society: does it belong with the West or the East?' reflects Bychkov. 'And that, in fact, is a feature that makes this opera incredibly modern, because that conflict hasn't disappeared.'

Khovanshchina also marks an evolution in Mussorgsky's music, as he turned away from the recitative style of the earlier *Boris Godunov* in favour of writing led more by melody. Yet the composer died before he finished the piece. 'It was thanks to Rimsky-Korsakov that the opera came to the world's attention,' explains Bychkov, 'and then Shostakovich, who re-orchestrated it. Rimsky-Korsakov had prettified the music but in Shostakovich's orchestration *Khovanshchina* emerges at once as something very harsh but something very noble.'

'From the first note to the last, everything is a musical highlight. If you say "highlight", then it presupposes lowlights. There aren't any!'

MONDAY 7 AUGUST

PROMS AT... CADOGAN HALL, PCM 4
1.00pm–c2.00pm • Cadogan Hall

For ticket prices, see page 159

IL POMO D'ORO

Hasse
Adagio and Fugue in G minor   7'

Platti Cello Concerto in D major   12'

Vivaldi
Cello Concerto in A minor, RV 419   9'

Telemann
Divertimento in B flat major   10'

Boccherini
Cello Concerto in D major, G479   15'

Edgar Moreau *cello*

Il Pomo d'Oro
Maxim Emelyanychev *director*

There will be no interval

Still in his early twenties, French cellist Edgar Moreau is already making his mark with the exuberant virtuosity of his playing. Here he joins the Baroque ensemble Il Pomo d'Oro for a programme focusing on 18th-century concertos. Charged with all the rhetorical and emotional intensity of opera arias, these wonderfully expressive and colourful works range from the fretful melancholy of Vivaldi's Cello Concerto in A minor to the poised elegance of Boccherini's Concerto in D major and the irrepressible joy of Platti's Concerto in D major.

MONDAY 7 AUGUST

PROM 30
7.30pm–c9.45pm • Royal Albert Hall

PRICE BAND **A**

KIRILL KARABITS

Beethoven
Symphony No. 1 in C major   26'

R. Strauss Die Frau ohne Schatten –
Symphonic Fantasy   21'

INTERVAL

Prokofiev Seven, They Are Seven   8'

Walton Belshazzar's Feast   36'

David Butt Philip *tenor*
James Rutherford *baritone*

National Youth Choir of Great Britain
Bournemouth Symphony Orchestra
Kirill Karabits *conductor*

A concert of musical legends and fairy tales. Based on an ancient Mesopotamian text, Prokofiev's 1917 mini-cantata *Seven, They Are Seven* is a disquieting work that conjures both the fantasies and the realities of the Russian Revolution. Divine wrath crashes down upon Mesopotamia in Walton's choral spectacular *Belshazzar's Feast* – whose premiere in 1931 was conducted by Malcolm Sargent, later chief conductor of the Proms – while morality gets altogether more ambiguous in Strauss's richly scored fairy-tale allegory *Die Frau ohne Schatten* ('The Woman Without a Shadow'). See 'Russian Revolutions', pages 20–25.

PROMS EXTRA TALK
5.45pm–6.30pm • Imperial College Union Irving Finkel of the British Museum talks about the Babylonian history behind *Belshazzar's Feast* and the stories he has deciphered from cuneiform tablets.
Edited version broadcast on BBC Radio 3 during tonight's interval

TUESDAY 8 AUGUST

PROM 31
7.30pm–c10.10pm • Royal Albert Hall

PRICE BAND **C**

ANN HALLENBERG

Berlioz The Damnation of Faust   125'
(sung in French)

Michael Spyres *Faust*
Ann Hallenberg *Marguerite*
Ashley Riches *Brander*

Trinity Boys Choir
Monteverdi Choir
National Youth Choir of Scotland
Orchestre Révolutionnaire et Romantique
Sir John Eliot Gardiner *conductor*

There will be one interval

Sir John Eliot Gardiner returns to the Proms with *The Damnation of Faust*, continuing his multi-season Berlioz series. Part opera, part cantata, this 'dramatic legend' is an epic retelling of the Faust story that captures the extremes of man's ambition and folly in music by turns exquisite and grotesque. American tenor Michael Spyres returns to the Proms in the title-role, with Swedish mezzo-soprano Ann Hallenberg as the innocent victim, Marguerite.

PROMS EXTRA TALK
5.45pm–6.30pm • Imperial College Union Peter Stanford, writer of *The Devil: A Biography*, discusses the devil in music ahead of tonight's performance of Berlioz's *The Damnation of Faust*.
Edited version broadcast on BBC Radio 3 during tonight's interval

WEDNESDAY 9 AUGUST

PROM 32
7.00pm–c9.05pm • Royal Albert Hall

PRICE BAND Ⓐ

RYAN WIGGLESWORTH

Britten Ballad of Heroes   17'

Brian Elias Cello Concerto   c25'
BBC commission: world premiere

INTERVAL

Purcell, arr. Elgar
Jehova, quam multi sunt hostes mei   7'

Elgar 'Enigma' Variations   30'

Toby Spence *tenor*
Natalie Clein *cello*

BBC National Chorus of Wales
BBC National Orchestra of Wales
Ryan Wigglesworth *conductor*

Ryan Wigglesworth joins the BBC National
Orchestra and Chorus of Wales for a programme
that spans four centuries, from Purcell's dramatic
choral motet *Jehova, quam multi sunt hostes mei*, to
the world premiere of Brian Elias's Cello Concerto,
whose intricate, spiral structure creates a dream-like
musical narrative. The concert opens with Britten's
most overtly political work – an impassioned musical
stand against fascism that anticipates the composer's
War Requiem; and reaches its culmination with Elgar's
'Enigma' Variations, which includes the much-loved
'Nimrod'. *See 'New Music', pages 66–71.*

PROMS EXTRA READING
5.15pm–6.00pm • Imperial College Union A literary
complement to tonight's Prom, with readings from and
about some of the great revolutionary heroes of the 20th
century, with a particular focus on the Spanish Civil War.
Edited version broadcast on BBC Radio 3 during tonight's interval

SPOTLIGHT ON ...
Natalie Clein • Prom 32

When Natalie Clein heard Brian Elias's music
for the first time, she was immediately taken
by its descriptive, serious quality. 'Brian and I
became friends and I was thrilled when he asked
me if I'd like a cello concerto from him. A year
later he handed me a draft,' she explains. I feel
incredibly honoured and lucky.'

'Brian wanted to explore the lyrical qualities
of the cello, although there are virtuosic and
difficult moments,' says Clein. 'There is a
beautiful slow opening and third section.
The third section is a playful Sestina [an ancient
poetic form rich in word-play] – a virtuosic
challenge for the mind and fingers – and the
last movement has a sense of returning to the
beginning.' And like Elgar, who wrote one of
the best-loved cello concertos, Elias has included
a puzzle: 'Brian has told me rather enigmatically
that, as we're friends, he has written something
about me into the piece, which I have to find.'

A former BBC Radio 3 New Generation Artist,
Clein loves the challenge of performing a new
piece. 'There are no-one's footsteps to walk in,
which is both exciting and daunting,' she says.
'And for me it has also been liberating,
because Brian is so open to suggestions. It is
a lot of fun too, not least because Brian is an
absolute wizard in the kitchen. He cooks the
most incredible Indian curries, so that is another
really good reason to do lots of work with him!'

THURSDAY 10 AUGUST

PROM 33
7.30pm–c9.50pm • Royal Albert Hall

PRICE BAND Ⓐ

LISE DAVIDSEN

Sibelius
Karelia Suite   15'
Luonnotar   9'

Grieg Peer Gynt – excerpts   21'

INTERVAL

Schumann
Cello Concerto in A minor   22'

Hindemith
Symphony 'Mathis der Maler'   24'

Lise Davidsen *soprano*
Alban Gerhardt *cello*

BBC Philharmonic
John Storgårds *conductor*

Norwegian soprano Lise Davidsen makes her Proms
debut in excerpts from Grieg's *Peer Gynt* and Sibelius's
tone-poem *Luonnotar*. The sophisticated orchestral
textures and sensuous melodies of the latter
couldn't be further from the rough-hewn folk music
of the composer's buoyant *Karelia Suite*. Linked to
his opera about historical events at the time of the
Protestant Reformation, Hindemith's *Mathis der
Maler* was denounced by the Nazi regime as
'degenerate'. Alban Gerhardt is the soloist for
Schumann's Cello Concerto, which rejects overt
solo virtuosity in favour of a dialogue between cello
and orchestra. *See 'To Sing a New Tune', pages 26–31.*

PROMS EXTRA TALK
5.45pm–6.30pm • Imperial College Union Musicologist
and broadcaster Erik Levi discusses the music of Hindemith.
Edited version broadcast on BBC Radio 3 during tonight's interval

Benjamin Ealovega (Wigglesworth); Neda Navaee (Clein); Charlotte Gundersen (Davidsen)

FRIDAY 11 AUGUST

PROMS 34 & 35
Prom 34 2.00pm–c5.30pm • Royal Albert Hall
Prom 35 7.30pm–c11.00pm • Royal Albert Hall

PRICE BAND **D**
WEEKEND PROMMING PASS PROM 35 *see page 159*

JOHN WILSON

Rodgers & Hammerstein
Oklahoma! *(semi-staged)*   *180'*

Cast to be announced

John Wilson Orchestra
John Wilson *conductor*
Rachel Kavanaugh *stage director*

There will be one interval

'Oklahoma! really is different – beautifully different,'
wrote one reviewer of the 1943 musical. Bursting
not just with tunes but also with emotions, this
first collaboration between Richard Rodgers and
Oscar Hammerstein II brought new dramatic
depth to the Broadway musical, creating a smash
hit in the process. Proms favourites John Wilson
and his orchestra return to bring their signature
energy and swagger to this beloved classic.
See 'Broadway's Gift to Opera', pages 88–89.

📻 *Broadcast live on BBC Radio 3 (Prom 35)*

📺 *Broadcast on BBC Four this evening (Prom 35)*

PROMS EXTRA TALK
5.45pm–6.30pm • Imperial College Union Critic and
Broadway expert Edward Seckerson introduces Rodgers
& Hammerstein's *Oklahoma!*
Edited version broadcast on BBC Radio 3 during tonight's interval

---

SATURDAY 12 AUGUST

PROMS AT...
SOUTHWARK CATHEDRAL
3.00pm–c4.30pm

For ticket prices, see page 159

DAVID HILL

Palestrina
Offertorium 'Confitebor tibi, Domine'   *2'*
Missa 'Confitebor tibi, Domine'   *32'*
Judith Weir In the Land of Uz   *c35'*
BBC commission: world premiere

Adrian Thompson *tenor*

BBC Singers
Nash Ensemble
David Hill *conductor*

There will be no interval

'I will praise thee, O Lord, with my whole heart.'
Palestrina's joyous Passiontide motet provides the
starting point for the Proms's first ever visit to
Southwark Cathedral in a programme that sets faith
against doubt and 16th-century Italian polyphony
against a world premiere by British composer
and Master of the Queen's Music Judith Weir.
Palestrina's radiant Mass glows with spiritual
certainty, whether in its dancing Hosanna or
long-limbed Sanctus. The BBC Singers are joined
by the Nash Ensemble and tenor Adrian Thompson
for Weir's *In the Land of Uz*, which takes inspiration
from the story of Job, whose faith in God is shaken
repeatedly through suffering and disaster.
See 'New Music', pages 66–71.

SATURDAY 12 AUGUST

PROM 36
7.30pm–c9.45pm • Royal Albert Hall

PRICE BAND **A**
WEEKEND PROMMING PASS *see page 159*

THOMAS DAUSGAARD

Schubert
Symphony No. 8 in B minor, 'Unfinished' *26'*

INTERVAL

Mahler, compl. Cooke
Symphony No. 10   *74'*

BBC Scottish Symphony Orchestra
Thomas Dausgaard *conductor*

How do you solve a problem like an unfinished
symphony? In his first Proms appearance as
Chief Conductor of the BBC Scottish Symphony
Orchestra, Thomas Dausgaard offers two
contrasting answers. Although Schubert started
work on his Eighth Symphony nearly six years
before his death, he never completed it and the
two existing movements of this lyrical, proto-
Romantic work are mostly performed without a
scherzo or finale. Mahler's final symphony grapples
with darkness and doubt in music of rare anguish
and intensity. It is presented tonight in the
performing version by Deryck Cooke, which
allows us to hear the work complete, in all its
knotty, generous invention.

PROMS EXTRA FAMILY
10.00am–12.15pm • Royal Albert Hall Create music
inspired by *Oklahoma!* onstage at the Royal Albert Hall with
conductor Tim Steiner and professional musicians. *Suitable
for all the family (ages 7-plus). See pages 76–78 for details.*

PROMS EXTRA TALK
5.45pm–6.30pm • Imperial College Union In the second
of David Owen Norris's musical explorations, he discusses
unfinished works and composers who complete them.
Edited version broadcast on BBC Radio 3 during tonight's interval

SUNDAY 13 AUGUST

PROM 37
6.00pm–c8.45pm • Royal Albert Hall

PRICE BAND A
WEEKEND PROMMING PASS *see page 159*

ALEXANDER GAVRYLYUK

Rachmaninov
Piano Concerto No. 3 in D minor   *41'*

INTERVAL

Symphony No. 2 in E minor   *60'*

Alexander Gavrylyuk *piano*

Latvian Radio Choir
BBC Scottish Symphony Orchestra
Thomas Dausgaard *conductor*

In tonight's all-Rachmaninov Prom prize-winning pianist Alexander Gavrylyuk makes his Proms debut in the composer's demanding Third Piano Concerto (continuing our cycle of the composer's complete piano concertos), while the BBC Scottish Symphony Orchestra steps into the spotlight for the mercurial Second Symphony, with its hauntingly beautiful Adagio and impassioned finale. The Latvian Radio Choir complements each work with Russian Orthodox chant, illuminating these blazing orchestral works with the hypnotic sound-world that seeped into Rachmaninov's works (including, possibly, the opening 'Russian Hymn' theme of the Third Concerto). These chants also formed the basis of Rachmaninov's glorious *All-Night Vigil* (*Vespers*), which follows in this evening's Late Night Prom. *See 'Russian Revolutions', pages 20–25.*

Broadcast on BBC Four this evening

PROMS EXTRA TALK
4.15pm–5.00pm • Imperial College Union Writer and broadcaster David Nice discusses traditional Russian music. *Edited version broadcast on BBC Radio 3 during tonight's interval*

SUNDAY 13 AUGUST

PROM 38 • LATE NIGHT
9.45pm–c11.00pm • Royal Albert Hall

PRICE BAND E
WEEKEND PROMMING PASS *see page 159*

LATVIAN RADIO CHOIR

Rachmaninov
All-Night Vigil (Vespers)   *63'*

Latvian Radio Choir
Sigvards Kļava *director*

There will be no interval

Hailed as 'the greatest musical achievement of the Russian Orthodox Church', Rachmaninov's *All-Night Vigil* (*Vespers*) is also one of the loveliest works of any faith – a profoundly moving statement of belief and the last major work the composer completed before he left Russia. Sung unaccompanied, the *Vigil* is a choral tour de force, pushing the singers to the limits of both range and dynamics. The effect is strikingly dramatic, encompassing the ecstatic choral celebration of the Resurrection Hymn 'Today salvation has come' and the infinite tenderness of the 'Ave Maria'. The Latvian Radio Choir returns following its performance of Orthodox chant in tonight's earlier Prom. *See 'Russian Revolutions', pages 20–25.*

Every Prom broadcast
live on BBC Radio 3

SPOTLIGHT ON ...

Latvian Radio Choir • Prom 38

'There's a saying in Latvia that half of the population are singers and the other half are dancers. And then there are some people who manage both!' Tenor Kārlis Rūtentāls *(above)* from the Latvian Radio Choir is understandably proud of his country's huge passion for singing: 'In Riga alone there are more than 100 choirs – we have bank choirs, ministry choirs, petrol station choirs, lawyers' choirs, university choirs – you name it. And we have a Song and Dance Festival every five years that brings 13,000 singers onto one stage.'

That's not quite the number that will be visiting the Proms for the Latvian Radio Choir's three concerts, the centrepiece of which is a late-night performance of Rachmaninov's *All-Night Vigil* (*Vespers*). 'We are in a privileged position with Russian music,' explains Rūtentāls, 'in that historically and geographically we are, in a way, bound up with Russian culture, which allows us to understand and perform this music with less effort. Rachmaninov's music is like the Russian soul itself, with all its greatness and also its subtlety – great choral chords against fragile solo parts.'

He's proud, too, of his choir's versatility. 'In Latvia we sing everything from Bach and Brahms to contemporary and experimental music – and even theatrical performances. We even did a Halloween concert recently with exploding singers' heads!'

Mika Bovan (Gavrylyuk); Dace Buša (Latvian Radio Choir); Jānis Deinats (Rūtentāls)

MONDAY 14 AUGUST

PROMS AT...CADOGAN HALL, PCM 5
1.00pm–c2.00pm • Cadogan Hall

For ticket prices, see page 159

ALEXANDER MELNIKOV

Shostakovich
Ten Poems on Texts by Revolutionary
Poets – excerpts   21'
Preludes and Fugues, Op. 87 –
Nos. 1–4 & 7–8   34'

Alexander Melnikov *piano*

Latvian Radio Choir
Sigvards Kļava *director*

There will be no interval

'Our family discussed the Revolution of 1905
constantly … The stories deeply affected my
imagination.' Born in the shadow of one of
Russia's darkest hours – the slaughter of over
1,000 peaceful protesters outside the Winter
Palace in St Petersburg – Shostakovich carried its
ghosts with him throughout his life. They are given
voice here in a concert that brings together the
wordless songs of the composer's Preludes and
Fugues with the more explicit homage of the
Ten Poems on Texts by Revolutionary Poets. In the last
of its three appearances this season, the Latvian
Radio Choir is joined by Russian pianist Alexander
Melnikov. See 'Russian Revolutions', pages 20–25.

MONDAY 14 AUGUST

PROM 39
7.30pm–c9.40pm • Royal Albert Hall

PRICE BAND Ⓐ

KAZUSHI ONO

Debussy
Prélude à l'après-midi d'un faune   10'
Ravel Piano Concerto in G major   22'

INTERVAL

Mark-Anthony Turnage
Hibiki   50'
European premiere

Inon Barnatan *piano*
Sally Matthews *soprano*
Mihoko Fujimura *mezzo-soprano*

Finchley Children's Music Group
New London Children's Choir
BBC Symphony Orchestra
Kazushi Ono *conductor*

Sunlight and sensuality dominate Debussy's ravishing
Prélude à l'après-midi d'un faune. The cooler shades of
jazz shoot through Ravel's blistering Piano Concerto
in G major, while Mark-Anthony Turnage's *Hibiki*
('beautiful sound') introduces a more meditative
mood. See 'New Music', pages 66–71.

PROMS EXTRA INSPIRE CONCERT
5.00pm–6.00pm • **Radio Theatre, New Broadcasting
House** The Aurora Orchestra performs the winning pieces
of the 2017 BBC Proms Inspire Young Composers'
Competition. *Tickets available from 9 June from BBC Studio
Audiences: bbc.co.uk/showsandtours.*

PROMS EXTRA TALK
5.45pm–6.30pm • **Imperial College Union** Ahead of
tonight's European premiere of *Hibiki*, Mark-Anthony
Turnage talks to Kate Molleson.
Edited version broadcast on BBC Radio 3 during tonight's interval

TUESDAY 15 AUGUST

PROM 40
7.00pm–c9.25pm • Royal Albert Hall

PRICE BAND Ⓐ

CHRISTIAN TETZLAFF

Brahms Tragic Overture   14'
Berg Violin Concerto   27'

INTERVAL

Thomas Larcher
Nocturne – Insomnia   15'
UK premiere
Schumann Symphony No. 3
in E flat major, 'Rhenish'   32'

Christian Tetzlaff *violin*

Scottish Chamber Orchestra
Robin Ticciati *conductor*

Brahms's *Tragic Overture* is not so much tragic as a
'serious' follow-up to his more frivolous *Academic
Festival Overture*. Dedicated 'To the memory of
an angel', Berg's luminous Violin Concerto is an
intensely moving personal testament to the death
of a young woman, quoting Bach's funeral chorale
'Es ist genug'. Thomas Larcher's nocturnal
wanderings receive their UK premiere before a
joyous journey down the Rhine in Schumann's
Third Symphony, which climaxes in a musical
homage to Cologne Cathedral. See 'New Music',
pages 66–71.

PROMS EXTRA TALK
5.15pm–6.00pm • **Imperial College Union** Nick Littlehales,
sports sleep coach and chair of the Sleep Council, talks with
novelist A. L. Kennedy about sleep and insomnia.
Edited version broadcast on BBC Radio 3 during tonight's interval

TUESDAY 15 AUGUST

PROM 41 • LATE NIGHT ☽ 📺
10.15pm–c11.30pm • Royal Albert Hall

PRICE BAND **E**

KAREN KAMENSEK

Ravi Shankar & Philip Glass

Passages   65'
first complete live performance

Anoushka Shankar *sitar*

Britten Sinfonia
Karen Kamensek *conductor*

There will be no interval

In the mid-1960s a rising star of Western classical
music met the 'Godfather' of the Indian classical
tradition. The result was a collision of musical
worlds and – some 25 years later – a studio album
that combined Glass's American Minimalism with
Shankar's sitar and the traditions of Hindustani
classical music. A hypnotic flow of sound, blending
cello, saxophone and other Western instruments
with the glittering pulse of the sitar, *Passages* is
presented here in its first complete live performance.
The Britten Sinfonia and Karen Kamensek are joined
by Shankar's daughter, sitar virtuoso Anoushka
Shankar. See *'Maximal Minimalists', pages 32–35.*

📺 *Broadcast on BBC Four on 18 August*

SPOTLIGHT ON …

Anoushka Shankar • Prom 41

'I have memories of it being recorded as a
child – I must have been aged about 9. It was
an album I was absolutely fascinated by.' Sitar
virtuoso Anoushka Shankar is talking about the
1990 album *Passages*, a collaboration between
her father Ravi Shankar and American composer
Philip Glass, in which each of the musical giants
came up with themes and allowed the other to do
what they liked with them. 'It now feels very
ahead of its time,' Anoushka Shankar continues.
'I'm sure it was a huge influence on me: to be able
to work between musical cultures in a way that's
respectful and authentic to both is pretty much
what I'm trying to do in my whole career. And
Passages is a beautiful example of that.'

Shankar's Late Night Prom is the first time that
Passages has been performed live and complete,
and brings together the Britten Sinfonia and
a raft of Indian musicians, alongside Shankar
herself as sitar soloist. 'I'm absolutely thrilled
to be doing it,' she says.

Does she feel any sense of responsibility to
continue her father's musical legacy, five years
after his death? 'I'm not sure I'd say it's a
responsibility – maybe more of a passion.
Obviously *Passages* is my teacher's work, but
it's also my father's work, so it's very close to
my heart. A project like this allows me to
immerse myself all over again in the roots of
my own music.'

WEDNESDAY 16 AUGUST

PROM 42
7.30pm–c9.50pm • Royal Albert Hall

PRICE BAND **B**

CÉDRIC TIBERGHIEN

Saint-Saëns
La princesse jaune – overture   7'
Delibes Lakmé – ballet music   6'
Saint-Saëns Piano Concerto No. 5
in F major, 'Egyptian'   25'

INTERVAL

Franck Les Djinns   12'
Lalo Namouna – Suites Nos. 1 & 2
(excerpts)   22'
Saint-Saëns
Samson and Delilah – Bacchanal   8'

Cédric Tiberghien *piano*

Les Siècles
François-Xavier Roth *conductor*

An all-French programme inspired by the East, from
the fragrant Indian gardens of Delibes's *Lakmé* and
the eroticism of *Samson and Delilah*, to Corfu with
the adventures of Lalo's *Namouna*. Oriental demons
surface in *Les Djinns*, complementing the vibrantly
coloured music of Java and the Middle East that
suffuses Saint-Saëns's 'Egyptian' Piano Concerto.

PROMS EXTRA TALK
5.45pm–6.30pm • Imperial College Union Turkish novelist
Elif Şafak and BBC Radio 3 New Generation Thinker
Shahidha Bari discuss the figure of the djinni (genie) in
Arabic mythology with Ian McMillan.
Edited version broadcast on BBC Radio 3 during tonight's interval

THURSDAY 17 AUGUST

PROM 43
6.30pm–c8.45pm • Royal Albert Hall

PRICE BAND **B**

JOSHUA BELL

Falla El amor brujo   24'
Lalo Symphonie espagnole   34'

INTERVAL

Saint-Saëns
Symphony No. 3 in C minor, 'Organ'   36'

Stéphanie d'Oustrac *mezzo-soprano*
Joshua Bell *violin*
Cameron Carpenter *organ*

Royal Philharmonic Orchestra
Charles Dutoit *conductor*

Tonight's celebration of the sun-scorched landscapes of Spain opens with Falla's flamenco ballet *El amor brujo*, rich in Andalusian folk melodies and featuring the famous 'Ritual Fire Dance'. Joshua Bell is the soloist in Lalo's *Symphonie espagnole*, whose title conceals a virtuosic violin concerto steeped in the sounds of Spain, while Cameron Carpenter takes to the organ console in Saint-Saëns's mighty 'Organ' Symphony. 'With it I have given all I could,' observed the composer. 'What I did I could not achieve again.'

PROMS EXTRA FAMILY
4.45pm–5.30pm • Imperial College Union (Dining Hall)
Join professional musicians for a family-friendly introduction to this evening's Prom. Bring your instrument and join in!
Suitable for all the family (ages 7-plus). See pages 76–78 for details.

PROMS EXTRA TALK
4.45pm–5.30pm • Imperial College Union (Concert Hall)
Musicologist Richard Langham Smith discusses the music of Saint-Saëns.
Edited version broadcast on BBC Radio 3 during tonight's interval

THURSDAY 17 AUGUST

PROM 44 • LATE NIGHT
10.15pm–c11.30pm • Royal Albert Hall

PRICE BAND **E**

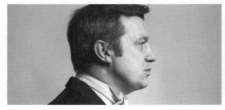

RUMON GAMBA

Michael Gordon Big Space*   c15'
BBC commission: world premiere

David Lang Sunray   12'
London premiere

Julia Wolfe
Big Beautiful Dark and Scary   9'
London premiere

Philip Glass Glassworks – Closing   6'

Louis Andriessen Workers Union   17'

BBC Proms Youth Ensemble
Bang on a Can All-Stars
***Rumon Gamba** conductor*

There will be no interval

Bang on a Can represents all that is most gleefully non-conformist and boundary-breaking in new music. Celebrating its 30th birthday this year, this pioneering American artistic collective and its three composer-directors, Michael Gordon, David Lang and Julia Wolfe, bring their signature energy to this Late Night Prom, together with their six-piece amplified ensemble. The All-Stars perform classic works by Wolfe, Lang and Louis Andriessen alongside an 80th-birthday tribute to Philip Glass and a world premiere by Michael Gordon, performed by the Proms Youth Ensemble. Expect propulsive rhythms and plenty of big grooves. See 'Maximal Minimalists', pages 32–35; 'New Music', pages 66–71; 'Summer Adventures', pages 76–78.

Lisa-Marie Mazzuca (Bell); Andreas Nilsson (Gamba); Peter Serling (Bang on a Can All-Stars)

SPOTLIGHT ON ...

Bang on a Can All-Stars
Prom 44

'We're part rock band (drum kit, electric guitar and keyboards) and part classical ensemble (cello, clarinet, piano and double bass).' Bang on a Can All-Stars bassist Robert Black has a neat way of summing up his group – and its famously genre-straddling identity. 'We have a reputation for playing rhythmically driving, hard-edged music, but we also have a lot of very gentle, mellow pieces,' he continues, providing perfect descriptions for two of the works the group is bringing to its Late Night Prom: Louis Andriessen's powerful *Workers Union* and Philip Glass's sweetly consolatory 'Closing' (from his early bestseller *Glassworks*).

But the backbone of the All-Stars' concert comes from Bang on a Can's own founding trio of New York-based composers – Michael Gordon, David Lang and Julia Wolfe. 'It feels great to have a close working relationship with them,' Black says. 'It's also rather unique in that it's been going on for 30 years. We really understand each other – the composers are very aware of the way we play and we have a fundamental understanding of their musical thinking too.' Alongside a brand-new piece from Gordon, Black is looking forward to two established classics from Wolfe and Lang: '*Big Beautiful Dark and Scary* and *Sunray* are a couple of our favourite pieces. They really capture the essence of their composers – they're sort of sonic portraits.'

FRIDAY 18 AUGUST

PROM 45
7.30pm–c9.05pm • Royal Albert Hall

PRICE BAND **A**

WEEKEND PROMMING PASS *see page 159*

ELIZABETH WATTS

Mahler Symphony No. 2 in C minor, 'Resurrection'   85'

Elizabeth Watts *soprano*
Elisabeth Kulman *mezzo-soprano*

The Bach Choir
BBC Symphony Chorus
BBC Symphony Orchestra
Sakari Oramo *conductor*

There will be no interval

In this season's second Mahler symphony, the composer wrestles with the essential questions of humanity in a work that took over six years to complete. Faith, mortality and the hope of resurrection are the subject of this epic musical exploration, which culminates in a glowing, transcendent choral finale. The BBC Symphony Orchestra and its Chief Conductor Sakari Oramo are joined by soloists Elizabeth Watts and Elisabeth Kulman as well as the combined forces of the BBC Symphony Chorus and The Bach Choir for a work whose scale and scope come into their own in the Royal Albert Hall.

PROMS EXTRA FILM
6.00pm–6.30pm • Imperial College Union Norman Lebrecht investigates the extraordinary obsession of Wall Street economist Gilbert Kaplan, who made his millions and then realised his ambition to conduct Mahler's 'Resurrection' Symphony.

SATURDAY 19 AUGUST

PROM 46
7.30pm–c9.20pm • Royal Albert Hall

PRICE BAND **C**

WEEKEND PROMMING PASS *see page 159*

SIR SIMON RATTLE

Schoenberg Gurrelieder   99'

Eva-Maria Westbroek *Tove*
Simon O'Neill *Waldemar*
Karen Cargill *Wood-Dove*
Peter Hoare *Klaus the Fool*
Christopher Purves *Peasant*
Thomas Quasthoff *Speaker*

CBSO Chorus
Orfeó Català
London Symphony Chorus
London Symphony Orchestra
Sir Simon Rattle *conductor*

There will be no interval

Gurrelieder is a tale of a love that even death cannot vanquish, of rage against the heavens, and ultimately of consolation in a closing musical sunrise of unparalleled beauty. What started out as a modest song-cycle grew into one of the most opulent musical giants of the 20th century – a cantata of Wagnerian ambition and proportions. The LSO and its Music Director Designate Sir Simon Rattle are joined by an outstanding line-up of soloists.

📺 *Broadcast on BBC Four on 3 September*

PROMS EXTRA SING
2.00pm–4.00pm • Imperial College Union (Concert Hall)
Join Simon Halsey in an exploration of Schoenberg's seminal work. An experience of sight-reading is recommended. *Open to ages 16-plus. See pages 72–73 for details.*

PROMS EXTRA TALK
5.45pm–6.30pm • Imperial College Union (Concert Hall)
Musicologist Julian Johnson on Schoenberg's epic *Gurrelieder*. *Edited version broadcast on BBC Radio 3 after tonight's Prom*

SPOTLIGHT ON ...

Thomas Quasthoff • Prom 46

'I have the smallest role in the whole piece!' German singer and actor Thomas Quasthoff is being modest about his crucial contribution to Schoenberg's massive *Gurrelieder* – 'an incredible, monumental, late-Romantic piece for a huge choir and orchestra, with beautiful music, and about love, death and everything in between,' as he describes it. For the climax of Schoenberg's gargantuan creation, he's very much centre stage, following the tragedy of the lovers' deaths with his joyous account of the coming of summer. 'It's an incredible piece for everyone involved,' he continues, 'and my section culminates in a wonderful sunrise, which ends the whole work – a truly amazing moment.'

One of the most admired singers of recent times, Quasthoff retired from the classical concert stage in 2012 but continues as a jazz vocalist, actor and speaker – recently, he even played Feste in the Berliner Ensemble's *Twelfth Night*. 'To be honest, I had to learn the technique of narrating in this way – it's tempting simply to turn it back into singing. But, if you're interpreting the meaning of the text, the speaking line follows those emotions anyway. It's a wonderful role – very colourful, a little bit kitsch, but I love it.'

He's particularly looking forward to working with Sir Simon Rattle again, too. 'He's my musical hero – I've done so many wonderful, challenging things with him. He actually lives in the next street to me in Berlin – we're pretty much neighbours!'

Marco Borggreve (Watts); Oliver Helbig (Rattle); Bernd Brundert (Quasthoff)

SUNDAY 20 AUGUST

PROM 47
1.00pm–c2.00pm • Royal Albert Hall

PRICE BAND **E**

WEEKEND PROMMING PASS *see page 159*

WILLIAM WHITEHEAD

REFORMATION DAY – 1

Programme to include:

Cheryl Frances-Hoad
Chorale Prelude 'Ein feste Burg ist unser
Gott'   c3'
BBC commission: world premiere

Jonathan Dove Chorale Prelude
'Christ unser Herr zum Jordan kam'   c3'
BBC commission: world premiere

Daniel Saleeb
Chorale Prelude 'Erhalt uns, Herr, bei
deinem Wort'   c3'
world premiere

Toccata on 'Erhalt uns, Herr, bei deinem
Wort'   5'

and chorale preludes from Bach's 'Orgelbüchlein', his
'St Anne' Fugue, Mendelssohn's Organ Sonata No. 3
and other Bach-related works by Schumann and
Samuel Wesley

William Whitehead *organ*
Robert Quinney *organ*

There will be no interval

Organists William Whitehead and Robert Quinney
launch our Reformation Day with a recital featuring
the great Lutheran chorale preludes of Bach's
Orgelbüchlein at its heart, alongside three brand-new
chorale preludes by British composers. See *'To Sing
a New Tune'*, pages 26–31; *'New Music'*, pages 66–71.

SUNDAY 20 AUGUST

PROM 48
3.30pm–c5.00pm • Royal Albert Hall

PRICE BAND **A**

WEEKEND PROMMING PASS *see page 159*

SOFI JEANNIN

REFORMATION DAY – 2

The story of the Crucifixion told through five centuries
of music

BBC Singers
City of London Sinfonia
Sofi Jeannin *conductor*

There will be no interval

A journey through five centuries of Western
classical music in an afternoon with the BBC Singers
and Swedish-French choral director Sofi Jeannin.
Together they tell the familiar Passion story as
you've never heard it before, moving from the
earliest-known responsorial setting by Johann
Walter (1496–1570) through Passion music by
Schütz, Bach, Handel, Mendelssohn and Stainer,
right up to contemporary settings by Sofia
Gubaidulina and Sir James MacMillan. This promises
to be a musical experience unlike any other, and a
perfect partner to tonight's complete performance
of Bach's *St John Passion*. See *'To Sing a New Tune'*,
pages 26–31.

**Every Prom broadcast
live on BBC Radio 3**

SUNDAY 20 AUGUST

PROM 49   📺
7.45pm–c10.45pm • Royal Albert Hall

PRICE BAND **B**

WEEKEND PROMMING PASS *see page 159*

SOPHIE BEVAN

REFORMATION DAY – 3

J. S. Bach St John Passion   130'

Nicholas Mulroy *Evangelist*
Matthew Brook *Jesus*
Sophie Bevan *soprano*
Tim Mead *counter-tenor*
Andrew Tortise *tenor*
Konstantin Wolff *bass*

Dunedin Consort
John Butt *harpsichord/director*

There will be one interval

The climax of the Proms Reformation Day is a
complete performance of Bach's *St John Passion*.
'More daring, forceful and poetic' than the
St Matthew Passion, according to Schumann, this is
a work of almost operatic vividness that brings both
a humanity and a painful immediacy to the Passion
narrative. Bach specialist John Butt and his Dunedin
Consort make their Proms debut in a performance
that offers the audience the chance to join in the
chorale-singing, reflecting how the work might
originally have been heard in a church setting.
See *'To Sing a New Tune'*, pages 26–31.

7.15pm–7.35pm: The audience is invited to take part in a
sing-through of the three chorales (hymn tunes) in which they
can optionally participate as part of tonight's performance.

📺 *Broadcast on BBC Four this evening*

PROMS EXTRA TALK
6.00pm–6.45pm • Imperial College Union The Revd Lucy
Winkett discusses Bach's *St John Passion*.
Edited version broadcast on BBC Radio 3 during tonight's interval

SPOTLIGHT ON ...
John Butt • Prom 49

It's no ordinary *St John Passion* that John Butt and his Scottish-based Dunedin Consort bring to the Proms – if there is such a thing, of course. As on his acclaimed 2013 recording of the work, Butt surrounds Bach's majestic choral masterpiece with organ music and choral motets, with the intention of recreating the context of a Passion performance as it might have been experienced in Bach's lifetime.

'It's a matter of hearing the *St John Passion* as part of a continuum,' Butt explains, 'where it rises out of something and falls back into it again. And it makes you more aware of the structures and symmetries within the piece itself. It also recalibrates the way we experience listening time – instead of starting at the beginning and going through to the end, this sense of time is more cyclical.'

The *St John Passion* is often described as the closest Bach came to an opera. However, for Butt, it's actually the other way round. 'A lot of people say that this piece is Bach leaning towards opera, but I'd say that, here, Bach has already seen opera, and is in fact turning it into something else.' What might that 'something else' be? 'There's still drama akin to opera that's happening, but it's happening not on the stage, but within each individual audience member.' A new form of drama for the inner self, perhaps – nothing if not an intriguing prospect.

MONDAY 21 AUGUST

PROMS AT... CADOGAN HALL, PCM 6
1.00pm–*c*2.00pm • Cadogan Hall

For ticket prices, see page 159

CHRISTIANE KARG

Duparc L'invitation au voyage	5'
Guridi Seis canciones castellanas	17'
Ravel Cinq mélodies populaires grècques	5'
Hahn Études latines – 'Lydé'; 'Vile potabis'; 'Tyndaris'	6'
Koechlin Shéhérazade – 'Chanson d'Engaddi'; 'La chanson d'Ishak de Mossoul'; 'Le voyage'	7'
Poulenc Voyage à Paris; Montparnasse; Hyde Park; Hôtel	7'

Christiane Karg *soprano*
Malcolm Martineau *piano*

There will be no interval

With triumphant performances for the Royal Opera and Glyndebourne behind her, rising German soprano Christiane Karg now makes her Proms debut. She is joined by pianist Malcolm Martineau for a musical voyage in song. They visit Greece in the heady love songs of Ravel's 'Greek popular songs', the exotic East in Koechlin's *Shéhérazade* settings and Spain in Guridi's darkly beautiful Castilian songs, before heading closer to home with a jaunty stroll in Hyde Park courtesy of Poulenc.

MONDAY 21 AUGUST

PROM 50
7.30pm–*c*9.30pm • Royal Albert Hall

PRICE BAND **A**

MIRGA GRAŽINYTĖ-TYLA

Beethoven Overture 'Leonore' No. 3	14'
Stravinsky Violin Concerto	22'
INTERVAL	
Gerald Barry Canada	*c*10'
BBC commission: world premiere	
Beethoven Symphony No. 5 in C minor	31'

Leila Josefowicz *violin*
Allan Clayton *tenor*

City of Birmingham Symphony Orchestra
Mirga Gražinytė-Tyla *conductor*

The CBSO and Mirga Gražinytė-Tyla explore the theme of political and artistic freedom. Beethoven's *Leonore* overture No. 3, written for his rescue opera *Fidelio*, celebrates the triumph of truth over tyranny in music of radiant beauty, while his Fifth Symphony rewrites the rules for the Classical symphony. In his new work, maverick composer Gerald Barry is inspired by revolutionary events in Canada's history, also setting the text from *Fidelio*'s Prisoners' Chorus; and violinist Leila Josefowicz amps up the drama in the fierce brilliance of Stravinsky's neo-Classical concerto. See 'New Music', pages 66–71.

Broadcast on BBC Four on 27 August

PROMS EXTRA TALK
5.45pm–6.30pm • Imperial College Union Ahead of tonight's premiere of *Canada*, composer Gerald Barry talks to Andrew McGregor.
Edited version broadcast on BBC Radio 3 during tonight's interval

TUESDAY 22 AUGUST

PROM 51
7.30pm–c9.55pm • Royal Albert Hall

PRICE BAND Ⓐ

JAVIER PERIANES

Sibelius
Scènes historiques – Suite No. 1   18'
Saint-Saëns
Piano Concerto No. 2 in G minor   24'

INTERVAL

Elgar–Payne Symphony No. 3   58'

Javier Perianes piano

BBC Symphony Orchestra
Sakari Oramo conductor

This year's cycle of Elgar symphonies concludes
with the unfinished Third Symphony. Elaborated
and completed by composer Anthony Payne from
the sketches Elgar left at his death, the music heard
here is as much Payne as it is Elgar, a symphony
of chivalric swagger and surging power that Payne
himself has described as 'different in its sheer
breadth of emotion from any of Elgar's other
symphonic works'. The swagger continues in the
insouciant virtuosity of Saint-Saëns's Second Piano
Concerto, performed here by soloist Javier Perianes,
and the concert opens with the patriotic musical
miniatures of Sibelius's Scènes historiques, marking
the centenary of Finnish independence. See
'Darkness and Light', pages 46–49.

PROMS EXTRA TALK
5.45pm–6.30pm • Imperial College Union Novelist
Meg Rosoff and art curator Karen Serres talk to BBC Radio 3
presenter Ian McMillan about unfinished works in literature
and in painting and whether it is always a good idea for
other people to finish them.
Edited version broadcast on BBC Radio 3 during tonight's interval

---

WEDNESDAY 23 AUGUST

PROM 52
7.30pm–c9.50pm • Royal Albert Hall

PRICE BAND Ⓐ

HENRY GOODMAN

**BEYOND THE SCORE®:
DVOŘÁK SYMPHONY NO. 9,
'FROM THE NEW WORLD'**

Henry Goodman actor
Rodney Earl Clarke bass-baritone

Hallé
Sir Mark Elder conductor
Gerard McBurney creative director
Mike Tutaj projection design

There will be one interval

Have you ever wondered about the story behind
Dvořák's haunting Symphony No. 9, with its
yearning Largo and its ebullient, dancing Scherzo?
Originally devised by Gerard McBurney and
the Chicago Symphony Orchestra, this newly
remounted Beyond the Score® performance
combines actors, projections and live musical
examples to explore the history of this enduringly
popular orchestral classic. In the second half,
Sir Mark Elder and the Hallé give a complete
performance of the symphony. A fascinating,
dramatic insight into one of the great works
of the symphonic repertoire.

*Beyond the Score® is a production of the
Chicago Symphony Orchestra*

PROMS EXTRA READING
5.45pm–6.30pm • Imperial College Union A literary
complement to tonight's Prom, with readings reflecting
impressions of America, from the earliest settlers to
latter-day travellers.
Edited version broadcast on BBC Radio 3 during tonight's interval

---

THURSDAY 24 AUGUST

PROM 53   📺
7.30pm–c10.00pm • Royal Albert Hall

PRICE BAND Ⓒ

SHABAKA HUTCHINGS

**BENEATH THE UNDERDOG:
CHARLES MINGUS
REVISITED**

Shabaka Hutchings saxophones
Christian Scott trumpet
Kandace Springs singer

Metropole Orkest
Jules Buckley conductor

There will be one interval

A giant of jazz, Charles Mingus (1922–79) combined
the classic style of Duke Ellington and Jelly Roll
Morton with the radical spirit of black music of the
1950s, 1960s and 1970s, and has influenced artists
from Joni Mitchell and Elvis Costello to Debbie
Harry. Following sell-out Quincy Jones and Jamie
Cullum Proms last year, Jules Buckley returns –
with his Metropole Orkest – to celebrate the life
and music of this legendary composer, bandleader
and bass-player. The Prom features Mingus
favourites including 'Better Git It in Your Soul',
'Moanin'' and 'Goodbye Pork Pie Hat', performed
by a starry line-up of artists.

📺 *Broadcast on BBC Four on 25 August*

PROMS EXTRA TALK
5.45pm–6.30pm • Imperial College Union An introduction
to the music of Charles Mingus with BBC Radio 3 presenter
Geoffrey Smith.
Edited version broadcast on BBC Radio 3 during tonight's interval

FRIDAY 25 AUGUST

PROM 54
6.30pm–c8.40pm • Royal Albert Hall

PRICE BAND (C)
WEEKEND PROMMING PASS *see page 159*

RICCARDO CHAILLY

Brahms
Violin Concerto in D major   42'
INTERVAL
Respighi
Fountains of Rome   16'
Pines of Rome   23'

Leonidas Kavakos *violin*

Orchestra of La Scala, Milan
Riccardo Chailly *conductor*

Riccardo Chailly returns to the Proms, this time as Music Director of the Orchestra of La Scala, Milan, which makes its Proms debut. They bring with them a little piece of Italy in two of Respighi's Rome-inspired tone-poems. Richly vivid in orchestral colour, these works delight in the kind of huge sonorities that come into their own in the Royal Albert Hall. The concert opens with one of the great violin concertos – Brahms's joyous, virtuosic musical homage to his friend and mentor, the virtuoso violinist Joseph Joachim.

PROMS EXTRA TALK
4.45pm–5.30pm • Imperial College Union Writer and historian Tom Holland talks about Ancient Rome and how its ruins and history have inspired writers and artists through the centuries.
Edited version broadcast on BBC Radio 3 during tonight's interval

Silvia Lelli (Chailly)

FRIDAY 25 AUGUST

PROM 55 • LATE NIGHT   ☾ ▭
10.15pm–c12.50am • Royal Albert Hall

PRICE BAND (E)
WEEKEND PROMMING PASS *see page 159*

ANANTHA R. KRISHNAN

CLASSICAL MUSIC OF INDIA AND PAKISTAN

Pandit Budhaditya Mukherjee *sitar*
Soumen Nandy *tabla*

Kumaresh Rajagopalan *Carnatic violin*
Jayanthi Kumaresh *Saraswati veena*
Anantha R. Krishnan *mridangam*

Fareed Ayaz, Abu Muhammad Qawwal & Brothers

This performance will be in three 45-minute sets with no interval

The Proms marks the 70th anniversary of partition and independence on the Indian subcontinent with a concert curated by the culture heritage trust Darbar representing the classical music of India and Pakistan. Explore the region's diverse musical culture in performances celebrating three very different traditions. Sitar and tabla dominate the rhythmically charged Hindustani music of North India, while South India's Carnatic music is more strongly melodic, coloured by the distinctive timbre of the Carnatic violin. The Sufi music of Pakistan provides an ecstatic climax to this Late Night Prom, weaving rich, mesmeric tapestries of sound.

▭ *Recorded for future broadcast on BBC TV*

SPOTLIGHT ON ...
Jayanthi Kumaresh • Prom 55

It's been 70 years since India and Pakistan gained independence – an anniversary whose celebrations are tempered by painful memories of the trauma of Partition. A special Late Night Prom sets out to celebrate the full breadth of the subcontinent's music, with performers from both of India's classical traditions – northern Hindustani and southern Carnatic – as well as the intense spirituality of Sufi devotional qawwali singing from Pakistan.

Representing the south of India is eminent veena (plucked stringed instrument) virtuoso Jayanthi Kumaresh. 'The veena dates back over 3,000 years and it has a lot of mystical significance,' she explains. 'Saraswati, goddess of learning, is always depicted with a veena in her hand, and it's designed in the shape of the human body, with a head and 24 frets representing the 24 vertebrae in our spines.'

Jayanthi is the sixth generation in an ancient family lineage of musicians. 'It means that expectations are very high, but I think it helps me a lot – I feel like I have the music in my genes.'

For her Proms performance she'll be appearing with her husband, violinist Kumaresh Rajagopalan. 'It's not something we do very often – only for special occasions. Our playing styles are very different, but when we play together it's as though we create a new musical space where we meet for our collaboration.'

SATURDAY 26 AUGUST

**PROMS AT... BOLD TENDENCIES
MULTI-STOREY CAR PARK, PECKHAM**
12.00pm–c1.15pm • 3.00pm–c4.15pm 📻

For ticket prices, see page 159

RUBY HUGHES

J. S. Bach, orch. Bantock
Chorale Prelude 'Wachet auf, ruft uns
die Stimme', BWV 645   5'

Kate Whitley I am I say   13'

John Adams Harmonielehre   40'

Ruby Hughes *soprano*
Michael Sumuel *bass-baritone*

The Multi-Story Youth Choir
The Multi-Story Orchestra
Christopher Stark *conductor*

There will be no interval

Following the success last year of their Proms debut
on their home turf in Peckham, Christopher Stark
and The Multi-Story Orchestra return for a
programme that picks up two of the threads
running through this year's Proms, and continues
our showcase for talented young musicians. The
classical symphony gets an appropriately urban,
contemporary makeover in the pulsing rhythms
and metallic glitter of John Adams's *Harmonielehre*,
while Kate Whitley's *I am I say*, written for local
schoolchildren to perform, is inspired by nature
but also firmly rooted in the sounds and communities
of the city. The concert opens with Bach's 'Wachet
auf' (Sleepers, Awake) in Granville Bantock's
unexpectedly rich orchestration. *See 'To Sing a
New Tune', pages 26–31; 'Maximal Minimalists',
pages 32–35.*

📻 *Broadcast live on BBC Radio 3 (3.00pm performance)*

SATURDAY 26 AUGUST

PROM 56
7.30pm–c9.50pm • Royal Albert Hall

PRICE BAND Ⓐ
WEEKEND PROMMING PASS *see page 159*

JAKUB HRŮŠA

THE BOHEMIAN
REFORMATION

Hussite Chorale 'Ktož jsú Boži bojovníci'
(You Who Are Warriors of God)   2'

Smetana Má vlast – Tábor; Blaník   27'

Martinů Field Mass   26'

INTERVAL

Dvořák Hussite Overture   14'

Janáček The Excursions of Mr Brouček –
Song of the Hussites   4'

Suk Prague   25'

Svatopluk Sem *baritone*

BBC Singers (men's voices)
BBC Symphony Orchestra
Jakub Hrůša *conductor*

Tonight's all-Czech programme opens with a
Hussite war song, whose melody reappears in
Dvořák's *Hussite Overture* (depicting the struggles
of Czech Reformation pioneer Jan Hus), Smetana's
symphonic poems from *Má vlast* and Martinů's
elegiac *Field Mass*, composed as a prayer for his
homeland after the German invasion in 1939.
See 'To Sing a New Tune', pages 26–31.

PROMS EXTRA TALK
5.45pm–6.30pm • Imperial College Union Author and
musicologist Jan Smaczny discusses Czech music ahead
of tonight's Prom.
Edited version broadcast on BBC Radio 3 during tonight's interval

---

SUNDAY 27 AUGUST

PROM 57   📻 📺
3.00pm–c5.45pm • Royal Albert Hall

PRICE BAND Ⓑ
WEEKEND PROMMING PASS *see page 159*

CLARE TEAL

SWING NO END

Clare Teal *singer/presenter*

Guy Barker Big Band
Guy Barker *bandleader*

Winston Rollins Big Band
Winston Rollins *bandleader*

There will be one interval

From stomps and shuffles to boogie-woogie and
blues, from bebop to Latin, this Sunday matinee
Prom presents a slice of musical action from the
1930s and 1940s. Two roaring big bands battle
against each other, joined by special guests and led
by Guy Barker and Winston Rollins. Singer and
broadcaster Clare Teal is our guide on a journey
that celebrates the triumphs of big band greats,
including Duke Ellington, Count Basie, Benny
Goodman, Tommy Dorsey, Jimmie Lunceford,
Boyd Raeburn, Machito, Stan Kenton and Woody
Herman. Tribute is also paid to a highly respected
but unassuming giant of the big band world –
pianist, arranger and composer Mary Lou Williams.

📻 *Recorded for future broadcast on BBC Radio 2*

📺 *Broadcast on BBC Four on 1 September*

PROMS EXTRA FAMILY
1.15pm–2.00pm • Imperial College Union Join professional
musicians for a family-friendly introduction to this afternoon's
Prom. Bring your instrument and join in! *Suitable for all the
family (ages 7-plus). See pages 76–78 for details.*

Barry Hole (Hughes); Zbyněk Maděryč (Hrůša)

SUNDAY 27 AUGUST

PROM 58
7.45pm–c9.50pm • Royal Albert Hall

PRICE BAND **C**
WEEKEND PROMMING PASS *see page 159*

LOUIS LANGRÉE

Bernstein
On the Waterfront – symphonic suite *22'*

Copland Lincoln Portrait *15'*

INTERVAL

Tchaikovsky
Symphony No. 5 in E minor *45'*

Cincinnati Symphony Orchestra
Louis Langrée *conductor*

The Cincinnati Symphony Orchestra makes its Proms debut with Music Director Louis Langrée, bringing works by two celebrated American composers. Bernstein's symphonic suite drawn from his soundtrack to *On the Waterfront* is a cinematic journey through the docks and slums of post-war New Jersey, telling the story of one man's heroic fight against corruption and intimidation. In a year in which America has inaugurated a new president, Copland's *Lincoln Portrait* offers a musical homage to another. Lincoln's greatest speeches are set against a stirring orchestral tone-poem: America in music. The climax of the concert is another passionate statement of musical nationalism: Tchaikovsky's Symphony No. 5.

PROMS EXTRA TALK
6.00pm–6.45pm • Imperial College Union Professor Kathleen Burk, University College London, reflects on Abraham Lincoln with BBC Radio 3 New Generation Thinker Joanna Cohen.
Edited version broadcast on BBC Radio 3 during tonight's interval

---

MONDAY 28 AUGUST

PROMS AT… CADOGAN HALL, PCM 7
1.00pm–c2.00pm • Cadogan Hall

For ticket prices, see page 158

PAVEL KOLESNIKOV

Chopin
Waltz in A flat major, Op. 69 No. 1	*3'*
Impromptu in A flat major, Op. 29	*4'*
Waltz in C sharp minor, Op. 64 No. 2	*3'*
Fantasy-Impromptu in C sharp minor, Op. 66	*5'*
Fantasy in F minor/A flat major, Op. 49	*14*
Mazurkas – selection	*12'*
Scherzo in E major, Op. 54	*10'*

Pavel Kolesnikov *piano*

There will be no interval

Still in his twenties, award-winning pianist and former BBC Radio 3 New Generation Artist Pavel Kolesnikov has been praised for the sensitivity and maturity of his playing. Fresh from a critically acclaimed recording of Chopin's Mazurkas, he performs an all-Chopin recital at Cadogan Hall, including the brooding Fantasy, Op. 49, the mercurial Scherzo in E major and the ever popular Waltz in A flat major, Op. 69 No 1, alongside a selection of Mazurkas – one of the forms in which Chopin most deeply expressed his feelings for his Polish homeland.

> **Every Prom broadcast
> live on BBC Radio 3**

MONDAY 28 AUGUST

PROM 59
7.00pm–c9.55pm • Royal Albert Hall

PRICE BAND **C**
WEEKEND PROMMING PASS *see page 159*

ALICE COOTE

Mozart La clemenza di Tito *132'*
(semi-staged; sung in Italian)

Steve Davislim *Titus*
Alice Coote *Vitellia*
Joélle Harvey *Servilia*
Kate Lindsey *Sextus*
Anna Stéphany *Annius*
Clive Bayley *Publius*

Glyndebourne Festival Opera
Orchestra of the Age of Enlightenment
Robin Ticciati *conductor*

There will be one interval

The collision of love and ambition in Mozart's morally conflicted final opera, and the compassion of a wronged emperor, make for a scenario as relevant today as in the ancient Rome where it is set. Blending ravishing arias with intricate human psychology, *La clemenza di Tito* ranks among the finest of Mozart's mature works. Mezzo-soprano Alice Coote leads an all-star cast as the vengeful Vitellia under Glyndebourne's Music Director Robin Ticciati.

PROMS EXTRA SING
12.30pm–3.30pm • Imperial College Union Join Mary King and members of the BBC Singers to rehearse excerpts from Mozart's *La clemenza di Tito*. Experience in sight-reading or a knowledge of the piece is an advantage but not essential. *Suitable for ages 16-plus. See pages 72–73 for details.*

PROMS EXTRA TALK
5.15pm–6.00pm • Imperial College Union Musicologist Timothy Jones introduces Mozart's *La clemenza di Tito*. *Edited version broadcast on BBC Radio 3 during tonight's interval*

Benoît Lintero (Langrée); Colin Way (Kolesnikov); Benjamin Ealovega (Coote)

TUESDAY 29 AUGUST

PROM 60
7.30pm–c9.50pm • Royal Albert Hall

PRICE BAND **C**

LEIF OVE ANDSNES

Stravinsky The Firebird – suite
(revised version, 1919)   21'

Rachmaninov Piano Concerto No. 4
in G minor (revised version, 1941)   24'

INTERVAL

Shostakovich Symphony No. 12
in D minor, 'The Year 1917'   41'

Leif Ove Andsnes *piano*

Oslo Philharmonic
Vasily Petrenko *conductor*

It would be impossible to mark this year's centenary
of the Russian Revolution without a performance
of Shostakovich's Symphony No. 12 – subtitled
'The Year 1917'. Its sweeping, filmic music paints a
portrait of Lenin, both as a man and a political force.
Acclaimed Shostakovich interpreter Vasily Petrenko
conducts the Oslo Philharmonic in an all-Russian
programme also featuring Stravinsky's ever-popular
suite from *The Firebird* and Rachmaninov's mercurial
Fourth Piano Concerto (continuing our cycle of the
composer's complete piano concertos). Norwegian
pianist Leif Ove Andsnes, whose Beethoven
concerto cycle was a highlight of the 2015 Proms,
returns as soloist. See 'Russian Revolutions',
pages 20–25.

PROMS EXTRA TALK
5.45pm–6.30pm • Imperial College Union Historians
Helen Rappaport and Victor Sebestyen consider the
figure of Lenin, as the Proms marks the 100th anniversary
of the Russian Revolution.
Edited version broadcast on BBC Radio 3 during tonight's interval

---

WEDNESDAY 30 AUGUST

PROM 61
7.00pm–c9.00pm • Royal Albert Hall

PRICE BAND **C**

SAKARI ORAMO

Andrea Tarrodi Liguria   12'
UK premiere

Barber Knoxville: Summer of 1915   16'

INTERVAL

R. Strauss Daphne – Transformation
Scene, 'Ich komme – ich komme'   11'

Nielsen Symphony No. 2, 'The Four
Temperaments'   33'

Renée Fleming *soprano*

Royal Stockholm Philharmonic Orchestra
Sakari Oramo *conductor*

Star American soprano Renée Fleming returns
to join Sakari Oramo and the Royal Stockholm
Philharmonic Orchestra for the shimmering
'transformation' music that closes Richard
Strauss's opera *Daphne*, and Samuel Barber's
Knoxville: Summer of 1915, a nostalgic portrait of the
America of a simpler age. The RSPO also brings
music by its Swedish compatriot Andrea Tarrodi –
Liguria, a vivid musical 'walking tour' through Italian
fishing villages as well as Nielsen's Second Symphony,
'The Four Temperaments', whose four movements
offer different character portraits, from a choleric
opening Allegro to a melancholic slow movement.
See 'New Music', pages 66–71.

PROMS EXTRA TALK
5.15pm–6.00pm • Imperial College Union Musicologist
Daniel Grimley introduces Nielsen's Second Symphony.
Edited version broadcast on BBC Radio 3 during tonight's interval

---

SPOTLIGHT ON ...

Renée Fleming • Prom 61

'No risk, no gain,' says Renée Fleming.
'You always have to take risks to keep people
interested in what you're doing.' It's a principle
the world-famous American soprano has
followed for her Prom this summer, which sees
her singing both Barber's *Knoxville: Summer
of 1915* and the final scene from Strauss's opera
Daphne. 'It's a very challenging scene, but it's
exquisitely beautiful,' Fleming explains, 'and it
really gives the orchestra a chance to shine.'

If Strauss is, for Fleming, her 'Desert Island
composer', Barber also holds an important place
in her heart. '*Knoxville* is probably our best
American work for orchestra with soprano, and
it's such an iconic piece,' she says. Commissioned
by another American soprano, Eleanor Steber,
who premiered it in 1948, *Knoxville* sets parts
of a prose-poem by James Agee. 'What appears
at first to be a very nostalgic and positive piece
is actually laced with tremendous melancholy,'
says Fleming. 'He's remembering a time when
he was a fully innocent young child, but then
his father died in a car crash within a year.
From this text, Barber made this beautiful work.'
And Fleming has also followed Steber's example.
'I thought, wow, this is a way a performer can
contribute to the art form. I've premiered Anders
Hillborg's *The Strand Settings* and also *Letters
from Georgia* by Kevin Puts. I think I was
inspired by *Knoxville*.'

WEDNESDAY 30 AUGUST

PROM 62 • LATE NIGHT 🌙 📺
10.15pm–c11.30pm • Royal Albert Hall

PRICE BAND **E**

KEVIN JOHN EDUSEI

Hannah Kendall
The Spark Catchers   c10'
BBC commission: world premiere

Dvořák Rondo in G minor, Op. 94   7'

Popper, orch. M. Schlegel
Hungarian Rhapsody, Op. 68   10'

George Walker Lyric for Strings   6'

Handel Arias   15'

Rimsky-Korsakov
Capriccio espagnol   16'

Sheku Kanneh-Mason *cello*
Jeanine De Bique *soprano*

Chineke!
Kevin John Edusei *conductor*

There will be no interval

Hailed by critics as 'fresh' and 'brilliant', the UK's
first BME orchestra Chineke! makes its Proms
debut in a programme including works by Pulitzer
Prize-winning George Walker and young British
composer Hannah Kendall, whose *The Spark
Catchers* takes inspiration from the urgent energy
of Lemn Sissay's poem of the same name. Cellist
Sheku Kanneh-Mason, winner of the 2016 BBC
Young Musician competition, also makes his
Proms debut here as soloist in music by Dvořák
and David Popper. See *'Natural Reflection'*,
pages 50–51; 'New Music', pages 66–71.

📺 *Broadcast on BBC Four on 8 September*

SPOTLIGHT ON …

Sheku Kanneh-Mason • Prom 62

'Life has changed immeasurably since BBC
Young Musician,' admits Nottingham-based
cellist Sheku Kanneh-Mason, winner of the 2016
competition. He now has an agent, a record deal
and invaluable mentors and friends in the music
world – including Guy Johnston, Julian Lloyd
Webber and Nicola Benedetti. 'I also have
bookings two years ahead now and I'm very busy
with engagements. And I'm still working towards
my A levels and going to school in between.'

Amid this hectic schedule, he sees his BBC Proms
debut as an unforgettable occasion. 'It seems like
such an iconic event, to play at the Proms, and it
holds a very special meaning. To be playing on such
a stage, with all the atmosphere and magic that this
involves, is very exciting.' The pieces he's playing,
too, are particular favourites. 'Dvořák's *Rondo* is
a beautiful work, combining tenderness with poise
and precision. Popper's *Hungarian Rhapsody*
covers almost everything a cello can do: singing
phrases, haunting melodies, virtuoso passages –
all the things I love about the cello!'

Kanneh-Mason is making his debut alongside
the orchestra Chineke!. 'Playing with Chineke!
has always been significant for me. It's a fantastic
group, bringing together the very best of black
and minority ethnic musicians and proving they
stand among the best orchestral players in the
world. On this occasion I won't be playing in
the orchestra myself – although I usually do!'

THURSDAY 31 AUGUST

PROM 63
7.30pm–c10.00pm • Royal Albert Hall

PRICE BAND **A**

KIRILL GERSTEIN

Taneyev Overture 'The Oresteia'   19'

Rachmaninov
Piano Concerto No. 1 in F sharp minor   27'

INTERVAL

Tchaikovsky Manfred   53'

Kirill Gerstein *piano*

BBC Symphony Orchestra
Semyon Bychkov *conductor*

Continuing his season-long Tchaikovsky Project,
which included performances earlier this summer
with the BBC Symphony Orchestra, Semyon Bychkov
conducts an all-Russian programme that climaxes
with the composer's vividly programmatic symphony
Manfred. Translating the struggles of Byron's hero
(who celebrates his 200th anniversary this year)
into music proved a challenging task for the
composer but the result is a glorious musical epic,
full of drama and colour. Kirill Gerstein is the soloist
for Rachmaninov's youthful Piano Concerto No. 1,
concluding our cycle of the composer's piano
concertos with a work whose stormy beauty is
a natural companion for Taneyev's brooding
Oresteia overture.

PROMS EXTRA TALK
5.45pm–6.30pm • Imperial College Union Novelist
Benjamin Markovits and BBC Radio 3 New Generation
Thinker Corin Throsby discuss Lord Byron and his
dramatic poem *Manfred*.
Edited version broadcast on BBC Radio 3 during tonight's interval

PRICE BAND **C**
WEEKEND PROMMING PASS *see page 159*

DANIELE GATTI

Wolfgang Rihm In-Schrift   17'

INTERVAL

Bruckner
Symphony No. 9 in D minor   65'

Royal Concertgebouw Orchestra
Daniele Gatti *conductor*

Amsterdam's mighty Royal Concertgebouw
Orchestra is regularly named as one of the world's
finest orchestras. Here it returns to the Proms for
the first time in almost a decade, under its new
Chief Conductor Daniele Gatti. The main work on
their programme is Bruckner's Ninth Symphony –
the composer's great, unfinished farewell to the
form, and his final testament of faith. Written in
1995 for St Mark's Basilica in Venice, Rihm's *In-Schrift*
is an exploration of space and its sonic possibilities.
With no high strings and additional low brass,
Rihm creates a sound-world of striking darkness,
illuminated only by the piercing brilliance of
percussion.

PROMS EXTRA READING
4.45pm–5.30pm • Imperial College Union A literary
complement to tonight's Prom, with readings on the
theme of unfinished works.
Edited version broadcast on BBC Radio 3 during tonight's interval

SPOTLIGHT ON ...
Daniele Gatti • Proms 64 & 66

By the time they arrive at the Proms, Daniele Gatti
and the Royal Concertgebouw Orchestra will have
just reached the end of their second season together.
For its London appearances, the world-famous
orchestra will be bringing music that's at the heart
of its repertoire. 'All my predecessors have been
crucial performers of Mahler and Bruckner,'
explains Gatti, who follows Mariss Jansons,
Riccardo Chailly and Bernard Haitink as the
ensemble's Chief Conductor. 'I feel I am part
of such an extraordinary performing tradition.'

'It's always difficult to choose something to put
next to Bruckner's Ninth Symphony, which is a
very mysterious work,' says the Italian conductor.
'This time I thought about including something by
a living German-speaking composer.' The choice?
Wolfgang Rihm's *In-Schrift*. 'Rihm plays with the
German language,' says Gatti, ' "Inschrift" means
"inscription", while "in Schrift" means "in writing".'

While the first of the orchestra's Proms under Gatti
features Bruckner at the end of his life – the Ninth
Symphony is incomplete and Gatti is 'convinced
that only silence can follow such a miraculous
third movement' – its second appearance (Prom
66) turns to Mahler's Fourth Symphony. 'Its
originality is stupefying,' says Gatti. It's the most
chamber-like of Mahler's symphonies and it
seemed obvious to Gatti to pair it with Haydn:
'The RCO has a great history of performing
Haydn. And "The Bear" is a masterpiece.'

PRICE BAND **F**
WEEKEND PROMMING PASS *see page 159*

JOOLS HOLLAND

THE SOUND OF SOUL: STAX RECORDS

William Bell *singer*
Eddie Floyd *singer*
Steve Cropper *guitar*

**Jools Holland and His Rhythm &
Blues Orchestra**

There will be no interval

Founded in 1959, Memphis-based Stax Records
was synonymous with Southern Soul – a distinctive
blend of funk, gospel and R & B that brought
listeners across America together at a time of racial
conflict and political unrest. In this Late Night Prom
Jools Holland and His Rhythm & Blues Orchestra
pay tribute to the pioneering label and celebrate
the 50th anniversary of the Stax/Volt Revue's first
tour of the UK, in a concert featuring some of the
label's greatest surviving artists alongside a number
of British artists inspired by the likes of Otis Redding,
Isaac Hayes, Rufus Thomas and the Staple Singers.

Recorded for future broadcast on BBC Radio 2

Broadcast on BBC Four this evening

Anne Dokter, Marco Borggreve (Gatti) Wolfgang Rohrflinke-images (Holland)

SATURDAY 2 SEPTEMBER

PROMS AT...
WILTON'S MUSIC HALL
3.00pm–c4.30pm • 7.30pm–c9.00pm

For ticket prices, see page 159

SIAN EDWARDS

John Luther Adams
songbirdsongs – excerpts   *14'*

Messiaen Le merle noir   *6'*

Handel
Rinaldo – 'Augelletti, che cantate'   *5'*

Rebecca Saunders
Molly's Song 3   *11'*

Davies
Eight Songs for a Mad King   *32'*

Jennifer France *soprano*
Marcus Farnsworth *baritone*

Birmingham Contemporary Music Group
Sian Edwards *conductor*
Olivia Fuchs *stage director*

There will be no interval

Dating from the mid-19th century, Wilton's is the world's oldest surviving music hall. With its tumbledown beauty and colourful history, it's the perfect space for a staged performance of Peter Maxwell Davies's *Eight Songs for a Mad King* – a dramatic monologue exploring the crazed fantasies and crumbling visions of George III. The fluttering and chattering of the king's pet bullfinches which run through the work find an echo in bird-inspired pieces by Messiaen and Handel, as well as Pulitzer Prize-winning American composer John Luther Adams. Sian Edwards conducts the Birmingham Contemporary Music Group, with exciting young British soloists Jennifer France and Marcus Farnsworth.

SPOTLIGHT ON ...

Marcus Farnsworth
Proms at ... Wilton's Music Hall

'It's one of the most visceral pieces of music I've ever performed. You have to approach it totally differently from anything else in the repertoire.' British baritone Marcus Farnsworth is talking about Peter Maxwell Davies's *Eight Songs for a Mad King*, an astonishingly powerful piece of music theatre from 1969 that portrays the derangement and confusion of George III in a notoriously demanding vocal part bringing together all manner of extreme effects, even including singing whole chords at once. 'It's really about exploring the emotions of madness, the internal turmoil of someone in that situation,' he continues. 'There's lots of pastiche in the music and plenty of references to Handel, as well as tunes from a mechanical organ the King owned. He also kept birds and there are lots of interesting little bits of birdsong throughout the piece, conversations that the King has with himself through the birds.'

It's a piece that has lost none of its power to startle in the almost half-century since its premiere, but for Farnsworth – who has been performing it since 2012 – it's about far more than shock value. 'It can be a very unusual experience for the audience, because it's so emotionally direct. And there are plenty of moments that are quite amusing. But I think it's very moving too, and it's given me a very different perspective on what we call madness and how we treat people we might call mad.'

SATURDAY 2 SEPTEMBER

PROM 66
7.30pm–c9.30pm • Royal Albert Hall

PRICE BAND C
WEEKEND PROMMING PASS *see page 159*

CHEN REISS

Haydn
Symphony No. 82 in C major, 'The Bear'   *26'*

INTERVAL

Mahler Symphony No. 4 in G major   *56'*

Chen Reiss *soprano*

Royal Concertgebouw Orchestra
Daniele Gatti *conductor*

From its jingling opening sleigh bells to its charming closing song for soprano and orchestra, Mahler's Fourth Symphony is one of the composer's sunniest and most appealing works, lively with birdsong and youthful energy. It's a mood it shares with Haydn's ebullient and richly orchestrated Symphony No. 82, nicknamed 'The Bear' for the lurching melody of its final movement, with its suggestion of dancing bears at a country fair. For their second concert, the Royal Concertgebouw Orchestra and Daniele Gatti are joined by Israeli soprano Chen Reiss, making her Proms debut.

PROMS EXTRA TALK
5.45pm–6.30pm • **Imperial College Union** An interview with Booker Prize-winning novelist Alan Hollinghurst about his forthcoming novel, *The Sparsholt Affair*.
Edited version broadcast on BBC Radio 3 during tonight's interval

SUNDAY 3 SEPTEMBER

PROM 67
1.00pm–c2.55pm • Royal Albert Hall

PRICE BAND **B**
WEEKEND PROMMING PASS see page 159

PABLO HERAS-CASADO

Mendelssohn
Overture 'The Hebrides' ('Fingal's Cave') 10'
Violin Concerto in E minor 27'
INTERVAL
Symphony No. 5 in D major, 'Reformation' 27'

Isabelle Faust *violin*

Freiburg Baroque Orchestra
Pablo Heras-Casado *conductor*

The dynamic Freiburg Baroque Orchestra brings
authentic period-instrument colour to three of
Mendelssohn's best-loved orchestral works in a
Proms matinee directed by rising young conductor
Pablo Heras-Casado. Violinist Isabelle Faust makes
her second appearance this season, as soloist in
Mendelssohn's Violin Concerto – the composer's
last completed orchestral work, and perhaps the
loveliest of all the Romantic violin concertos. The
500th anniversary of the Reformation continues
to be marked with Mendelssohn's Fifth Symphony,
whose final movement quotes movingly from
Luther's chorale 'Ein feste Burg ist unser Gott',
while the concert opens with the composer's
glorious overture *The Hebrides*, inspired by a
visit to Fingal's Cave on the Scottish Isle of Staffa.
See 'To Sing a New Tune', pages 26–31.

PROMS EXTRA FAMILY
11.15am–12.00pm • Imperial College Union Join
professional musicians for a family-friendly introduction
to this afternoon's Prom. Bring your instrument and join in!
Suitable for all the family (ages 7-plus). See pages 76–78 for details.

SPOTLIGHT ON ...

Isabelle Faust • Proms 3 & 67

There are two chances to hear Isabelle Faust at this
year's Proms, playing two miraculous concertos
with two very different orchestras. It's Mozart first
(Prom 3): the G major Concerto, K216, which is,
says the German violinist, 'especially impulsive,
full of ideas and happy to be alive!' And it's fair
to say that Faust is excited about working again
with the Chamber Orchestra of Europe and the
legendary conductor Bernard Haitink. 'I worship
Bernard Haitink! I would want to make music
with this refined, noble, heartwarming musician
every day, if I could. And the COE is the perfect
partner for both of us.'

We jump from the Classical to the Romantic era
for her second appearance (Prom 67), but move
from a modern to a period-instrument ensemble.
Faust has already worked with the distinctive
Freiburg Baroque Orchestra and conductor
Pablo Heras-Casado on Schumann, and now
they turn to Mendelssohn. 'I am sure we will find
a passionate and sparkling approach to the concerto
and take a fresh look at one of the most popular
pieces of violin repertoire,' says Faust. 'I am
especially focusing on the available sources to find
out how Mendelssohn's violinist contemporaries
played this piece, which is highly interesting.'
And what makes the piece such a joy? 'It combines
new, innovative ideas with ideal shape, lyricism
with virtuosity, lightness and wit with depth
and tenderness. It's simply the perfect concerto.'

SUNDAY 3 SEPTEMBER

PROM 68
7.30pm–c10.05pm • Royal Albert Hall

PRICE BAND **C**
WEEKEND PROMMING PASS see page 159

VALERY GERGIEV

Prokofiev Cantata for the 20th
Anniversary of the October Revolution 39'
Tchaikovsky
Piano Concerto No. 3 in E flat major 13'
INTERVAL
Shostakovich
Symphony No. 5 in D minor 49'

Denis Matsuev *piano*

Mariinsky Chorus
Mariinsky Orchestra
Valery Gergiev *conductor*

Who better than Russia's foremost opera orchestra
and chorus to mark the centenary of the Russian
Revolution? Along with Artistic Director Valery
Gergiev they perform Prokofiev's epic *Cantata for
the 20th Anniversary of the October Revolution* – a
work that captures the violence of the Bolshevik
Revolution and the birth of the Soviet Union in bold
orchestral textures and rich, folk-infused choral
writing. The cruelty of the Stalinist regime is
captured in Shostakovich's evocative Fifth
Symphony, and regular collaborator Denis Matsuev
joins the orchestra as soloist in Tchaikovsky's final
work – the single-movement Piano Concerto No. 3.
See 'Russian Revolutions', pages 20–25.

PROMS EXTRA THE LISTENING SERVICE
6.00pm–6.30pm • Imperial College Union Tom Service
presents a revolutionary edition of BBC Radio 3's
The Listening Service. Tickets available from BBC Studio Audiences:
bbc.co.uk/showsandtours.
Edited version broadcast on BBC Radio 3 later this evening

Fernando Sancho (Heras-Casado); Felix Broede (Faust); Alberto Venzago (Gergiev)

MONDAY 4 SEPTEMBER

PROMS AT…CADOGAN HALL, PCM 8
1.00pm–c2.00pm • Cadogan Hall

For ticket prices, see page 159

ELIAS STRING QUARTET

Schubert String Quintet in C major *53'*

Elias String Quartet
Alice Neary *cello*

There will be no interval

Schubert's final chamber work is a piece of sublime beauty, a masterpiece of the repertoire composed only two months before the composer's death at the age of just 31. Instead of the additional viola preferred by Mozart and Beethoven in their string quintets, Schubert adds a second cello, to create a work of sonorous beauty. From its expansive opening Allegro and the fragile beauty of the Adagio to its exuberant Scherzo and good-humoured closing Allegretto, this is a work of boundless invention and charm. Former BBC Radio 3 New Generation Artists the Elias String Quartet are joined by cellist Alice Neary.

> **Every Prom broadcast
> live on BBC Radio 3**

MONDAY 4 SEPTEMBER

PROM 69
7.30pm–c9.55pm • Royal Albert Hall

PRICE BAND **B**

ANNE-SOPHIE MUTTER

John Adams Lollapalooza *7'*
Dvořák Violin Concerto in A minor *33'*
INTERVAL
Mahler Symphony No. 1 in D major *56'*

Anne-Sophie Mutter *violin*

Pittsburgh Symphony Orchestra
Manfred Honeck *conductor*

Following hot on the heels of the Cincinnati Symphony Orchestra is a visit from another great American ensemble. The Pittsburgh Symphony Orchestra and Music Director Manfred Honeck continue this season's strand of Mahler symphonies with the First, a work that started life as a tone-poem and retains all of that narrative energy. A young hero sets out, hopeful, into the world, only to have his ambitions dashed by cruel fate. Anne-Sophie Mutter makes a welcome Proms return as soloist in Dvořák's vivacious Violin Concerto, and the concert opens with a nod to great American Minimalist John Adams's 70th birthday, with his joyous orchestral dance *Lollapalooza*. *See 'Maximal Minimalists', pages 32–35.*

See 'Maximal Minimalists', pages 32–35.

PROMS EXTRA TALK
5.45pm–6.30pm • Imperial College Union David Owen Norris explores how composers have brought the influence of the natural world into their music.
Edited version broadcast on BBC Radio 3 during tonight's interval

---

TUESDAY 5 SEPTEMBER

PROM 70
7.30pm–c9.45pm • Royal Albert Hall

PRICE BAND **A**

KARINA CANELLAKIS

Missy Mazzoli
Sinfonia (for Orbiting Spheres) *12'*
European premiere of orchestral version

Bartók Piano Concerto No. 2 *28'*
INTERVAL
Dvořák
Symphony No. 8 in G major *36'*

Jeremy Denk *piano*

BBC Symphony Orchestra
Karina Canellakis *conductor*

Following her recent UK debut, American conductor Karina Canellakis now makes her first visit to the Proms, joining the BBC Symphony Orchestra and fellow American Jeremy Denk for Bartók's ferociously brilliant Second Piano Concerto. Dvořák's Symphony No. 8, by contrast, is a work of genial lyricism. 'Melodies simply pour out of me,' wrote the composer, and the result is a pastoral symphony in all but name. The concert opens with the European premiere of Missy Mazzoli's mesmeric *Sinfonia* — music 'in the shape of the solar system' that weaves and coils itself in a sequence of pulsing loops. *See 'New Music', pages 66–71.*

See 'New Music', pages 66–71.

Broadcast on BBC Four on 8 September

PROMS EXTRA TALK
5.45pm–6.30pm • Imperial College Union Ahead of the performance of her *Sinfonia (for Orbiting Spheres)* Missy Mazzoli talks to BBC Radio 3 presenter Andrew McGregor.
Edited version broadcast on BBC Radio 3 during tonight's interval

WEDNESDAY 6 SEPTEMBER

PROM 71
7.00pm–c9.40pm • Royal Albert Hall

PRICE BAND **B**

ALINA IBRAGIMOVA

Stravinsky Funeral Song   *12'*

arr. Stravinsky
Song of the Volga Boatmen   *2'*

Prokofiev
Violin Concerto No. 1 in D major   *22'*

INTERVAL

Britten Russian Funeral   *7'*

Shostakovich Symphony No. 11
in G minor, 'The Year 1905'   *65'*

Alina Ibragimova *violin*

London Philharmonic Orchestra
Vladimir Jurowski *conductor*

Alina Ibragimova joins Vladimir Jurowski and the
London Philharmonic Orchestra in a Russian-
themed programme. The Proms pays tribute to the
centenary of the Russian Revolution with Prokofiev's
lyrical First Violin Concerto, composed amid the
growing turmoil of 1917. Shostakovich's Symphony
No. 11 harks back to another crisis, the failed
revolution of 1905; its brooding cinematic
landscapes are punctuated by bright flecks of
instrumental colour. The concert opens with
Stravinsky's youthful *Funeral Song*, lost for over a
century and given its first modern performance
only last year. See 'Russian Revolutions', pages 20–25.

PROMS EXTRA TALK
4.45pm–5.30pm • Imperial College Union Join Director
of the BBC Proms David Pickard and Craig Hassall, Chief
Executive of the Royal Albert Hall, as they look back over
the 2017 Proms season.

WEDNESDAY 6 SEPTEMBER

**PROMS AT... THE TANKS AT
TATE MODERN • LATE NIGHT** ☾
10.15pm–c11.30pm

For ticket prices, see page 159

ACTRESS

OPEN EAR PROM

Actress *electronics*
Rodrigo Constanzo *drums/electronics/lights*

Exaudi
London Contemporary Orchestra
Robert Ames *director*
Hugh Brunt *director*

There will be no interval

Join BBC Radio 3 presenter Sara Mohr-Pietsch and
the London Contemporary Orchestra for a specially
curated Prom in the industrial surroundings of
The Tanks at Tate Modern. In a link-up with
BBC Radio 3's new music series *Open Ear*,
cutting-edge experimental music sits side by side
with brand-new sounds and free improvisation.
The programme includes a collaboration between
the LCO and London-based electronic artist
Actress; new work by Catherine Lamb; Cassandra
Miller's evocative, folk-inspired *Guide* performed by
vocal ensemble Exaudi; and Rodrigo Constanzo's
dynamic performances with light and sound.

SPOTLIGHT ON ...
Sara Mohr-Pietsch
Proms at ...
The Tanks at Tate Modern

It's an unconventional space for a concert –
and it's set to host some equally unconventional
music. The Tanks at Tate Modern – which stored
oil during the gallery's former life as a power
station and have now been converted into a
raw, industrial space for the newest of art –
is the venue for an unpredictable Late Night
Prom curated by BBC Radio 3 presenter
Sara Mohr-Pietsch.

'This is an *Open Ear* concert,' she explains,
referring to the BBC Radio 3 series that started
last year, 'to showcase the huge variety of practice
in contemporary music. We've had everything
from a chamber orchestra playing traditionally
notated music to turntable artists, improvisation
and performance art. There's a growing audience
of adventurous listeners for whom the usual
distinctions between music, art, architecture, even
theatre and dance, just don't exist in the same way.'

Mohr-Pietsch is delighted to have on board the
London Contemporary Orchestra, and she's
particularly excited about the Tanks' remarkable
space. 'It has such an extraordinary atmosphere,'
she continues, 'with the extremity of the concrete,
and its huge, sweeping walls. It feels like a space
that's just waiting to have people come in and
make weird noises!'

THURSDAY 7 SEPTEMBER

PROM 72
6.30pm–c8.10pm • Royal Albert Hall

PRICE BAND D

DANIEL HARDING

Mahler Symphony No. 6 in A minor *82'*

Vienna Philharmonic
Daniel Harding conductor

There will be no interval

If the Ninth Symphony is Mahler's musical 'dark night of the soul', then the Sixth is the afternoon, dark with storm clouds, that preceded it. Although written at the happiest time of the composer's life, the work builds gradually into a shattering frenzy of despair. 'The hero,' wrote Mahler, 'is assaulted by three hammer-blows of fate, the last of which fells him as a tree is felled.' It was a musical vision that was to prove all too prescient for a composer who would soon suffer a series of life-changing personal heartbreaks. The Sixth Symphony is a Viennese work, and who better to champion it than the Vienna Philharmonic, conducted here – in the first of its two appearances this season – by regular collaborator Daniel Harding.

PROMS EXTRA POETRY COMPETITION
5.15pm–6.00pm • Imperial College Union Jacob Polley, winner of this year's T. S. Eliot poetry prize, and Judith Palmer, Director of the Poetry Society, join BBC Radio 3 presenter Ian McMillan to announce the winners of the 2017 Proms Poetry Competition.
Edited version broadcast on BBC Radio 3 after tonight's Prom

THURSDAY 7 SEPTEMBER

PROM 73 • LATE NIGHT 🌙 📺
9.30pm–c11.30pm • Royal Albert Hall

PRICE BAND C

SIR ANDRÁS SCHIFF

J. S. Bach The Well-Tempered Clavier – Book 1 *111'*

Sir András Schiff piano

There will be no interval

The two volumes of Bach's *The Well-Tempered Clavier* together represent one of Western music's greatest achievements. Once described as the 'Old Testament' of the keyboard repertoire, these two sequences of 24 Preludes and Fugues – one in every key – represent a wealth of musical invention, ingenuity and delight. A supreme technical challenge for any performer, they also offer an astonishing experience for every listener. Eminent Bach specialist Sir András Schiff, whose discography includes Bach's complete keyboard repertoire, here performs Book 1 – embarking upon a cycle that he will conclude next year with Book 2.

📺 *Broadcast on BBC Four this evening*

FRIDAY 8 SEPTEMBER

PROM 74
7.30pm–c9.45pm • Royal Albert Hall

PRICE BAND D

MICHAEL TILSON THOMAS

Brahms
Variations on the St Anthony Chorale *18'*
Mozart
Piano Concerto No. 14 in E flat major *23'*
INTERVAL
Beethoven
Symphony No. 7 in A major *40'*

Emanuel Ax piano

Vienna Philharmonic
Michael Tilson Thomas conductor

Michael Tilson Thomas and pianist Emanuel Ax join the Vienna Philharmonic for the orchestra's second concert this season – a programme filled with song and dance. Wagner famously described Beethoven's Symphony No. 7 as 'the apotheosis of the dance', and it's hard to hear the breathless Scherzo or exuberant finale without becoming swept up in the work's restless energy. That energy also invigorates Brahms's Variations, taking a theme once thought to be by Haydn and transforming it by turns into a graceful sicilienne and a swaying, syncopated dance. For Mozart it is song that offers the inspiration for his dramatic Piano Concerto No. 14, with its arching melodies and almost operatic musical dialogues between soloist and orchestra.

PROMS EXTRA TALK
5.45pm–6.30pm • Imperial College Union Ahead of tonight's visit from the Vienna Philharmonic, Gavin Plumley discusses the cultural context of Vienna.
Edited version broadcast on BBC Radio 3 during tonight's interval

Julian Hargreaves (Harding); Nadia F. Romanini (Schiff); Chris Wahlberg (Tilson Thomas)

SATURDAY 9 SEPTEMBER

PROM 75
7.15pm–c10.30pm • Royal Albert Hall

PRICE BAND G

NINA STEMME

LAST NIGHT OF THE PROMS 2017

Lotta Wennäkoski Flounce   c5'
BBC commission: world premiere

Kodály Budavári Te Deum   21'

Sargent
An Impression on a Windy Day   7'

Sibelius Finlandia (choral version)   8'

Wagner Tristan and Isolde –
Prelude and Liebestod   17'

INTERVAL

John Adams
Lola Montez Does the Spider Dance   5'
London premiere

Songs by Weill and Gershwin   15'

arr. Wood
Fantasia on British Sea-Songs   18'

Arne, arr. Sargent
Rule, Britannia!   5'

Elgar
Pomp and Circumstance March No. 1
in D major ('Land of Hope and Glory')   8'

Parry, orch. Elgar
Jerusalem   3'

The National Anthem   3'

Trad., arr. Thorpe Davie
Auld Lang Syne   2'

Nina Stemme *soprano*
Lucy Crowe *soprano*
Christine Rice *mezzo-soprano*
Ben Johnson *tenor*
John Relyea *bass*

BBC Singers
BBC Symphony Chorus
BBC Symphony Orchestra
Sakari Oramo *conductor*

Sakari Oramo and the BBC Symphony Orchestra weave together many of this season's musical strands into the exuberant celebration that is the Last Night of the Proms. They mark the 50th anniversaries of the deaths of composers Zoltán Kodály and Malcolm Sargent (better known as the longtime chief conductor of the Proms), and celebrate John Adams's 70th birthday with the London premiere of his exhilarating *Lola Montez Does the Spider Dance*. Music by Sibelius marks the 100th anniversary of Finnish Independence, and Nina Stemme, arguably the world's greatest living Wagnerian soprano, leads the end-of-season festivities. See 'Maximal Minimalists', pages 32–35; 'New Music', pages 66–71; 'Staff Sargent', pages 80–83.

📺 *First half live on BBC Two, second half live on BBC One*

PROMS EXTRA THE CHOIR
4.30pm–5.45pm • Imperial College Union Join us for a special edition of BBC Radio 3's *The Choir*, presented by Sara Mohr-Pietsch. *Tickets available from BBC Studio Audiences: bbc.co.uk/showsandtours.*
Edited version broadcast on BBC Radio 3 on 10 September

BBC
Last Night of the
Proms

Kristian Schuller (Stemme); Chris Christodoulou (Last Night of the Proms)

SATURDAY 9 SEPTEMBER

PROMS IN THE PARK 📻 📺

Gates open 3.00pm • Entertainment from 5.15pm • Hyde Park, London

THE ROYAL PARKS

For ticket prices, see page 159

SIR BRYN TERFEL

Sir Bryn Terfel *bass-baritone*
Michael Ball *presenter*

BBC Concert Orchestra
Richard Balcombe *conductor*

Join in the Last Night of the Proms celebrations in Hyde Park, hosted by Michael Ball. The open-air concert features a host of musical stars, including Proms in the Park favourites the BBC Concert Orchestra under the baton of Richard Balcombe, and special guest Sir Bryn Terfel.

Listen to BBC Radio 2 from Monday 1 May for announcements of headline artists and special guests.

📻 *Broadcast live on BBC Radio 2*

The BBC Proms in the Park events offer live concerts featuring high-profile artists, well-loved presenters and BBC Big Screen link-ups to the Royal Albert Hall, when you can join with audiences across the nations. So gather your friends and your Last Night spirit for an unforgettable evening.

Keep checking bbc.co.uk/promsinthepark for announcements of artists, venue and booking information.

Highlights of the Last Night celebrations around the UK will feature as part of the live television coverage of the Last Night and you can watch more at bbc.co.uk/proms.

You can also access Proms in the Park content via the red button.

EXPERIENCE THE LAST NIGHT MAGIC AROUND THE UK!

Hyde Park, London

❖

Northern Ireland

❖

Scotland

❖

Wales

Booking tickets Tickets available from 11.00am on Friday 5 May from the Royal Albert Hall. Ticket requests may also be included in the Proms Planner submitted from 9.00am on Saturday 13 May. See below for details of how to book.

Online bbc.co.uk/promsinthepark.

By telephone from the Royal Albert Hall on 0845 401 5040 † (a booking fee of 2% of the total value, plus £2.00 per ticket up to a maximum of £25.00, applies for telephone bookings).

In person at the Royal Albert Hall Box Office (no fees apply to tickets bought in person).

By post see page 160.

For details of how to order a picnic hamper for collection on the day, or to find out about VIP packages and corporate hospitality, visit bbc.co.uk/promsinthepark.

ODRADEK

PEERLESS MUSICIANS. PEER REVIEWED.

17 ensembles – 17 women – 17 men – 24 countries – and counting!

5

YEARS

ODRADEK

www.odradek-records.com

GEORGE ENESCU
FESTIVAL

Enescu Festival in a New Light!

MAGIC EXISTS

2 - 24.09.2017
festivalenescu.ro/en

Honorary President: Zubin Mehta
Artistic Director: Vladimir Jurowski

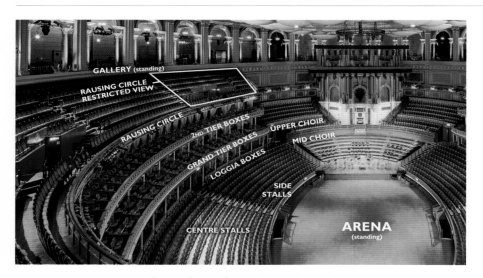

Royal Albert Hall

Seated tickets are available for all BBC Proms concerts at the Royal Albert Hall and fall into one of eight price bands, indicated beside each concert listing on pages 118–155.

Up to 1,350 Promming (standing) places are available in the Arena and Gallery for each concert on the day for £6.00. Save by buying a Season or Weekend Promming Pass *(see opposite)*.

All tickets for the Relaxed Prom (Prom 19, 29 July) are priced £6.00 (no discounts are available on these tickets).

18s and under go half-price

Tickets for persons aged 18 and under can be purchased at half-price in any seating area for all Proms except the Last Night (Prom 75) and in any price band except for £6.00 tickets at any venue. This discount is available through all booking methods.

Great savings for groups

Groups of 10 or more attending concerts at the Royal Albert Hall can claim a 5% discount on the price of Centre/Side Stalls or Rausing Circle Front/Mid/Rear tickets (excluding the Last Night), subject to availability. To make a group booking, or for more information, call the Group Booking Information Line on 020 7070 4408.

Tickets and discounts for disabled concert-goers

All disabled concert-goers (and one companion) receive a 50% discount on all ticket prices (except Arena and Gallery areas) for concerts at the Royal Albert Hall and Cadogan Hall.

To book, call the Access Information Line on 020 7070 4410 or purchase in person at the Royal Albert Hall.

Please note that wheelchair spaces cannot be booked online or via the Proms Planner.

Discounts for disabled concert-goers cannot be combined with other ticket offers.

PRICE BANDS	A	B	C	D	E	F	G	H	
GRAND TIER BOXES 12 seats, price per seat*	£40.00	£50.00	£60.00	£70.00	£25.00	£35.00	£100.00	£20.00	
LOGGIA AND 2ND TIER BOXES Loggia: 8 seats, price per seat 2nd Tier: 5 seats, price per seat	£35.00	£45.00	£55.00	£65.00	£25.00	£35.00	£95.00	£20.00	**All tickets for Relaxed Prom £6.00**
CENTRE STALLS	£30.00	£42.00	£52.00	£62.00	£20.00	£30.00	£90.00	£16.00	
SIDE STALLS	£28.00	£38.00	£48.00	£58.00	£20.00	£30.00	£87.00	£16.00	
MID CHOIR	£25.00	£25.00	£34.00	£44.00	£20.00	£30.00	£65.00	£16.00	
UPPER CHOIR	£19.50	£22.00	£29.00	£37.00	£15.00	£20.00	£62.00	£16.00	
RAUSING CIRCLE FRONT	£19.50	£22.00	£29.00	£37.00	£15.00	£20.00	£62.00	£12.00	
RAUSING CIRCLE MID	£17.00	£20.00	£24.00	£29.00	£15.00	£20.00	£58.00	£12.00	
RAUSING CIRCLE REAR	£12.50	£15.50	£19.50	£24.50	£15.00	£20.00	£47.00	£12.00	
RAUSING CIRCLE RESTRICTED VIEW	£7.50	£9.50	£14.00	£18.00	£7.50	£10.00	£27.00	£7.50	

Please note: a booking fee of 2% of the total value – plus £2.00 per ticket (£1.00 per ticket for the Relaxed Prom) up to a maximum of £25.00 – applies to all bookings (including Season and Weekend Promming Passes), other than those made in person at the Royal Albert Hall.

*As most Grand Tier Boxes are privately owned, availability is limited.

TICKETS AND DISCOUNTS

Season and Weekend Promming Passes

Frequent Prommers can save money by purchasing a Season Pass for either the Arena or the Gallery covering the whole Proms season at the Royal Albert Hall only, including the Last Night, or only the first or second half, or a Weekend Promming Pass *(exclusions apply, see box below)*.

Weekend Promming Passes must be purchased a minimum of two hours before the start of the first concert covered. Prices vary for each weekend depending on the number of concerts included – see box below.

BBC Proms in the Park, Hyde Park, London, Saturday 9 September

Tickets (standard admission) £44.00 *(booking fees apply)*. See page 155 for details.

Ticket exchange

Unwanted tickets for all Proms that have been purchased through the Royal Albert Hall Box Office may be exchanged for tickets to other Proms concerts (subject to availability). A fee of £1.00 per ticket will be charged for this service. Call the Royal Albert Hall Box Office (0845 401 5040†) for further details.

Proms at ... Cadogan Hall, Proms Chamber Music

Stalls: £15.00, Centre Gallery: £13.00 *(booking fees apply)*. Promming tickets are available on the day from Cadogan Hall.

Proms Chamber Music Series Pass

Hear all eight Monday-lunchtime Proms Chamber Music concerts at Cadogan Hall for just £40.00 *(booking fees apply)*.

Other 'Proms at ...' concerts

Advance tickets can only be bought from the Royal Albert Hall Box Office *(see prices below)*. A limited number of Promming tickets are available for cash only on the day from each venue one and a half hours before each performance, as listed below. Promming tickets are limited to two per transaction.

Stage@TheDock, Hull, Saturday 22 July, 12.30pm, 3.00pm and 5.30pm

Unreserved seats and standing tickets: £6.00 *(booking fees apply)*.

Southwark Cathedral, Saturday 12 August, 3.00pm

Reserved seats: £15.00 *(booking fees apply)*.

Bold Tendencies Multi-Storey Car Park, Peckham, Saturday 26 August, 12.00pm and 3.00pm

Reserved seats: £12.00, unreserved seats and standing tickets: £6.00 *(booking fees apply)*.

Wilton's Music Hall, Saturday 2 September, 3.00pm and 7.30pm

Reserved seats: £15.00 *(booking fees apply)*.

The Tanks at Tate Modern, Wednesday 6 September, 10.15pm

Standing tickets: £6.00 *(booking fees apply)*.

BOOKING

Royal Albert Hall Proms Passes	Concerts	Price
Whole season 14 July – 9 September	Proms 1–75 *(excluding Proms 11, 12, 19 and 34)*	£240.00
First Half 14 July – 13 August	Proms 1–38 *(excluding Proms 11, 12, 19 and 34)*	£144.00
Second Half 14 August – 8 September	Proms 39–74	£152.00
Weekend 1	Proms 1–4	£22.00
Weekend 2	Proms 9–10	£11.00
Weekend 3	Proms 18–21 *(excluding Prom 19)*	£16.50
Weekend 4	Proms 27–29	£16.50
Weekend 5	Proms 35–38	£22.00
Weekend 6	Proms 45–49	£27.50
Weekend 7	Proms 54–59	£33.00
Weekend 8	Proms 64–68	£27.50

†CALL COSTS
Calls cost up to 5p/min from most landlines (an additional connection fee may also apply). Calls from mobiles may cost considerably more. All calls may be recorded and may be monitored for training and quality-control purposes.

BOOKING FEES

A booking fee of 2% of the total value – plus £2.00 per ticket (£1.00 per ticket for the Relaxed Prom) up to a maximum of £25.00 – applies to all bookings (including Season and Weekend Promming Passes), other than those made in person at the Royal Albert Hall.

HOW TO BOOK

ONLINE
at bbc.co.uk/proms or
royalalberthall.com

—

BY TELEPHONE
on 0845 401 5040†

IN PERSON
at the Royal Albert Hall
Box Office

—

BY POST

When does booking open?
General booking opens at 9.00am on
Saturday 13 May

Season and Weekend Promming Passes
are available to purchase from 9.00am
on Thursday 11 May.

Proms Chamber Music Series Passes
are available to purchase from 9.00am
on Thursday 11 May.

Tickets for the **Ten Pieces Presents … Proms**
(Proms 11 and 12) are available to purchase
from 9.00am on Friday 12 May.

Tickets for the **Relaxed Prom** (Prom 19),
including a limited number of Promming tickets,
are available to purchase from 9.00am on
Friday 12 May.

Tickets for the **'Proms at …'** series are available
from 9.00am on Friday 23 June.

For **Last Night of the Proms** tickets, see page 163.

For **Promming** tickets, see page 162.

For **Proms in the Park** tickets, see page 155.

Online
Between Thursday 20 April (2.00pm) and
Friday 12 May (11.59pm) use the Proms Planner,
accessible via bbc.co.uk/proms to create your
personal Proms Plan.

From 9.00am on Saturday 13 May you can
redeem your plan and submit your booking.
If you do not have a Proms Plan, you can just
book online at royalalberthall.com.

The following tickets are not part of the Proms
Planner. See opposite for how to book:

– Season and Weekend Promming Passes
– Proms Chamber Music Series Passes
– Ten Pieces Presents … Proms
  (Proms 11 and 12)
– Relaxed Prom (Prom 19)
– 'Proms at …' series

PLEASE NOTE
It is not possible to book entire boxes online.
If you would like to book a full box, call the
Box Office on 0845 401 5040†.

The 'Select Your Own Seat' option is not available
via the Proms Planner or during the first few
days that Proms tickets are on sale. You will be
allocated the best available places within your
chosen seating area.

By telephone
From 9.00am on Saturday 13 May, call the Royal
Albert Hall Box Office on 0845 401 5040†
(open 9.00am–9.00pm daily). From outside
the UK, please call +44 20 7589 8212.

In person
From 9.00am on Saturday 13 May, visit the
Royal Albert Hall Box Office at Door 12.
(Open 9.00am–9.00pm daily.)

PLEASE NOTE
No booking fees apply to tickets bought in
person.

By post
Please write to BBC Proms, Box Office, Royal
Albert Hall, London SW7 2AP with the
following details:

– your name, address, telephone number(s)
  and email address (if applicable)
– the concerts you wish to attend
– number of tickets required
– preferred seating area, preferably with
  alternatives (see *ticket prices and seating plan
  on pages 158–159*)
– applicable discounts (see *page 159*)
– a cheque, payable to 'Royal Albert Hall' and
  made out for the maximum amount (including
  booking fees); or your credit card details,
  including type of card, name on the card, card
  number, issue number (Maestro only), start
  date, expiry date and security code (last three
  digits on back of Visa/Mastercard or last four
  digits on front of American Express). Your
  details will be held securely.

General postal bookings will start to be
processed from 9.00am on Saturday 13 May,
when booking opens.

PLEASE NOTE
following the start of booking, all postal
applications are processed in random order, not
the order in which they are received.

Postal bookings for Season and Weekend
Promming Passes must be made separately to
other booking requests. Please mark your
envelope 'Proms Season Pass' or 'Weekend
Promming Pass' as appropriate. These bookings will
be processed from 9.00am on Thursday 11 May.

†CALL COSTS
Calls cost up to 5p/min from most landlines
(an additional connection fee may also apply).
Calls from mobiles may cost considerably more.
All calls may be recorded and may be monitored
for training and quality-control purposes.

HOW TO BOOK

Season and Weekend Promming Passes
are available to purchase from 9.00am on
Thursday 11 May.

Postal bookings for Season and Weekend
Promming Passes *(see 'By post' opposite)*
will be processed in random order from
9.00am on Thursday 11 May.

PLEASE NOTE
Season Passes are non-transferable and two
passport-sized photographs must be provided
before tickets can be issued. ID may be requested
upon entry.

You may purchase a maximum of four Weekend
Promming Passes per weekend.

There is no Weekend Promming Pass covering
Proms 74 and 75.

Season and Weekend Promming Passes are valid
for concerts at the Royal Albert Hall only.

Season and Weekend Promming Passes are
subject to availability.

Proms Chamber Music Series Passes
are available to purchase from 9.00am on
Thursday 11 May. Two passport-sized
photographs must be provided.

PLEASE NOTE
Proms Chamber Music Series Passes cannot be
purchased from Cadogan Hall and are subject
to availability.

**Tickets for the Ten Pieces
Presents ... Proms**
are available from 9.00am on Friday 12 May.

Tickets for the Relaxed Prom
are available from 9.00am on Friday 12 May.

Tickets for the 'Proms at ...' series
are available from 9.00am on Friday 23 June.

BOOKING FEES
A booking fee of 2% of the total value – plus
£2.00 per ticket (£1.00 per ticket for the
Relaxed Prom) up to a maximum of £25.00 –
applies to all bookings (including Season and
Weekend Promming Passes), other than those
made in person at the Royal Albert Hall.

CREATE YOUR PROMS PLAN

From 2.00pm on Thursday
20 April go to bbc.co.uk/proms
and fill in your Proms Planner

BOOK YOUR PASSES

From 9.00am on Thursday
11 May book your Season and
Weekend Promming Passes for
the Royal Albert Hall or Proms
Chamber Music Series Passes
for Cadogan Hall (these are not
included in the Proms Planner)

BOOK YOUR TICKETS

From 9.00am on Saturday 13 May
submit your Proms Planner or book
online via bbc.co.uk/proms,
in person or on the phone

DON'T MISS OUT

on the Ten Pieces Presents ...
Proms, Relaxed Prom, or the
'Proms at ...' series – see
opposite for how to book

What Is Promming?

The popular tradition of Promming (standing in the Arena or Gallery areas of the Royal Albert Hall) is central to the unique and informal atmosphere of the BBC Proms.

Up to 1,350 standing places in the Arena and Gallery are available for each Proms concert at the Royal Albert Hall, although the capacity may vary for each Prom.

How to Prom

Book a Season or Weekend Promming Pass and benefit from guaranteed entry (until 30 minutes before each concert) as well as great savings – prices can work out at less than £3.50 per concert. See page 159 for details.

PLEASE NOTE

Season and Weekend Promming pass-holders arriving at the Hall less than 30 minutes before a concert are not guaranteed entry and should join the back of the Day queue.

Prom on the day – tickets can be purchased in person with cash or contactless payment card. Ticket purchases are made as you enter, in queue order, through the relevant doors. Tickets for Late Night Proms are available on the doors from 30 minutes before the performance.

A limited number of Promming tickets will be available on the day to purchase online between 9.00am and 12.00pm for main-evening and Late Night Proms. Tickets are limited to one per person, with the exception of the Ten Pieces Presents … Proms (Proms 11 and 12) for which four tickets per person will be available.

Promming tickets for the Ten Pieces Presents … Proms will be available to purchase online from 9.00am on the day before the concerts.

A limited number of Promming tickets for the Relaxed Prom (Prom 19) will be available to purchase online from 9.00am on Friday 12 May.

Prommers who have purchased tickets online should join the relevant Arena or Gallery ticket-holders queue and are guaranteed entry only until the concert starts.

Promming tickets for wheelchair-users

The Gallery can accommodate up to four wheelchair-users. On arrival at the Royal Albert Hall, ask a steward (on duty from 9.00am) for assistance. Wheelchair-users will be issued a queue number and can leave and return in time for doors opening (see page 164), at which point all Prommers will enter in queue order. Please note that the Arena is not accessible to wheelchair-users.

Promming tickets for ambulant disabled concert-goers: Seat Reservation Card

A limited number of seats will be available for reservation each day by ambulant disabled concert-goers (disabled concert-goers who do not use a wheelchair) who wish to Prom.

On arrival at the Royal Albert Hall, ambulant disabled concert-goers should ask a steward (on duty from 9.00am) for a Seat Reservation Card, along with a queue number.

You can then leave the queue, returning in time for doors opening (see page 164), at which point you can purchase your ticket as Prommers begin to enter the Hall in queue order. If you secure a Promming ticket with a Seat Reservation Card, a seat will have been reserved for you.

Between 9.00am and 12.00pm on the day of the concert, ambulant disabled Season and Weekend Promming Pass-holders and Online Promming ticket-holders can also request Seat Reservation Cards by telephone only (one per call) by phoning 020 7070 4410. You will need to collect your Seat Reservation Card from the Box Office before joining the appropriate Prommers' queue (stewards will direct you). After 12.00pm Seat Reservation Cards can be requested in person only – please ask a steward for a Seat Reservation Card along with a queue number.

You must be in the queue, having collected your Seat Reservation Card, no less than 30 minutes before the concert to guarantee entry, and a seat will have been reserved for you.

PLEASE NOTE

A Seat Reservation Card does not guarantee entry on its own – you must also purchase a Promming ticket.

Proms at … Cadogan Hall
Proms Chamber Music Series Pass

Book a Proms Chamber Music Series Pass and benefit from guaranteed entry to the Side Gallery until 12.40pm. See page 159 for details.

Prom on the day – tickets can be purchased in person at Cadogan Hall from 10.00am.

Other 'Proms at …' concerts

Promming tickets for the other 'Proms at …' concerts are available on the day from each venue as detailed on page 159.

ONLINE PROMMING TICKETS

All Promming tickets purchased online are subject to a booking fee of 2% of the total value plus £1.00 per ticket.

QUEUING

Queuing arrangements will differ from previous years, while the Royal Albert Hall undergoes the next phase of its development.

Stewards will be on hand to assist Prommers from 9.00am. Visit royalalberthall.com/promsqueue from Thursday 11 May for details.

Owing to high demand, the majority of tickets for the Last Night of the Proms are allocated by ballot.

THE FIVE-CONCERT BALLOT

Customers who purchase tickets for at least five other concerts at the Royal Albert Hall are eligible to enter the Five-Concert Ballot.

How to enter

When booking online, tick the Ballot opt-in box, or when booking by telephone, in person or by post, inform the Box Office that you wish to enter this ballot.

You must do this before the Five-Concert Ballot closes on Thursday 1 June.

If you require a wheelchair space for the Last Night of the Proms, you will still need to book for five other concerts but you must phone the Access Information Line (020 7070 4410) by Thursday 1 June and ask to be entered into the separate Ballot for wheelchair spaces. This Ballot cannot be entered online.

Successful applicants will be informed by Friday 9 June.

PLEASE NOTE
You can apply to buy a maximum of two tickets for the Last Night. If you are successful in the Ballot, you will not be obliged to buy Last Night tickets should your preferred seating area not be available.

If you are successful, your Last Night tickets will be issued from Friday 1 September.

We regret that, if you are unsuccessful in the Five-Concert Ballot, no refunds for other tickets purchased will be payable.

THE OPEN BALLOT

One hundred Centre Stalls seats (priced £90.00 each plus booking fee) and 100 Front Circle seats (priced £62.00 each plus booking fee) for the Last Night of the Proms at the Royal Albert Hall will be allocated by Open Ballot.

How to enter

Please complete the official Open Ballot Form for 2017, which is available to download from bbc.co.uk/promstickets; or call 020 7765 2044 to receive a copy by post.

The completed form should be sent by post only – to arrive no later than Thursday 29 June – to:

BBC Proms Open Ballot
Box Office
Royal Albert Hall
London SW7 2AP

PLEASE NOTE
No other ticket purchases are necessary. Only one application (for a maximum of two tickets) may be made per household.

The Open Ballot application envelopes should contain only the official 2017 Open Ballot Form.

The Open Ballot takes place on Friday 30 June and successful applicants will be contacted by Thursday 6 July.

If you are successful in the Five-Concert Ballot, you will not be eligible for Last Night tickets via the Open Ballot.

GENERAL AVAILABILITY FOR THE LAST NIGHT

Any remaining tickets for the Last Night will go on sale on Friday 7 July at 9.00am, by telephone or online only. There is exceptionally high demand for Last Night tickets, but returns occasionally become available, so it is always worth checking with the Box Office.

PLEASE NOTE
For all Last Night bookings, only one application (for a maximum of two tickets) can be made per household.

BOOKING FEES
A booking fee of 2% of the total value – plus £2.00 per ticket (£1.00 per ticket for the Relaxed Prom) up to a maximum of £25.00 – applies to all bookings (including Season and Weekend Promming Passes), other than those made in person at the Royal Albert Hall.

PROMMING AT THE LAST NIGHT

Whole Season Promming Passes include admission to the Last Night.

A limited allocation of Last Night tickets (priced £6.00) is also reserved for Prommers who have attended five or more concerts (in either the Arena or the Gallery). They are eligible to purchase one ticket each for the Last Night on presentation of their used tickets (which will be retained) at the Box Office. Tickets will be available to buy from the Box Office from the following dates:

— Tuesday 18 July for First Half Season Pass-holders, Weekend Promming Pass-holders and Day Prommers with five used tickets
— Friday 18 August for Second Half Season Pass-holders, Weekend Promming Pass-holders and Day Prommers with five used tickets
— Monday 4 September for both First and Second Half Season Pass-holders, Weekend Promming Pass-holders and Day Prommers with five used tickets.

ON THE NIGHT

A limited number of Promming tickets will be available on the Last Night itself (priced £6.00, one per person). No previous ticket purchases are necessary.

QUEUING
Please note that queuing arrangements for the Last Night of the Proms will differ from other Proms, but stewards will be on hand to assist Prommers from 9.00am.

Visit royalalberthall.com/promsqueue from Thursday 24 August for details.

ROYAL ALBERT HALL

Kensington Gore, London SW7 2AP • www.royalalberthall.com

FOOD AND DRINK

With a number of restaurants and bars, as well as box catering, there is a wide range of food and drink to enjoy at the Royal Albert Hall, from two and a half hours before each concert. Booking in advance is recommended. Visit royalalberthall.com or call the Box Office on 0845 401 5040[†] to make your reservation.

Bars are located throughout the building and open two hours before each concert. Interval drinks are available from any bar and, to beat the queues, you can order before the concert.

Restaurants
- **Verdi – Italian Kitchen** (First Floor, Door 12)
- **Elgar Bar & Grill** (Circle level, Door 9)
- **Coda Restaurant** (Circle level, Door 3)
- **Cloudy Bay and Seafood Bar** (Second Tier, Door 3)
- **Berry Bros. & Rudd No. 3** (Basement level, Doors 1 & 6)
- **Café Bar** (Ground Floor, Door 12)

Grand Tier, Second Tier and Loggia Box seats If you have seats in one of the Royal Albert Hall's boxes, you can pre-order food and drinks to be served upon arrival or at the interval. Visit boxcatering.royalalberthall.com and please order at least 36 hours before the concert that you are attending. Please note that the consumption of your own food and drink in the Hall is not permitted. Glasses and bottles are permitted in boxes, as part of box catering ordered through the Royal Albert Hall.

YOUR VISIT

Auditorium doors open one hour before the start of each concert (two and a half hours for restaurant and bar access) and 30 minutes before each late-night concert. Tickets and passes will be scanned upon entry. Please have them ready, one per person.

Latecomers will not be admitted into the auditorium unless or until there is a suitable break in the performance.

Bags and coats may be left in the cloakrooms at Door 9 (ground level) and at basement level beneath Door 6. A charge of £1.00 per item applies (cloakroom season tickets priced £20.40, including a 40p payment-handling fee, are also available). Conditions apply – see royalalberthall.com. For reasons of safety and comfort, only one small bag per person is permitted in the Arena.

Security In the interests of safety, bags may be searched upon entry.

Children under 5 are not allowed in the auditorium out of consideration for both audience and artists, with the exception of the Ten Pieces Presents … Proms (Proms 11 and 12) and the Relaxed Prom (Prom 19).

Dress code Come as you are: there is no dress code at the Proms.

'Story of the Proms' tours of the Royal Albert Hall lasting approximately one hour run throughout the Proms season. Other tours also run regularly For bookings and further information, including the Royal Albert Hall's other regular tours, call 0845 401 5045 or visit royalalberthall.com. For group bookings of 15 people or more, call 020 7959 0558. Special group rates apply.

Proms and Royal Albert Hall gifts and merchandise are available inside the porches at Doors 6 and 12 and on the Circle level at Doors 4 and 8. BBC Proms programmes are available outside the auditorium before every concert.

ACCESS

Access Information Line, 020 7070 4410 (9.00am–9.00pm daily).

The Royal Albert Hall has a Silver award from the Attitude is Everything Charter of Best Practice. Full information on the facilities offered to disabled concert-goers (including car parking) is available online at royalalberthall.com. Information is also available through the Access Information Line.

Provision for disabled concert-goers includes:

- 20 spaces bookable for wheelchair-users with adjacent companion spaces. For more details and to book call the Access Information Line
- six additional Side Stalls wheelchair spaces available for Proms 19, 20 and 55–75
- seats available in the Arena and Gallery for reservation each day by ambulant disabled Prommers. For details see page 162
- ramped access, located at Doors 1, 3, 8, 9 and 12. For arrival by car, taxi, minibus or Dial-a-Ride, the most convenient set-down point is at Door 1, which is at the rear of the building and has ramped access.
- public lifts located at Doors 1 and 8 with automatic doors, Braille and tactile numbering and voice announcements
- accessibility for wheelchair-users to all bars and restaurants.

A limited number of parking spaces for disabled concert-goers will be reserved close to the Hall; please contact the Access Information Line for more information.

Wheelchair spaces can be booked by calling the Access Information Line or in person at the Royal Albert Hall Box Office. For information on wheelchair spaces available for the Last Night of the Proms via the Five-Concert Ballot, see page 163.

Other services available on request are as follows:

- The Royal Albert Hall auditorium has an infra-red system with a number of personal headsets for use with or without hearing aids. Headsets can be collected on arrival from the Information Desk at Door 6.
- If you have a guide or hearing dog, the best place to sit in the Royal Albert Hall is in a box, where your dog may stay with you. If you prefer to sit elsewhere, stewards will be happy to look after your dog while you enjoy the concert.

FOR TICKET PRICES, SEE PAGES 158–159

BEIT VENUES, IMPERIAL COLLEGE UNION

Prince Consort Road, London SW7 2BB • www.beitvenues.org

- Transfer wheelchairs are available for customer use.
- A Royal Albert Hall steward will be happy to read your concert programme to you.

To request any of the above services, please call the Access Information line or complete an accessibility request form online at royalalberthall.com 48 hours before you attend. Alternatively you can make a request upon arrival at the Information Desk at Door 6 on the Ground Floor, subject to availability.

Following the success of the signed Proms in past years, a British Sign Language interpreter will guide you through the Ten Pieces Presents … Prom on Sunday 23 July at 2.00pm (Prom 11) and the Relaxed Prom on Saturday 29 July (Prom 19). Please book your tickets online in the usual way (see page 161). If you require good visibility of the signer, please choose the 'Stalls Signer Area' online when selecting your tickets, or call the Access Information Line and request this area.

GETTING THERE

The nearest Tube stations are Gloucester Road (Piccadilly, Circle & District Lines), High Street Kensington (Circle & District Lines) and South Kensington (Piccadilly, Circle & District Lines). These are all a 10- to 15-minute walk from the Hall.

The following buses serve the Royal Albert Hall and Imperial College Union (via Kensington Gore, Queen's Gate, Palace Gate and/or Prince Consort Road): 9/N9, 10 (24-hour service), 49, 52/N52, 70, 360 & 452. Coaches 701 and 702 also serve this area.

† CALL COSTS
Calls cost up to 5p/min from most landlines (an additional connection fee may also apply). Calls from mobiles may cost considerably more. All calls may be recorded and may be monitored for training and quality-control purposes.

Proms Extra Proms Extra pre-concert events will be held in the Concert Hall at Beit Venues, Imperial College Union. Family Intros will be held in the Dining Hall. Entry for all events is through Beit Quad, Prince Consort Road.

Proms Extra events are free of charge and unticketed (seating is unreserved), with the exception of the First Night live *In Tune* event on Friday 14 July, *The Listening Service* on Sunday 3 September and *The Choir* on Saturday 9 September, for which free tickets will be available from BBC Studio Audiences (bbc.co.uk/showsandtours/shows).

Places must be reserved in advance for all Proms Extra Family Orchestra & Chorus events and most Proms Extra Sing events (visit bbc.co.uk/proms or call 020 7765 0557).

PLEASE NOTE
Prommers who join the Royal Albert Hall queue before the Proms Extra event should make sure they take a numbered slip from one of the Royal Albert Hall stewards to secure their place back in the queue in time for doors opening.

Access Beit Venues, Imperial College Union has a range of services to assist disabled visitors, including:
- a limited number of spaces for wheelchair-users in the Concert Hall and Dining Hall
- an induction loop installed in the Concert Hall
- accessible lifts throughout the building
- wheelchair access points into the building via Prince Consort Road and Kensington Gore. (Please contact us prior to arrival for access via Kensington Gore.)

Guide dogs are welcome, but please contact us prior to arrival, so that any special arrangements can be made if necessary. Contact the Beit Venues team on 020 7594 8113 or email beitvenues@imperial.ac.uk.

PLEASE NOTE
Seating at Beit Venues, Imperial College Union is limited and all Proms Extra events are subject to capacity, so we advise arriving early for the more popular events. Latecomers will be admitted where possible but, as many of these events are recorded for broadcast, you may have to wait until a suitable break. The event stewards will guide you.

CADOGAN HALL

5 Sloane Terrace, London SW1X 9DQ
www.cadoganhall.com

Food and drink A selection of savouries, sandwiches and cakes is available from the Oakley Bar and Café. The café and bar will be open at 11.00am. Cadogan Hall's bars offer a large selection of champagne, wines, spirits, beer, soft drinks and tea and coffee.

Doors open at 11.00am (entry to the auditorium from 12.30pm).

Bags and coats may be left in the cloakroom on the lower ground level. A charge of £1.00 per item applies.

Access Cadogan Hall has a range of services to assist disabled customers, including:

– Three wheelchair spaces in the Stalls available for advance booking and one space reserved for sale as a day ticket from 10.00am on the day of the concert. Please note: there is no lift access to the Gallery.
– Box Office counter fitted with a loop system.
– An infra-red amplification system in the auditorium. This is not the same as a loop system, so you will need to use an amplification aid.

Guide dogs are welcome to access the Hall and auditorium but please contact Cadogan Hall prior to arrival, so that any special arrangements can be made, as necessary. For further information, call 020 7730 4500.

BOLD TENDENCIES MULTI-STOREY CAR PARK

95A Rye Lane, London SE15 4ST
www.boldtendencies.com

Food and drink Frank's Cafe on the rooftop of Bold Tendencies offers food and drink throughout the day. There are no advance reservations, so we advise early arrival. Refreshments will also be available in the performance area.

Doors open 30 minutes before the performance.

Personal items and valuables are the responsibility of the visitor. There is no cloakroom available on site.

Children under 5 are welcome, but parents are requested to show consideration to both artists and other audience members.

Getting there The following buses serve Bold Tendencies Peckham: 12, 37, 63, 78, 197, 343, 363, 484 and P12. Peckham Rye train station is a 5-minute walk from the car park.

Access Step-free access to the performance level is available via the lifts. If you require step-free access, please email access@boldtendencies.com between 10.00am and 5.00pm, Monday–Friday.

SOUTHWARK CATHEDRAL

London Bridge, London SE1 9DA
www.cathedral.southwark.anglican.org

Food and drink The Refectory offers a selection of savouries, sandwiches, cakes and hot lunches, as well as champagne, wines, beer and tea and coffee, throughout the day.

Doors open 45 minutes before the performance.

Personal items and valuables are the responsibility of the visitor. There is no cloakroom available on site.

Children under 5 are welcome, but parents are requested to show consideration to both artists and other audience members.

Getting there Both London Bridge train and Tube stations are less than 5 minutes' walk from the Cathedral.

Access Southwark Cathedral has a range of services to assist disabled visitors, including:

– access to all levels available via lifts or fixed and portable ramps
– accessible toilets at the West end (Ground floor)
– a loop system: please turn your hearing aid to the 'T' position
– a wheelchair is available upon request.

STAGE@THEDOCK, HULL

High Street, Hull HU1 1UU
www.stageatthedock.co.uk

Food and drink Stage@TheDock is positioned in the Fruit Market quarter of Hull, within easy reach of many cafés and bars.

Doors open 30 minutes before the performance.

Personal items and valuables are the responsibility of the visitor. There is no cloakroom available on site.

Children under 5 are welcome, but parents are requested to show consideration to both artists and other audience members.

Getting there Hull Paragon Interchange Rail and Bus station is less than 20 minutes' walk from Stage@TheDock. If you are arriving by car, you should follow signs to Fruit Market from Castle Street (A63), or use post code HU1 1UU for GPS devices.

Access Stage@TheDock has step-free access and wheelchair spaces are available.

Guide dogs are welcome to access the venue.

THE TANKS AT TATE MODERN

Bankside, London SE1 9TG
www.tate.org.uk

Food and drink A selection of wines, beers, soft drinks, tea, coffees and snacks is available from Tate Modern's Terrace Bar.

Doors open 45 minutes before the performance.

Personal items A limited number of lockers are available on site.

Children under 5 will not be admitted to this concert out of consideration for both audience and artists.

Getting there The nearest tube and train stations are Southwark, Blackfriars, St Paul's and London Bridge. The following buses serve Tate Modern: 45, 63, 100, 344, 381 and RV1.

Access The Switch House Entrance provides step-free access to the Terrace Bar and Level 1, Switch House. From here, there is lift access to the performance level.

There are 12 parking spaces for disabled visitors, located on the south side of the building and accessed via Park Street. These spaces must be booked ahead: email ticketing@tate.org.uk (with your name, contact details, date and time of visit) or call 020 7887 8888 (open 9.45am–6.00pm daily).

WILTON'S MUSIC HALL, LONDON

1 Graces Alley, London, E1 8JB
www.wiltons.org.uk

Food and drink A wide-selection of food and drink is provided by in-house caterers, Gatherers (table service available in the Cocktail Bar and snacks in the Mahogany Bar).

Doors open 45 minutes before the performance.

Personal items and valuables are the responsibility of the visitor. There is no cloakroom available on site. Please do not bring any large bags.

Children under 5 are welcome, but parents are requested to show consideration to both artists and other audience members.

Getting there The nearest tube and train stations are Aldgate East, Tower Hill, Shadwell and Fenchurch Street.

Access Wheelchair spaces in the Stalls are available for advanced booking and one space is reserved for sale on the day until 30 minutes before the performance – to book, call the Box Office on 020 7702 2789.

Guide Dogs are welcome but please contact the Box Office prior to arrival so that any special arrangements can be made, as necessary.

BBC Proms

MORE WAYS TO ENJOY BBC PROMS PUBLICATIONS

This BBC Proms 2017 Festival Guide is also available in the following formats:

🔊 AUDIO CD   ⠿ BRAILLE

Audio CD (including readings by BBC Radio 3 presenters) and Braille versions of this Festival Guide are available in two parts, 'Article' and 'Concert Listings/Booking Information', priced £3.50 each. For more information and to order, call the RNIB Helpline on 0303 123 9999.

ᴀᴀ LARGE PRINT

A text-only large-print version of this Festival Guide is available, priced £7.00. Please allow 10 working days for delivery.

Large-print concert programmes can be made available on the night (at the same price as the standard programme) if ordered at least five working days in advance. Large-print sung texts and opera librettos (where applicable) can also be made available on the night if ordered in advance.

The programmes and texts will be left for collection at the Door 6 Information Desk one hour before the start of the concert.

To order large-print BBC Proms 2017 Festival Guide, programmes or texts, please call Deborah Fether on 020 7765 3246, or email PromsPublications@bbc.co.uk. Please note we can only accept payment by cheque, made payable to 'BBC'.

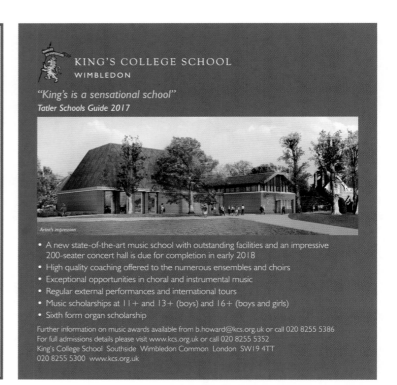
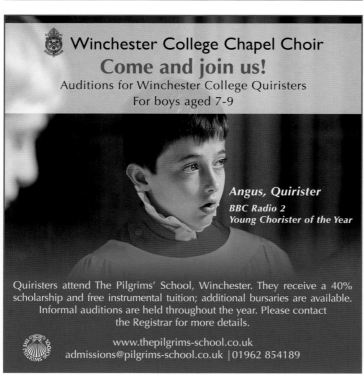

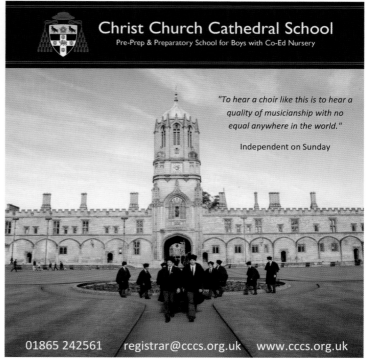

INDEX OF ARTISTS

Bold italic figures refer to Prom numbers
PCM indicates Proms Chamber Music concerts at Cadogan Hall
BTMCP Bold Tendencies Multi-Storey Car Park, Peckham, Saturday 26 August
SC Southwark Cathedral, Saturday 12 August
S@TD Stage@TheDock, Hull, Saturday 22 July
TTM The Tanks at Tate Modern, Wednesday 6 September
WMH Wilton's Music Hall, London, Saturday 2 September
*first appearance at a BBC Henry Wood Promenade Concert
†current / ‡former member of BBC Radio 3's New Generation Artists scheme

A

Behzod Abduraimov piano **5**
Actress* electronics **TTM**
Thomas Adès conductor **28**
Louise Alder soprano **9**
Robert Ames* director **TTM**
Virgile Ancely* bass **22**
Leif Ove Andsnes piano **60**
Ain Anger bass **29**
Emanuel Ax piano **74**

B

Daniel Barenboim conductor **2, 4**
Guy Barker bandleader **57**
Inon Barnatan* piano **39**
Lisa Batiashvili‡ violin **2**
Clive Bayley bass **59**
Joshua Bell violin **43**
William Bell* singer **65**
Nicola Benedetti violin **6**
Sophie Bevan soprano **49**
Vlada Borovko soprano **29**
Renaud Bres* bass **22**
Giuseppina Bridelli* soprano **22**
Matthew Brook bass-baritone **49**
Hugh Brunt* director **TTM**
Jules Buckley conductor **15, 53**
Jeremy Budd tenor **23**
Geoffroy Buffière* bass **22**
John Butt* harpsichord/director **49**
David Butt Philip tenor **30**
Semyon Bychkov conductor **29, 63**

C

Karina Canellakis* conductor **70**
Karen Cargill mezzo-soprano **46**
Cameron Carpenter organ **43**
Riccardo Chailly conductor **54**
William Christie conductor **23**
Rodney Earl Clarke bass-baritone **52**
Allan Clayton‡ tenor **50**
Natalie Clein‡ cello **32**
Jarvis Cocker **15**
Nicholas Collon conductor **10**

Rodrigo Constanzo* drums/ electronics/lights **TTM**
Alice Coote‡ mezzo-soprano **59**
Jessica Cottis conductor **11, 12**
Marianne Crebassa* mezzo-soprano **24**
Steve Cropper* guitar **65**
Lucy Crowe soprano **75**
Paul Curran stage director **29**

D

Thomas Dausgaard conductor **36, 37**
Lise Davidsen* soprano **33**
Iestyn Davies counter-tenor **21**
Sir Andrew Davis conductor **13**
Steve Davislim tenor **59**
Jeanine De Bique* soprano **62**
Jeremy Denk piano **70**
Anna Devin soprano **23**
Charles Dutoit conductor **43**

E

Kevin John Edusei* conductor **62**
Sian Edwards conductor **WMH**
Sir Mark Elder conductor **52**
Maxim Emelyanychev* director **PCM 4**
Norbert Ernst* tenor **29**

F

Marcus Farnsworth* baritone **WMH**
Isabelle Faust violin **3, 67**
Renée Fleming soprano **61**
Eddie Floyd* singer **65**
Jennifer France* soprano **WMH**
Vilde Frang violin **26**
Olivia Fuchs* stage director **WMH**
Mihoko Fujimura mezzo-soprano **39**

G

James Gaffigan* conductor **18**
George Gagnidze* baritone **29**
Rumon Gamba conductor **44**
Sir John Eliot Gardiner conductor **25, 31**

Edward Gardner conductor **1**
Daniele Gatti conductor **64, 66**
Alexander Gavrylyuk* piano **37**
Valery Gergiev conductor **68**
Alban Gerhardt‡ cello **33**
Kirill Gerstein piano **63**
Jess Gillam* saxophone **11, 12**
Emiliano Gonzalez Toro* tenor **22**
Henry Goodman* actor **52**
John Grant* **15**
Mirga Gražinytė-Tyla conductor **50**
Vsevolod Grivnov* tenor **29**

H

Bernard Haitink conductor **3**
Ann Hallenberg* mezzo-soprano **31**
Daniel Harding conductor **72**
Joélle Harvey soprano **9**
Pablo Heras-Casado* conductor **67**
David Hill conductor **SC**
Peter Hoare tenor **46**
Hannah Holgersson* soprano **18**
Robert Hollingworth* director **PCM 1**
Manfred Honeck conductor **69**
Stephen Hough piano **20**
Jakub Hrůša* conductor **56**
Ruby Hughes‡ soprano **BTMCP**
Benjamin Hulett tenor **9**
Shabaka Hutchings*‡ saxophones **53**

I

Alina Ibragimova violin **71**
Jacques Imbrailo baritone **21**

J

Paavo Järvi conductor **26**
Sofi Jeannin* conductor **48**
Ante Jerkunica* bass **29**
Ben Johnson‡ tenor **75**
Leila Josefowicz violin **50**
Colin Judson tenor **29**
Vladimir Jurowski conductor **71**

K

Karen Kamensek* conductor **41**
Sheku Kanneh-Mason* cello **62**
Kirill Karabits conductor **30**
Christiane Karg* soprano **PCM 6**
Leonidas Kavakos violin **54**
Rachel Kavanaugh* stage director **34, 35**
Kreeta-Maria Kentala* violin **PCM 3**
Sigvards Kļava* director **38, PCM 5**
Pavel Kolesnikov‡ piano **PCM 7**
Anu Komsi soprano **PCM 3**

Anantha R. Krishnan* mridangam **55**
Elisabeth Kulman mezzo-soprano **45**
Jayanthi Kumaresh* Saraswati veena **55**

L

Louis Langrée conductor **58**
Andrew Lawrence-King* harp/kantele/psaltery **PCM 3**
Igor Levit‡ piano **1**
Kathryn Lewek* soprano **11, 12**
Kate Lindsey* mezzo-soprano **59**
Grant Llewellyn conductor/presenter **19**
Keith Lockhart conductor **8**
Christopher Lowrey* counter-tenor **23**

M

Gerard McBurney creative director **52**
Nicholas McGegan conductor **S@TD**
Malcolm Martineau piano **PCM 6**
Denis Matsuev piano **68**
Sally Matthews‡ soprano **39**
John Mauceri conductor **27**
Elena Maximova* mezzo-soprano **29**
Tim Mead counter-tenor **49**
Alexander Melnikov‡ piano **PCM 5**
Juanjo Mena conductor **9, 17**
Ricarda Merbeth* soprano **9**
Sara Mohr-Pietsch* presenter **TTM**
Edgar Moreau* cello **PCM 4**
James Morrison* trumpet **27**
Pandit Budhaditya Mukherjee* sitar **55**
Nicholas Mulroy tenor **49**
Anne-Sophie Mutter violin **69**

N

Soumen Nandy* tabla **55**
Alice Neary* cello **PCM 8**

O

Simon O'Neill tenor **21, 46**
Kazushi Ono conductor **39**
Sakari Oramo conductor **45, 51, 61, 75**
Steven Osborne‡ piano **16**
Stéphanie d'Oustrac* mezzo-soprano **43**

P

Eero Palviainen* theorbo/guitar **PCM 3**
Javier Perianes* piano **51**
Vasily Petrenko conductor **60**
Raphaël Pichon* director **22**

Andy Pidcock* *presenter/musician* 19
Rowan Pierce* *soprano* 23
Lawrence Power‡ *viola* 26
Sonia Prina *mezzo-soprano* 21
Christopher Purves *baritone* 17, 46

Q
Thomas Quasthoff* *speaker* 46
Robert Quinney* *organ* 47

R
Kumaresh Rajagopalan*
  Carnatic violin 55
Beatrice Rana*† *piano* 13
Sir Simon Rattle *conductor* 46
Dianne Reeves* *singer* 27
Chen Reiss* *soprano* 66
John Relyea *bass* 75
Jennifer Rhys-Davies* *soprano* 29
Christine Rice‡ *mezzo-soprano* 75
Ashley Riches*† *bass-baritone* 31
Winston Rollins *bandleader* 57
Detlef Roth *bass-baritone* 9
François-Xavier Roth *conductor* 42
James Rutherford *baritone* 30

S
Esa-Pekka Salonen *conductor* 24
Sir András Schiff *piano* 73
Christian Scott* *trumpet* 53
Svatopluk Sem *baritone* 56
Tom Service *presenter* 10
Anoushka Shankar *sitar* 41
Brindley Sherratt *bass* 9
Stuart Skelton *tenor* 9
David Soar *bass* 9
Thomas Søndergård *conductor* 5, 6
Toby Spence *tenor* 32
Kandace Springs* *singer* 53
Michael Spyres *tenor* 31
Christopher Stark *conductor*
  BTMCP
Magnus Staveland* *tenor* 22
Nina Stemme *soprano* 75
Anna Stéphany *mezzo-soprano* 59
John Storgårds *conductor* 33
Michael Sumuel* *bass-baritone*
  BTMCP

T
Clare Teal *singer/presenter* 57
Christian Tetzlaff *violin* 40
Michael Tilson Thomas *conductor* 74
Adrian Thompson *tenor* SC
Callum Thorpe *bass* 23

Cédric Tiberghien‡ *piano* 42
Robin Ticciati *conductor* 40, 59
Andrew Tortise *tenor* 49
Mike Tutaj* *projection design* 52

V
Christopher Ventris *tenor* 29
Milla Viljamaa* *harmonium* PCM 3
Alexander Vinogradov* *bass* 21
Ilan Volkov *conductor* 16

W
Erin Wall *soprano* 21
Elizabeth Watts‡ *soprano* 45
Annelien Van Wauwe*† *clarinet*
  PCM 2
Alisa Weilerstein *cello* 7
Joshua Weilerstein* *conductor* 7
Eva-Maria Westbroek *soprano* 46
William Whitehead* *organ* 47
Mark Wigglesworth *conductor* 20
Ryan Wigglesworth *conductor* 32
John Wilson *conductor* 14, 34, 35
Ida Falk Winland *soprano* 18
Konstantin Wolff* *bass* 49

Y
Dingle Yandell* *bass-baritone* 23

Z
Eva Zaïcik* *mezzo-soprano* 22
Xian Zhang *conductor* 21

GROUPS
Aurora Orchestra 10
The Bach Choir 45
Bang on a Can All-Stars 44
BBC Concert Orchestra 8, 27
BBC National Chorus of Wales
  21, 32
BBC National Orchestra of Wales
  5, 6, 19, 21, 32
BBC Philharmonic 9, 17, 20, 33
BBC Proms Youth Choir 1
BBC Proms Youth Ensemble 44
BBC Scottish Symphony
  Orchestra 14, 16, 36, 37
BBC Singers 29, SC, 48, 56, 75
BBC Symphony Chorus 1, 18,
  45, 75
BBC Symphony Orchestra 1, 7,
  13, 18, 29, 39, 45, 51, 56, 63, 70, 75
Birmingham Contemporary Music
  Group WMH
Bournemouth Symphony
  Orchestra 30
Britten Sinfonia 41
CBSO Chorus 21, 46
CBSO Youth Chorus (female voices)
  14
Chamber Orchestra of Europe 3
Chineke!* 62
Choir of the Age of Enlightenment
  23
Cincinnati Symphony Orchestra*
  58
City of Birmingham Symphony
  Orchestra 50
City of London Sinfonia 48
Crouch End Festival Chorus 17
Deutsche Kammerphilharmonie
  Bremen 26
Dunedin Consort* 49
Elias String Quartet‡ PCM 8
English Baroque Soloists 25
Exaudi TTM
I Fagiolini PCM 1
Fareed Ayaz, Abu Muhammad
  Qawwal & Brothers* 55
Finchley Children's Music Group 39
Freiburg Baroque Orchestra 67
Glyndebourne Festival Opera 59
Guy Barker Big Band 57
Hallé 52
Heritage Orchestra 15
John Wilson Orchestra 34, 35
Jools Holland and His Rhythm
  & Blues Orchestra* 65

Latvian Radio Choir* 37, 38, PCM 5
London Contemporary
  Orchestra* TTM
London Philharmonic Orchestra 71
London Symphony Chorus 46
London Symphony Orchestra 46
London Voices 17
Mariinsky Chorus 68
Mariinsky Orchestra 68
Metropole Orkest 53
Monteverdi Choir 25, 31
Nash Ensemble SC
National Youth Choir of Great
  Britain 30
National Youth Choir of Scotland
  31
National Youth Orchestra of
  Great Britain 28
New London Children's Choir 39
Orchestra of La Scala, Milan* 54
Orchestra of the Age of
  Enlightenment 23, 59
Orchestre Révolutionnaire
  et Romantique 31
Orfeó Català* 46
Orfeón Donostiarra* 9
Oslo Philharmonic 60
Philharmonia Orchestra 24
Philharmonia Voices 24
Pittsburgh Symphony Orchestra 69
Il Pomo d'Oro* PCM 4
Pygmalion* 22
Royal Concertgebouw Orchestra
  64, 66
Royal Northern Sinfonia S@TD
Royal Philharmonic Orchestra
  11, 12, 43
Royal Stockholm Philharmonic
  Orchestra* 61
Schola Cantorum of the Cardinal
  Vaughan Memorial School 29
Scottish Chamber Orchestra 40
Les Siècles 42
Slovak Philharmonic Choir 29
Staatskapelle Berlin 2, 4
Ten Pieces Children's Choir 11, 12
The Multi-Story Orchestra
  BTMCP
The Multi-Story Youth Choir*
  BTMCP
Tiffin Boys' Choir 29
Trinity Boys Choir 31
Van Kuijk Quartet*† PCM 2
Vienna Philharmonic 72, 74
Winston Rollins Big Band 57

181

INDEX OF WORKS

Bold italic figures refer to Prom numbers
PCM indicates Proms Chamber Music concerts at Cadogan Hall
BTMCP Bold Tendencies Multi-Storey Car Park, Peckham, Saturday 26 August
SC Southwark Cathedral, Saturday 12 August
S@TD Stage@TheDock, Hull, Saturday 22 July
TTM The Tanks at Tate Modern, Wednesday 6 September
WMH Wilton's Music Hall, London, Saturday 2 September
*first performance at a BBC Henry Wood Promenade Concert

A

John Adams (born 1947)
Harmonielehre **BTMCP**
Harmonium **1**
Lola Montez Does the Spider Dance*
   London premiere **75**
Lollapalooza* **69**
Naïve and Sentimental Music **24**
John Luther Adams (born 1953)
songbirdsongs – excerpts* **WMH**
Thomas Adès (born 1971)
Polaris* **28**
Julian Anderson (born 1967)
Piano Concerto* BBC co-commission:
   world premiere **16**
Louis Andriessen (born 1939)
Workers Union* **44**
Thomas Arne (1710–78)
Rule, Britannia! (arr. Sargent) **75**

B

Johann Sebastian Bach (1685–1750)
Canonic Variations on 'Vom Himmel
   hoch, da komm' ich her', BWV 769
   (arr. Stravinsky) **24**
Cantata No. 79 'Gott der Herr ist Sonn
   und Schild' **25**
Cantata No. 80 'Ein feste Burg ist unser
   Gott' **25**
Chorale Prelude 'Wachet auf, ruft uns die
   Stimme', BWV 645 (orch. Bantock)*
   BTMCP
St John Passion **49**
The Well-Tempered Clavier – Book 1*
   73
Samuel Barber (1910–81)
Knoxville: Summer of 1915 **61**
Gerald Barry (born 1952)
Canada* BBC commission: world premiere
   50
Béla Bartók (1881–1945)
Piano Concerto No. 2 **70**
Ludwig van Beethoven (1770–1827)
Fidelio **9**
Overture 'Leonore' No. 3 **50**
Piano Concerto No. 3 in C minor **1**

Symphony No. 1 in C major **30**
Symphony No. 3 in E flat major, 'Eroica'
   10
Symphony No. 5 in C minor **50**
Symphony No. 7 in A major **74**
Symphony No. 9 in D minor, 'Choral' **21**
Alban Berg (1885–1935)
Violin Concerto **40**
Hector Berlioz (1803–69)
The Damnation of Faust **31**
Overture 'Le carnaval romain' **13**
Symphonie fantastique **7**
Leonard Bernstein (1918–90)
On the Waterfront – symphonic suite **58**
Sir Harrison Birtwistle (born 1934)
Deep Time* BBC co-commission:
   UK premiere **4**
Luigi Boccherini (1743–1805)
Cello Concerto in D major, G479 **PCM 4**
Johannes Brahms (1833–97)
Piano Concerto No. 1 in D minor **20**
Symphony No. 2 in D major **26**
Tragic Overture **40**
Variations on the St Anthony Chorale **74**
Violin Concerto in D major **54**
Benjamin Britten (1913–1976)
Ballad of Heroes* **32**
Russian Funeral* **71**
The Young Person's Guide to
   the Orchestra **13**
Anton Bruckner (1824–96)
Symphony No. 9 in D minor **64**

C

Frédéric Chopin (1810–49)
Fantasy in F minor/A flat major, Op. 49*
   PCM 7
Fantasy-Impromptu in C sharp minor,
   Op. 66 **PCM 7**
Impromptu in A flat major, Op. 29*
   PCM 7
Mazurkas – selection **PCM 7**
Scherzo in E major, Op. 54* **PCM 7**
Waltz in A flat major, Op. 69 No. 1*
   PCM 7

Waltz in C sharp major minor, Op. 64
   No. 2* **PCM 7**
Francisco Coll (born 1985)
Mural* London premiere **28**
Aaron Copland (1900–90)
Lincoln Portrait **58**
Tom Coult (born 1988)
St John's Dance* BBC commission:
   world premiere **1**

D

Peter Maxwell Davies (1934–2016)
Eight Songs for a Mad King **WMH**
Claude Debussy (1862–1918)
Prélude à l'après-midi d'un faune **39**
Léo Delibes (1836–91)
Lakmé – ballet music **40**
Frederick Delius (1862–1934)
On Hearing the First Cuckoo in Spring **13**
Summer Night on the River **S@TD**
Jonathan Dove (born 1959)
Chorale Prelude 'Christ unser Herr zum
   Jordan kam'* BBC commission: world
   premiere **47**
Henri Duparc (1848–1933)
L'invitation au voyage **PCM 6**
Laurent Durupt (born 1978)
Grids for Greed* BBC commission:
   world premiere **PCM 2**
Pascal Dusapin (born 1955)
Outscape* BBC co-commission:
   UK premiere **7**
Antonín Dvořák (1841–1904)
Hussite Overture **56**
Rondo in G minor, Op. 94 **62**
Symphony No. 8 in G major **70**
Symphony No. 9 in E minor, 'From the
   New World' **52**
Violin Concerto in A minor **69**

E

Edward Elgar (1857–1934)
'Enigma' Variations **32**
Overture 'Cockaigne (In London Town)'
   13
Pomp and Circumstance March No. 1
   in D major ('Land of Hope and
   Glory') **75**
Symphony No. 1 in A flat major **2**
Symphony No. 2 in E flat major **4**
Symphony No. 3 (elab. Payne) **51**
Brian Elias (born 1948)
Cello Concerto* BBC commission:
   world premiere **32**

F

Manuel de Falla (1876–1946)
El amor brujo **43**
Cheryl Frances-Hoad (born 1980)
Chorale Prelude 'Ein feste Burg ist unser
   Gott'* BBC commission: world premiere
   47
César Franck (1822–90)
Les Djinns **42**

G

George Gershwin (1898–1937)
Songs **75**
Philip Glass (born 1937)
Glassworks – Closing* **44**
Passages (with Ravi Shankar)*
   first complete live performance **41**
Michael Gordon (born 1956)
Big Space* BBC commission:
   world premiere **44**
Edvard Grieg (1843–1907)
Peer Gynt – excerpts **33**
Jesús Guridi (1886–1961)
Seis canciones castellanas* **PCM 6**

H

Reynaldo Hahn (1874–1947)
Études latines – 'Lydé'*; 'Vile potabis'*;
   'Tyndaris'* **PCM 6**
George Frideric Handel (1685–1759)
Arias **62**
Israel in Egypt* **23**
Rinaldo – 'Augelletti, che cantate' **WMH**
Water Music – Suites Nos. 2 & 3 **S@TD**
Johann Adolph Hasse (1699–1783)
Adagio and Fugue in G minor* **PCM 4**
Joseph Haydn (1732–1809)
Symphony No. 82 in C major, 'The Bear'
   66
Symphony No. 99 in E flat major **20**
Anders Hillborg (born 1954)
Sirens* UK premiere **18**
Paul Hindemith (1895–1963)
Symphony 'Mathis der Maler' **33**
Gustav Holst (1874–1934)
The Perfect Fool – ballet music **13**
The Planets **14**

J

Leoš Janáček (1854–1928)
The Excursions of Mr Brouček – Song
   of the Hussites* **56**

K

Hannah Kendall (born 1984)
The Spark Catchers* BBC commission:
  world premiere **62**
Zoltán Kodály (1882–1967)
Budavári Te Deum* **75**
Charles Koechlin (1867–1950)
Shéhérazade – 'Chanson d'Engaddi'*;
  'La chanson d'Ishak de Mossoul'*;
  'Le voyage'* **PCM 6**
Erich Wolfgang Korngold
  (1897–1957)
The Sea Hawk – overture **18**

L

Édouard Lalo (1823–92)
Namouna – Suites Nos. 1 & 2
  (excerpts)* **42**
Symphonie espagnole **43**
David Lang (born 1957)
Sunray* London premiere **44**
Thomas Larcher (born 1963)
Nocturne – Insomnia* UK premiere **40**
Franz Liszt (1811–86)
From the Cradle to the Grave* **16**
Hamlet* **16**

M

Sir James MacMillan (born 1959)
A European Requiem* European
  premiere **21**
Gustav Mahler (1860–1911)
Symphony No. 1 in D major **69**
Symphony No. 2 in C minor,
  'Resurrection' **45**
Symphony No. 4 in G major **66**
Symphony No. 6 in A minor **72**
Symphony No. 10 (compl. Cooke) **36**
Bohuslav Martinů (1890–1959)
Field Mass **56**
Missy Mazzoli (born 1980)
Sinfonia (for Orbiting Spheres)* European
  premiere of orchestral version **70**
Felix Mendelssohn (1809–47)
Calm Sea and Prosperous Voyage **S@TD**
Overture 'The Hebrides' ('Fingal's Cave')
  67
Symphony No. 5 in D major,
  'Reformation' **67**
Violin Concerto in E minor **67**
Olivier Messiaen (1908–92)
Le merle noir **WMH**
Claudio Monteverdi (1567–1643)
Chiome d'oro* **PCM 1**
Cruda Amarilli* **PCM 1**

Laudate pueri Dominum a 5
  (concertato)* **PCM 1**
Longe da ta, cor mio* **PCM 1**
Orfeo – 'Possente spirto' **PCM 1**
Sfogava con le stelle* **PCM 1**
Vespers of 1610 **22**
Volgendo il ciel per l'immortal sentiero
  PCM 1
Vorrei baciarti, o Filli* **PCM 1**
Wolfgang Amadeus Mozart
  (1756–91)
La clemenza di Tito **59**
Piano Concerto No. 14 in E flat major **74**
Clarinet Quintet in A major **PCM 2**
Sinfonia concertante in E flat major **26**
Symphony No. 38 in D major, 'Prague' **3**
Violin Concerto No. 3 in G major **3**
Modest Mussorgsky (1839–81)
Khovanshchina (orch. Shostakovich)* **29**
Pictures at an Exhibition (orch. Ravel) **16**

N

Carl Nielsen (1865–1931)
Symphony No. 2, 'The Four
  Temperaments' **61**

P

Giovanni Pierluigi da Palestrina
  (c1525–1594)
Offertorium 'Confitebor tibi, Domine'*
  SC
Missa 'Confitebor tibi, Domine' **SC**
Hubert Parry (1848–1918)
Jerusalem (orch. Elgar) **75**
Giovanni Benedetto Platti
  (1697–1763)
Cello Concerto in D major* **PCM 4**
David Popper (1843–1913)
Hungarian Rhapsody, Op. 68
  (orch. M. Schlegel) **62**
Francis Poulenc (1899–1963)
Banalités – 'Voyage à Paris'; 'Hôtel'
  PCM 6
Montparnasse; Hyde Park (Deux
  mélodies de Guillaume Apollinaire)*
  PCM 6
Sergey Prokofiev (1891–1953)
Cantata for the 20th Anniversary of the
  October Revolution **68**
Seven, They Are Seven* **30**
Violin Concerto No. 1 in D major **71**
Henry Purcell (1659–95)
Jehova, quam multi sunt hostes mei
  (arr. Elgar)* **32**

R

Sergey Rachmaninov (1873–1943)
All-Night Vigil (Vespers) **38**
Piano Concerto No. 1 in F sharp minor **63**
Piano Concerto No. 2 in C minor **5**
Piano Concerto No. 3 in D minor **37**
Piano Concerto No. 4 in G minor
  (revised version, 1941) **60**
Symphony No. 2 in E minor **37**
Jean-Philippe Rameau (1683–1764)
Naïs – overture* **S@TD**
Maurice Ravel (1875–1937)
Cinq mélodies populaires grècques*
  PCM 6
Piano Concerto in G major **39**
Shéhérazade **24**
Jean-Féry Rebel (1666–1747)
Les élémens – Le cahos **7**
Ottorino Respighi (1879–1936)
Fountains of Rome **54**
Pines of Rome **54**
Wolfgang Rihm (born 1952)
In-Schrift **64**
Nikolay Rimsky-Korsakov
  (1844–1908)
Capriccio espagnol **62**
Scheherazade **18**
Richard Rodgers (1902–79)
Oklahoma! **34, 35**

S

Camille Saint-Saëns (1835–1921)
Piano Concerto No. 2 in G minor **51**
Piano Concerto No. 5 in F major,
  'Egyptian' **42**
La princesse jaune – overture **42**
Samson and Delilah – Bacchanal **42**
Symphony No. 3 in C minor, 'Organ' **43**
Daniel Saleeb (born 1985)
Chorale Prelude 'Erhalt uns, Herr, bei
  deinem Wort'* world premiere **47**
Toccata on 'Erhalt uns, Herr, bei deinem
  Wort'* **47**
Malcolm Sargent (1895–1967)
An Impression on a Windy Day **75**
Rebecca Saunders (born 1967)
Molly's Song 3* **WMH**
David Sawer (born 1961)
The Greatest Happiness Principle **20**
Arnold Schoenberg (1874–1951)
Gurrelieder **46**
Franz Schubert (1797–1828)
String Quintet in C major **PCM 8**
Symphony No. 8 in B minor, 'Unfinished'
  36

Robert Schumann (1810–56)
Cello Concerto in A minor **33**
Piano Concerto in A minor **13**
Symphony No. 2 in C major **3**
Symphony No. 3 in E flat major, 'Rhenish'
  40
Heinrich Schütz (1585–1672)
Danket dem Herren, denn er ist
  freundlich* **25**
Nicht uns, Herr, sondern deinem
  Namen **25**
Nun lob, mein Seel, den Herren* **25**
Ravi Shankar (1920–2012)
Passages (with Philip Glass)*
  first complete live performance **41**
Dmitry Shostakovich (1906–75)
October* **6**
Preludes and Fugues, Op. 87 – Nos. 1–4
  & 7–8* **PCM 5**
Symphony No. 5 in D minor **68**
Symphony No. 10 in E minor **5**
Symphony No. 11 in G minor,
  'The Year 1905' **71**
Symphony No. 12 in D minor,
  'The Year 1917' **60**
Ten Poems on Texts by Revolutionary
  Poets – excerpts* **PCM 5**
Violin Concerto No. 1 in A minor **6**
Jean Sibelius (1865–1957)
Finlandia (choral version) **75**
Karelia Suite **33**
Luonnotar **33**
Scènes historiques – Suite No. 1 **51**
Symphony No. 2 in D major **6**
Symphony No. 7 in C major **5**
Violin Concerto in D minor **2**
Mark Simpson (born 1988)
The Immortal* London premiere **17**
Bedřich Smetana (1824–84)
Má vlast – Tábor; Blaník **56**
Richard Strauss (1864–1949)
Daphne – Transformation Scene,
  'Ich komme – ich komme' **61**
Die Frau ohne Schatten – Symphonic
  Fantasy **30**
Metamorphosen **10**
Igor Stravinsky (1882–1971)
The Firebird – suite (revised version,
  1919) **60**
Funeral Song* **71**
The Rite of Spring **28**
Song of the Volga Boatmen* **71**
Violin Concerto **50**
Josef Suk (1874–1935)
Prague* **56**

T

Sergey Taneyev *(1856–1915)*
Overture 'The Oresteia'* **63**
Andrea Tarrodi *(born 1981)*
Liguria* *UK premiere* **61**
Pyotr Ilyich Tchaikovsky *(1840–93)*
Manfred **63**
Piano Concerto No. 3 in E flat major **68**
Symphony No. 5 in E minor **58**
Symphony No. 6 in B minor, 'Pathétique'
17
Georg Philipp Telemann
(1681–1767)
Divertimento in B flat major* **PCM 4**
Water Music – overture **S@TD**
Traditional
Auld Lang Syne (arr. Thorpe Davie) **75**
Hussite Chorale 'Ktož jsú Boži bojovníci'
('You Who Are Warriors of God)*
56
The National Anthem **75**
The National Anthem (arr. Wood) **13**
Mark-Anthony Turnage *(born 1960)*
Hibiki* *European premiere* **39**
Erkki-Sven Tüür *(born 1959)*
Flamma* *UK premiere* **26**

V

Ralph Vaughan Williams
(1872–1958)
Symphony No. 9 in E minor **14**
Antonio Vivaldi *(1678–1741)*
Cello Concerto in A minor, RV 419*
PCM 4

W

Richard Wagner *(1813–83)*
Tristan and Isolde – Prelude and
Liebestod **75**
George Walker *(born 1922)*
Lyric for Strings* **62**
William Walton *(1902–83)*
Belshazzar's Feast **30**
Façade Suite No. 1; Suite No. 2 –
Popular Song **13**
Anton Webern *(1883–1945)*
Langsamer Satz **PCM 2**
Kurt Weill *(1900–50)*
Songs **75**
Judith Weir *(born 1954)*
In the Land of Uz* *BBC commission:
world premiere* **SC**
Lotta Wennäkoski *(born 1970)*
Flounce* *BBC commission: world premiere*
75

Kate Whitley *(born 1989)*
I am I say* **BTMCP**
Grace Williams *(1906–77)*
Sea Sketches – High Wind; Calm Sea
in Summer **S@TD**
Roderick Williams *(born 1965)*
Là ci darem la mano* *BBC commission:
world premiere* **PCM 1**
Julia Wolfe *(born 1958)*
Big Beautiful Dark and Scary*
London premiere **44**
arr. Henry Wood *(1869–1944)*
Fantasia on British Sea-Songs **75**

MISCELLANEOUS

Beneath the Underdog: Charles Mingus
Revisited **53**
Beyond the Score®: Dvořák Symphony
No. 9, 'From the New World' **52**
Celebrating John Williams **8**
Classical Music of India and Pakistan **55**
Ella and Dizzy: A Centenary Tribute **27**
From the Kalevala to Kaustinen: Finnish
Folk and Baroque Music **PCM 3**
The 'Godlike Genius' of Scott Walker **15**
Malcolm Sargent's 500th Prom **13**
Open Ear Prom **TTM**
Reformation Day **47, 48, 49**
Relaxed Prom **19**
The Sound of Soul: Stax Records **65**
Swing No End **57**
Ten Pieces Presents … Sir Henry's
Magnificent Musical Inspirations!
11, 12

BBC Proms 2017

Director, BBC Proms David Pickard
Controller, BBC Radio 3 Alan Davey
Personal Assistant Yvette Pusey
Editor, BBC Radio 3 Emma Bloxham

Head of Marketing, Publications and Learning Kate Finch

Concerts and Planning Helen Heslop (Manager), Hannah Donat, Alys Jones, Helen White
(Producers), Alison Dancer, Victoria Gunn (Co-ordinators)
Press and Communications Madeleine Castell (Communications Manager),
Anna Hughes (Assistant Publicist), Kate Warnock (Publicity Assistant)

Marketing Louise Williams (Manager), Anna Brophy (Assistant)

Learning Ellara Wakely (Senior Learning Manager), Lauren Creed, Garth McArthur (Managers),
Rebecca Burns, Catherine Humphrey, Naomi Selwyn (Co-ordinators), Molly Gallagher
(Administrator)

Business Co-ordinator Jenny McHale

Music Television Jan Younghusband (Head of Commissioning, BBC Music TV), Mark Cooper
(Head of Music Television, BBC Studios), Francesca Kemp (Executive Producer, BBC Studios),
Michael Ledger (Series Production Manager, BBC Studios)

Digital Andrew Caspari (Head of Speech Radio and Classical Music, Multiplatform),
Andrew Downs (BBC Proms Digital Editorial Lead), Rhian Roberts (Digital Editor, BBC Radio 3)

BBC Music Library Natalie Dewar (Archive Collections Manager), Declan Kennedy (Proms
Co-ordinator), Tim Auvache, Anne Butcher, Raymond Howden, Michael Jones, Richard Malton,
David Vivian Russell (Music Librarians), Alison John, Claire Martin (Archive Assistants)

Business Affairs Emma Trevelyan (Head of Business Affairs), Mark Waring (Manager),
Catherine Grimes (Manager, Music Copyright), Sarah Bredl-Jones, Laura Davies, Sue Dickson,
Hilary Dodds, Pamela Wise (Executives)

Publications Editor Petra Abbam
Editorial Manager Edward Bhesania
Sub-Editor Úna-Frances Clarke
Publications Designers Reenie Basova (BBC Proms 2017 Festival Guide), Joanna Fezner-Williams
Publications Assistant Deborah Fether

Advertising John Good Ltd
Cover illustration BBC Creative/BBC
Published by BBC Proms Publications, Room 1045, Broadcasting House, London W1A 1AA
Distributed by Bloomsbury Publishing, 50 Bedford Square, London WC1B 3DP

Printed by APS Group

FSC
www.fsc.org
MIX
Paper from
responsible sources
FSC® C003270

ISBN 978-19-12114-00-9   © BBC 2017. All details correct at time of going to press.